PRACTICING THE ART OF LEADERSHIP

A Problem-based Approach to Implementing the ISLLC Standards

Second Edition

REGINALD LEON GREEN

The University of Memphis

Upper Saddle River, New Jersey
Columbus, Ohio

Library of Congress Cataloging-in-Publication Data

Green, Reginald Leon.
   Practicing the art of leadership : a problem-based approach to
implementing the ISLLC standards / Reginald Leon Green. — 2nd ed.
         p. cm.
   Includes bibliographical references.
ISBN 0-13-113253-9
 1.   Interstate School Leaders Licensure Consortium. 2.   Educational
leadership--Standards--United States. 3.   School management and
organization--United States. 4.   Problem-based learning--United States.
I. Title.
   LB2805.G687 2005
   371.2'00973--dc22   2004000396

Vice President and Executive Publisher: Jeffery W. Johnston
Executive Editor: Debra A. Stollenwerk
Editorial Assistant: Mary Morrill
Production Editor: Kris Roach
Production Coordination: nSight
Design Coordinator: Diane C. Lorenzo
Cover Designer: Jason Moore
Cover image: Getty One
Production Manager: Susan Hannahs
Director of Marketing: Ann Castel Davis
Marketing Manager: Darcy Betts Prybella
Marketing Coordinator: Tyra Poole

This book was set in Bembo by Laserwords. It was printed and bound by R.R. Donnelley & Sons Company.
The cover was printed by Coral Graphic Services, Inc.

Pearson Education Ltd.   Pearson Education Australia Pty. Limited
Pearson Education Singapore Pte. Ltd.   Pearson Education North Asia Ltd.
Pearson Education Canada, Ltd.   Pearson Educación de Mexico, S.A. de C.V.
Pearson Education—Japan   Pearson Education Malaysia Pte. Ltd.

10 9 8 7 6 5 4 3
ISBN: 0-13-113253-9

To my grandchildren,
may you develop an in-depth understanding of the value of
leadership and strive to become effective leaders

ABOUT THE AUTHOR

Reginald Leon Green is Associate Professor of Educational Leadership at The University of Memphis. He received the Ed.D. in Educational Administration and Supervision from the University of Missouri–Columbia. He has served at the teacher, principal, deputy superintendent, and superintendent levels of K–12 education, and has been in higher education for 11 years. In 1977, Dr. Green was one of five educators chosen nationally to participate in the Rockefeller Foundation's Superintendency Preparation Program, and, in 1996, he was selected as an associate to the Institute for Educational Renewal, under the leadership of Dr. John Goodlad.

Dr. Green has published a book on inner-city education and articles on educational restructuring, primary grade restructuring, gang violence, and other contemporary educational issues. He has completed national inquiries into nurturing characteristics that exist in schools and standards and assessment measures being established as a part of school reform. This work led to the development of The Center for Urban School Leadership at The University of Memphis, where Dr. Green administers programs to prepare principals for roles in urban school leadership, using a nontraditional approach. In addition to directing the Center, Dr. Green teaches courses in educational leadership with a focus on instructional leadership and participatory governance and change.

PREFACE

New Leaders for Today's Schools

The challenges in today's schools are increasing in frequency, complexity, and intensity, influencing a demand for a new level of excellence from schools' leaders. These demands have become so critical that there is a resurgence of leadership preparation programs. Many universities are renewing their leadership preparation programs to incorporate a practice-oriented approach based on standards and accountability measures. This type of renewal is being advocated by a number of national organizations and most state educational agencies. The organization that has laid the groundwork for this resurgence is the Interstate School Leaders Licensure Consortium (ISLLC). The program crafted by this organization defines and offers a "new leadership paradigm" that incorporates what the members believe is required behavior for today's school leaders.

Through a series of six standards, ISLLC presents a common core of knowledge, disposition, and performance indicators that link leadership behavior to productive schools and enhanced educational outcomes. The standards represent an effort to refine the skills of school leaders and to align leadership behavior with effective educational outcomes (ISLLC, 1996). They have influenced major changes in university leadership preparation programs and the development of related performance assessment instruments used by a number of states as part of their school leader licensure requirements.

Practicing the Art of Leadership: A Problem-based Approach to Implementing the ISLLC Standards is designed to support the new approach by providing a compilation of scenarios that incorporate the leadership behaviors informed by the ISLLC Standards. It is designed to assist prospective school leaders in understanding the standards and developing skills and attributes sufficient to put them into practice. Also, it is about theories and the processes leaders use to meet challenging school situations. Theory is connected to practice in a manner that allows the prospective school leader an opportunity to understand how theory can be used to resolve problems that confront school leaders. Notably, these theories are 30, 40, or 50 years old; however, their appropriateness has not changed. What has changed is the process of practice. Standards, accountability measures, and other societal demands have forced changes in the processes leaders use in responding to the principles of these theories.

A second, yet crucial, objective is to connect the standards, theory, and contemporary literature on school leadership to the scenarios. The approach used is significantly different from the traditional case study format, which probes issues that build on one another and need to be resolved. Instead, the text is written in a manner that recognizes that definitive action is extremely critical to the success of school leaders as they function on a day-to-day basis in a setting filled with complex challenges.

This text is designed for use in a capstone course of a leadership preparation program. Therefore, the content is written based on the assumption that individuals who utilize it have already developed a basic knowledge of administrative theories and concepts that inform leadership behavior. However, it has been recognized as being beneficial in earlier courses when used as a supplement to a text that treats the theoretical concepts of leadership in a comprehensive manner. The caution to be remembered in the use of this material (as with most behavioral material) is that there is no substitute for reflective reasoning. The reader must take care to select a solution to a school challenge based on the interrelationships between the people, the situation, the skills needed, and the environmental forces. An appropriate mix of theory, reflective thinking, and prescription must be identified.

The New Edition

The processes used by school leaders and the skills needed to implement those processes are continuously changing. In the course of revising this text, we have attempted to address those changes. Some of the revisions come as a result of comments and suggestions from reviewers and users of the first edition, and others were necessitated by my commitment to advance a text that fosters a problem-based approach to preparing school leaders. These revisions involved modifications in the format of the text, relocation of some major concepts and topics, creation of a new chapter, and the addition of several new features.

The New Format

Foundation for Leadership: The theoretical concepts forming the foundation section of each chapter have been strengthened, and new theoretical principles have been added.

Reflective Questions and Scenario Analysis: The reflective questions have been refined to assist the reader in focusing on the key issues in the scenarios and to enhance the identification of theoretical concepts and principles that inform solutions to the challenges posed.

Discussion of the Solution: The multiple choice questions for each scenario have been moved to a website to provide an end-of-chapter knowledge-based assessment. The discussion section that previously provided responses to these questions has been redesigned. Rather than providing a response to a series of individual questions, a comprehensive solution to the challenges posed in the scenarios is offered. The questions are posed and discussed, and a suggested solution is offered in a comprehensive format.

A New Chapter 1: This chapter sets the stage for the remaining six chapters of the text, providing a critical analysis of accountability measures and standards. It addresses the need for leadership accountability, the source of standards, and the importance of both to leadership for today's schools.

New End-of-Chapter Features

Additional Readings: The suggested readings have been updated, and additional sources have been added.

Web Surfing Addresses: Website addresses have been added. These sites provide support materials that can be used to enhance content understanding and inform the practical application of theoretical concepts.

Online Web Material

 To enhance classroom discussion and interaction and to provide another source of information for readers, a special website has been created. The following sources may be accessed via the website:

Deepening Your Understanding: The multiple-choice questions have been moved to the website in the form of an end-of-chapter assessment activity. This feature has been added to assist readers in assessing their understanding of the knowledge base necessary to meet the standards addressed in the chapter.

Educational and Leadership Theories: The theories used to form the foundation for each chapter have been grouped by theorist and are listed on the website. The listing contains a description of each theory and its application to the standards.

PowerPoints: A PowerPoint presentation has been developed on the key concepts of each chapter and contains the tables and figures from that chapter. These presentations can be used in class to stimulate discussion or they can be used in after-class review sessions.

Creating Scenarios: A process is presented that students can use to create scenarios for classroom discussion. The scenarios might capture local leadership behavior and issues, assisting students in resolving practical problems in the local setting.

Practice Performance Assessment: An assessment tool on the website allows readers to assess their knowledge bases, explore their dispositions, and judge their leadership performances. Taking this practice assessment prior to engaging in the national assessment examination that is required in most states for licensure is likely to be beneficial.

Appendixes

Appendix Section: Sections containing the ISLLC Standards and additional scenarios have been added as a quick reference for readers. Some of the scenarios were previously included in a chapter. These scenarios are not discussed in detail but can be used to motivate additional classroom discussion and activities.

I hope the prospective school leaders and the practitioners who read this text and work through the scenarios find it beneficial.

Acknowledgments

I hereby gratefully acknowledge the assistance, encouragement, support, and sacrifice given me by my wife, Jean; my son, Reginald, who developed the charts; and my daughters, Cynthia, Stephanie, and especially Reginique, who motivated me to write this book.

Obviously, the contents of a work of this nature come from a number of sources. First and foremost, I express appreciation to all my leadership students for their reflections, assistance, and support during the many class sessions in which these scenarios were refined. I am also grateful to Georgia Edwards and Shirley Johnson, District 89, Maywood, Illinois, for reviewing the scenarios and providing me with invaluable feedback. I am deeply indebted to Dr. Glynda Cryer, Memphis (Tennessee), who read and edited each and every draft.

In addition, the comments of the following reviewers were invaluable: Gina Doolittle, Rowan University; Ann Hassenpflug, University of Akron; Judith A. Kerrins, California State University, Chico; Rosemarye Taylor, University of Central Florida; and Jeffrey F. Zackon, Wilkes University.

EDUCATOR LEARNING CENTER:
AN INVALUABLE ONLINE RESOURCE

Merrill Education and the Association for Supervision and Curriculum Development (ASCD) invite you to take advantage of a new online resource, one that provides access to the top research and proven strategies associated with ASCD and Merrill—the Educator Learning Center. At **www.EducatorLearningCenter.com** you will find resources that will enhance your students' understanding of course topics and of current educational issues, in addition to being invaluable for further research.

How the Educator Learning Center will Help Your Students Become Better Teachers

With the combined resources of Merrill Education and ASCD, you and your students will find a wealth of tools and materials to better prepare them for the classroom.

Research

- More than 600 articles from the ASCD journal *Educational Leadership* discuss everyday issues faced by practicing teachers.
- A direct link on the site to Research Navigator™ gives students access to many of the leading education journals, as well as extensive content detailing the research process.
- Excerpts from Merrill Education texts give your students insights on important topics of instructional methods, diverse populations, assessment, classroom management, technology, and refining classroom practice.

Classroom Practice

- Hundreds of lesson plans and teaching strategies are categorized by content area and age range.
- Case studies and classroom video footage provide virtual field experience for student reflection.
- Computer simulations and other electronic tools keep your students abreast of today's classrooms and current technologies.

Look into the Value of Educator Learning Center Yourself

A four-month subscription to Educator Learning Center is $25 but is FREE when used in conjunction with this text. To obtain free passcodes for your students, simply contact your local Merrill/Prentice Hall sales representative, and your representative will give you a special ISBN to give your bookstore when ordering your textbooks. To preview the value of this website to you and your students, please go to www.EducatorLearningCenter.com and click on "Demo."

Discover the Companion
Website Accompanying This Book

The Prentice Hall Companion Website: A Virtual Learning Environment

Technology is a constantly growing and changing aspect of our field that is creating a need for content and resources. To address this emerging need, Prentice Hall has developed an online learning environment for students and professors alike—Companion Websites—to support our textbooks.

In creating a Companion Website, our goal is to build on and enhance what the textbook already offers. For this reason, the content for each user-friendly website is organized by chapter and provides the professor and student with a variety of meaningful resources.

For the Professor—

Every Companion Website integrates **Syllabus Manager™**, an online syllabus creation and management utility.

- **Syllabus Manager™** provides you, the instructor, with an easy, step-by-step process to create and revise syllabi, with direct links into Companion Website and other online content without having to learn HTML.
- Students may logon to your syllabus during any study session. All they need to know is the web address for the Companion Website and the password you've assigned to your syllabus.
- After you have created a syllabus using **Syllabus Manager™**, students may enter the syllabus for their course section from any point in the Companion Website.
- Clicking on a date, the student is shown the list of activities for the assignment. The activities for each assignment are linked directly to actual content, saving time for students.
- Adding assignments consists of clicking on the desired due date, then filling in the details of the assignment—name of the assignment, instructions, and whether or not it is a one-time or repeating assignment.
- In addition, links to other activities can be created easily. If the activity is online, a URL can be entered in the space provided, and it will be linked automatically in the final syllabus.
- Your completed syllabus is hosted on our servers, allowing convenient updates from any computer on the Internet. Changes you make to your syllabus are immediately available to your students at their next logon.

Common Companion Website features for students include:

For the Student—

> **Chapter Objectives**–Outline key concepts from the text.
> **Interactive Self-quizzes**–Complete with hints and automatic grading that provide immediate feedback for students.

After students submit their answers for the interactive self-quizzes, the Companion Website **Results Reporter** computes a percentage grade, provides a graphic representation of how many questions were answered correctly and incorrectly, and gives a question-by-question analysis of the quiz. Students are given the option to send their quiz to up to four email addresses (professor, teaching assistant, study partner, etc.).

> **Web Destinations** – Links to www sites that relate to chapter content.
> **Message Board** – Virtual bulletin board to post or respond to questions or comments from a national audience.

To take advantage of the many available resources, please visit the *Practicing the Art of Leadership* Companion Website at
www.prenhall.com/green

CONTENTS

Note: Every effort has been made to provide accurate and current Internet information in this book. However, the Internet and information posted on it are constantly changing, so it is inevitable that some of the Internet addresses listed in this textbook will change.

INTRODUCTION

A New Approach to Using Scenarios

Practicing the Art of Leadership: A Problem-based Approach to Implementing the ISLLC Standards is a new approach to problem-based instruction. In reviewing many educational-leadership case-based instruction books, you are likely to observe that writers offer no right answers to the challenges posed in the cases. In fact, in many instances, writers stress the point that there are no right answers. Yet case-based instruction is not hopelessly mired in relativism; there are certain points of view and approaches to issues in administrative practices that are more effective than others (Merseth, 1997, p. 5). What seems clear is the need to formulate a case scenario instructional approach that sensitizes the prospective leader to the problems of practice, rather than one that is simply a device to stimulate discussions (Hoy & Tarter, 1995). Classroom discussions that simply allow participants to foster opinions appear to be inconsistent with the new direction of school leader preparation.

Practicing the Art of Leadership: A Problem-based Approach to Implementing the ISLLC Standards uses this method. Though not an easy task, in this text an attempt has been made to develop a case scenario approach that provides suggested responses grounded in theory and best practices. It provides the prospective leader an opportunity to move beyond mere reflective discussions by analyzing suggested responses to the challenges posed in the scenarios. This is a practice common in case study textbooks used in other disciplines. By using such an approach, the prospective school leader has an opportunity to reflect, examine, compare, and make judgments about well-documented responses. Such an approach appears to be warranted, given the standards-based instruction advocated by the Interstate School Leaders Licensure Consortium (ISLLC).

The Composition of the Text

The text is specifically designed for use in a course that offers the students or practitioners capstone experiences in which they reflect on information previously acquired and use that information to solve complex school challenges. It is about people, processes, and outcomes. Scenarios depict the behavior of people affiliated with schools, theoretical principles offer an explanation for that behavior, and standards describe the preferred outcome. The text does not attempt to address all of the functions of a school leader; rather, it addresses five processes and procedures that contemporary literature (Bennis, Spreitzer, & Cummings, 2001; Conley, 1997; Fullan, 1999; Kouzes & Posner, 2002; Lashway, 1999; Sarason, 1996; Sergiovanni & Starratt, 1998; Yukl, 1994) suggests leaders must effectively use in fulfilling their roles and responsibilities. The five areas addressed are decision making, communication, change, conflict management, and the establishment of an effective teaching and learning climate.

The theoretical framework of the text is illustrated using a circular design, as depicted in the illustration. Leadership appears in the center of the inner circle and is surrounded by three triangles that encompass decision making, change, and conflict management. Adjacent to each triangle are the category indicators of the ISLLC Standards, denoting that a standard of excellence must be achieved in each of the identified areas. Leadership is presented in the center to characterize leadership as the focal point of the school. Each of the three triangles surrounding leadership identifies processes and procedures in which the effective leader must be proficient. Communication appears in an outer circle to indicate that it is the

The Theoretical Framework

linchpin, connecting all areas and providing the lifeblood that generates substance, allowing them to function. The internal field represents the internal environment of the school and the influences of internal forces. Then, there is the outer circle, reflecting the external environment that influences the school's teaching and learning processes. The chapters follow this theoretical framework.

The Scenarios

The scenarios in the text cover critical processes and procedures leaders must effectively use in fulfilling their responsibilities on a daily basis. They are about real-life situations that have occurred in central offices, schools, and classrooms. Scenarios are constructed to provoke thought, motivate reflections, and establish a setting in which prospective school leaders can explore multiple options and enhance their leadership skills before entering an actual school situation.

In addition, the performances specified by the ISLLC Standards appear in scenarios in both a negative and positive manner, allowing the reader to consider behaviors that are appropriate and inappropriate. To further accentuate the standards, those addressed within the context of the chapter are listed at the beginning of the chapter. An additional discussion will be held on the value of using scenarios and vignettes in Chapter 1.

A Framework for Using the Text

The text has multiple uses. It is structured in a manner that allows students to utilize it in the context of their total program. Purposes of the scenarios are to support presentations made by professors, as well as serve as a framework for group discussions, reflective questioning, individual problem analyses, and student interaction. The student is also provided an opportunity to examine values and beliefs and to formulate or refine leadership styles. The following is a description of an effective approach to using the text:

Reading the chapter introduction
Reviewing the professor's presentation
Reading the scenario
Interacting in small groups
Responding to the reflective questions
Participating in a general class discussion

The Theoretical Foundation

Each chapter begins with an introductory section that provides a theoretical foundation to inspire critical thinking and responses to questions about the scenarios that follow. This section places the scenarios into one of the five leadership process areas and assists the student in developing an appreciation for the practical application of related concepts and principles. The author does not intend for this section to be comprehensive or to introduce new concepts. Rather, the introductory section establishes a framework and builds a foundation for addressing issues in the scenarios, motivating the recall of concepts given in-depth treatment in class discussions or previous readings.

Professor's Presentation

Prior to reviewing a scenario in class, professors often present information or lead a discussion on the subject of the material addressed in the scenario. Students **may** use these presentations to revisit theoretical concepts and build a foundation for responding to the challenges posed in the scenario.

Reading the Scenario

It is recommended that a scenario be read two to three times. The first reading should be general to become familiar with the content and characters. During the second reading, key issues can be identified and a position formulated on how the issues relate to theoretical principles and the ISLLC Standards. Because of the comprehensiveness of the standards, multiple standards may be cross-referenced in a single chapter or scenario. Throughout this reading, it is advisable to take notes as ideas occur. This practice will facilitate the recall of key points.

A third reading allows students to develop tentative action plans for use in identifying appropriate solutions to the scenario challenges. In so doing, students should take care to respond to such questions as:

1. What should the principal do next?
2. What factors should the principal consider before responding?
3. What additional information, if any, will the principal need to develop an effective response?
4. What are the sources of additional information?

Small-Group Interaction

After a presentation by professors (if the professor elects to) and the reading of the scenario, students might engage their classmates in a discussion about the behavior of characters in the scenario. By participating in a small-group discussion, students have an opportunity to analyze the scenario using theoretical principles and make behavioral comparisons of the characters in the scenario with those advocated by the standards. It will also allow for reflective responses, the exchange of ideas, and the formulation of positions on the issues. It is suggested that students:

• Think about the scenario from multiple points of view.
• Identify the critical issues in the scenario.

- Determine the knowledge base necessary to address the issues (models).
- Project a course of action to be taken.
- Identify the probable consequences of the course of action selected.
- Identify the theoretical principles that apply to suggested alternative actions.
- Review the suggested response to each issue.
- Suggest alternative actions from those given in the text.
- Pose reflective questions to members of the group.

After an allotted time period, each group might make a presentation to the entire class, generating further discussion and analysis. Students may also elect to do extended activities outside of class. In such instances, these activities could include:

- Developing a written analysis of select questions.
- Relating select questions to an experience the student may have had in the past several years.
- Relating select questions to elements of school reform.
- Creating a newspaper article that focuses on some aspect of the issues.
- Developing a scenario of a similar nature.

Reflective Thinking

The reflective thinking section is heavily based on the ISLLC Standards and designed to provoke thoughtful discussion among class members. The reflective questions reveal many philosophical aspects of belief systems and suggest areas that warrant additional attention. Different points of view can be presented and a rationale provided for alternative responses. This type of discussion yields valuable information of a theoretical nature. The following principles of conversation tend to establish and maintain collegiality as issues are discussed:

- *Engage in conversation. Conversation* means sharing ideas and exchanging informed opinions. The key to an effective conversation is to share only informed opinions (a position taken as a result of past reading, writing, and discussion of an issue).
- *Exchange informed opinions.* State your ideas and beliefs and try to maintain an unbiased view. Be honest and foster open dialogue.
- *Don't argue.* Try to make the people around you feel comfortable.
- *Be a good listener.* Stay focused on the issues.

SUGGESTED READINGS

In addition to the theoretical foundation section of each chapter and the instruction the prospective leaders receive in the classroom, reading the references listed below will provide additional background information in administrative theories, research, and practice sufficient to understand the content issues and address the challenges posed in each scenario.

Bennis, W., Spreitzer, G., & Cummings, T. (Eds.). (2001). *The future of leadership: Today's top leadership thinkers speak to tomorrow's leaders*. San Francisco: Jossey-Bass.

Council of Chief State School Officers. (1996). *Interstate school leaders consortium standards for school leaders*. Washington, DC: Author.

Deal, T., & Peterson, K. (1999). *Shaping school culture: The heart of leadership*. San Francisco: Jossey-Bass.

Fullan, M. (1999). *Change forces: The sequel*. New York: Farmer Press.

Goodlad, J. I., & McMannon, T. J. (1997). *The public purpose of education and schooling*. San Francisco: Jossey-Bass.

Greenberg, J. (1996). *Managing behavior in organizations*. Upper Saddle River, NJ: Prentice Hall.

Interstate School Leaders Licensure Consortium of the Council of Chief State School Officers. (1997). *Candidate information bulletin for school leaders assessment*. Princeton, NJ: Educational Testing Service.

Lashway, L. (1999). *Preparing school leaders:* Research Roundup, Vol. 15(3) NAESP: Alexandria, VA.

National Policy Board for Educational Administration. (2002). *Instructions to implement standards for advancement in educational leadership for principals, superintendents, curriculum directors, and supervisors*. Arlington, VA: NPBEA.

Sirotnick, K., & Soder, R. (Eds.). (1999). *The beat of a different drummer: Essays on educational renewal in honor of John I. Goodlad*. New York: Peter Lang.

REFERENCES

Bennis, W., Spreitzer, G., & Cummings, T. (Eds.). (2001). *The future of leadership: Today's top leadership thinkers speak to tomorrow's leaders*. San Francisco: Jossey-Bass.

Conley, D. T. (1997). *Roadmap to restructuring: Charting the course of change in American education*. Eugene: University of Oregon (ERIC Clearinghouse on Educational Management).

Fullan, M. (1999). *Change forces: The sequel*. New York: Farmer Press.

Hoy, W. K., & Tarter, J. C. (1995). *Administrators solving the problem of practice: Decision-making concepts, cases, and consequences*. Boston: Allyn & Bacon.

Interstate School Leaders Licensure Consortium of the Council of Chief State School Officers. (1997). *Candidate information bulletin for school leaders assessment*. Princeton, NJ: Educational Testing Service.

Kouzes, J. M., & Posner, B. Z. (2002). *The leadership challenge*. San Francisco: Jossey-Bass.

Lashway, L. (1999). *Preparing school leaders*. Research Roundup, vol. 15(3) NAESP: Alexandria, VA.

Merseth, K. (1997). *Case studies in educational administration*. New York: Longman.

Sarason, S. (1996). *Revisiting the culture of the school and the problem of change*. New York: Teachers College Press.

Sergiovanni, T. J., & Starratt, R. J. (1998). *Supervision: A redefinition* (6th ed.). New York: McGraw-Hill.

Yukl, G. A. (1994). *Leadership in organizations* (3rd ed.). Upper Saddle River, NJ: Prentice Hall.

1

STANDARDS INFORMING SCHOOL
LEADERSHIP

As a result of the recent enactment of new federal and state laws, American education is faced with the renewed challenge of educating all of the children who attend today's schools. This challenge has caused many individuals and groups to seriously question the quality of existing schools and the individuals who lead them, ushering in a new wave of educational reform. The general public, state educational agencies, and politicians are demanding excellent schools and greater accountability from individuals who lead them (Riley, 2002).

This new reform movement has forged a stronger linkage between schools and their leadership, resulting in school leaders assuming the role of "chief learning officer" and being held accountable for individual student achievement (Bottoms & O'Neill, 2001). However, many national organizations argue that school leaders are not equipped to meet these demands, as traditional preparation programs have not prepared them to do so (NPBEA, 2002).

Increasingly, reformers agree that individuals entrusted with leading today's schools may be licensed but question whether they are highly capable of practicing the art of leadership in an effective manner (Hess, 2003). As a result of this stance, national standards have been designed and are being used to inform school leadership behavior and practices. New accountability measures for school leaders have been linked to high standards, and new investments to improve the quality of education for all children have been proposed for school districts in almost all states (Riley, 2002). The standards movement that started in the curriculum area of schools has broadened to the leadership of those schools.

While standards are quite distinct, it is arguable that national standards will enhance the quality of leadership performance in today's schools (Hess, 2003). Nevertheless, they have been set forth and are being used to inform the redesign of college and university leadership preparation programs, renew accreditation of those programs, as well as grant certification or license to prospective school leaders (Riley, 2002). Therefore, introducing standards to practicing and prospective school leaders and describing how they are being used to inform school leadership behavior appear warranted.

This chapter examines the case that is being made for using standards to inform school leader behavior, the way leaders should perform in schools. It summarizes the rationale for using standards, identifies organizations proposing them, presents the set of standards informing school leadership programs in more than 35 states, and describes how scenarios and vignettes are being used to transform the standards into practice.

The Emergence of Standards for School Leaders

There has been a major shift in thinking about the role, responsibility, and accountability of school leaders, which has caused the emergence of standards. The fundamental principles underlying the standards movement are high expectations for all children and the accountability of individuals accepting responsibility for their education (Riley, 2002). Standards are being used to build an infrastructure to measure school effectiveness and to ensure that individuals who lead have acquired the knowledge, disposition, and skills necessary to understand existing conditions, create collaborative environments, and build the capacity to prepare all children to live and work in a social and political democracy.

Measuring Effectiveness

Given the challenges of today's schools and the large numbers of academically challenged students, few, if any, individuals would oppose the assessment of the performance of schools and their leaders. Researchers have addressed and answered the question of what leaders of today's schools need to know and be able to do (Bottoms & O'Neill, 2001). Therefore, in this era of high-stakes accountability, it seems reasonable to identify a means of determining if individuals entering the schoolhouse with the charge to lead possess the knowledge and skills identified as necessary.

Clearly, leadership is situational and each individual leader is unique. However, there are patterns to effectively practicing the art of leadership that can be learned and assessed (Kouzes & Posner, 2002). For the assessment to be conducted fairly and effectively, standards of performance need to be established. A school leader may have a vision for the school, but the question becomes whether the leader's vision is adequate and if the approach used to communicate that vision to all stakeholders is appropriate.

If one accepts the premise that establishing clear objective standards that inform effective leader behavior is preferable to the ambiguity that exists without them, then, to ensure effectiveness, the standards must be defined (Reeves, 2002). When standards of leadership behavior are defined—what the school leader should know and be able to do—clear and consistent evaluation criteria can be established. Then, the behavior of prospective and/or practicing school leaders can be compared to an objective measure (Reeves, 2002).

Understanding Existing School Conditions

The new accountability measure established for school leaders emphasizes instructional leadership. This new thrust requires the school leader to support a collaborative school culture focused on teaching and learning, while providing professional development and using data to evaluate performance (Hess, 2003). In order to fulfill these responsibilities, the leader needs to be well versed in processes and procedures that can be used to align professional development activities with plans for school improvement, involve stakeholders in school-related decisions, and analyze data to enhance student performance. Tantamount to the successful implementation of these activities is developing an understanding of the existing conditions of the school. Once that understanding is acquired, a vision of instructional leadership can be identified and shared with stakeholders, and a collaborative environment that moves current reality toward the vision can be established.

Clearly, building a collaborative environment is key to effective leadership. The school leader must be able to establish a climate of trust and mutual respect in which individuals feel empowered and free to be creative and offer suggestions for the enhancement of organizational goals. By transforming the school into a collaborative environment, the leader empowers individuals and builds a team that is committed to goal attainment.

Building Capacity

Building capacity means utilizing best practices to enhance the academic achievement of students. It means sustaining professional development programs to ensure that all personnel have the necessary knowledge to use test data in making instructional decisions that help all children succeed (Riley, 2002). Building capacity also means utilizing highly developed skills in the areas of planning, organization, communication, interpersonal relations, group processes, problem solving, and the change process (NPBEA, 2002).

The standards movement has emerged to ensure that school leaders are skilled in these areas and a number of others. The National Policy Board for Educational Administration (NPBEA, 2002), a strong advocate of standards for school leaders, sums it up in this manner:

> Educational leaders must be able to work with diverse groups and to integrate ideas to solve a common flow of problems. They must study their craft as they practice their

craft, reflecting and then applying what they have learned to people and institutions and the achievement task. This requires patience and perspective, the exercise of judgment and wisdom, and the development of new technical and analytical skills. It also demands sensitivities to other cultures and highly developed communication skills. Finally, it requires personal values that integrate the ethical dimensions of decision making with those of a more technical variety. (p. 3)

The NPBEA proffers that the enactment of standards will establish accountability measures and enhance student achievement. To achieve this end, educational organizations and institutions are using standards in multiple ways.

The Use of Standards and Organizations That Create Them

Among the multiple ways standards are being used, two are of paramount importance. First, many college and university leadership preparation programs are moving from a strict course-based program to a standards-driven program. According to a literature review on the subject, a leadership preparation program falls short if it does not have at its core the requirement of high standards (Lashway, 1999). Second, standards are being used to inform the development of assessment instruments for school leaders. These assessment instruments attempt to measure the extent to which the prospective school leader has reached proficiency in a variety of areas. Also, some states are currently using these instruments in their leadership certification or licensure process.

The National Policy Board for Educational Administration

The essential questions being addressed by standards, and necessarily so, are what does an individual need to know and be able to do in order to be an effective leader in today's schools? What type of disposition is needed, and what are the practices that enable a school leader to perform effectively? To respond to these questions in general and to specifically inform the type of leadership that is required for today's schools, the NPBEA provided the impetus for the development of a set of standards that are being used to govern school leadership developmental programs as well as the behavior of practitioners in the field. A listing of associations holding membership in this organization appears in Table 1.1.

The purpose of the NPBEA is to use the collective action of its member organizations to advance the professional standards of educational administration. Initially, the organization adopted two goals: (a) to develop common and higher standards for the state licensure of principals and (b) to develop a common set of guidelines for the National Council for Accreditation of Teacher Education (NCATE) for advanced programs in educational leadership (NPBEA, 2002). The work of the NPBEA, coupled with the work of its member organizations, led to the development and implementation of The Interstate School Leader Licensure Consortium Standards.

TABLE 1.1 National Policy Board for Educational Administration Members

American Association of Colleges For Teacher Education (AACTE)
American Association of School Administrators (AASA)
Association for Supervision and Curriculum Development (ASCD)
Council of Chief State School Officers (CCSSO)
National Association of Elementary School Principals (NAESP)
National Association of Secondary School Principals (NASSP)
National Council for Accreditation of Teacher Education (NCATE)
National Council of Professors of Educational Administration (NCPEA)
National School Boards Association (NSBA)
University Council for Educational Administration (UCEA)

SOURCE: NPBEA, 2002.

These nationally recognized standards describe a new vision for school leaders, one that speaks to what they should know and be able to do.

The Interstate School Leader Licensure Consortium Standards

The Interstate School Leader Licensure Consortium (ISLLC) Standards is a program of the Council of Chief State School Officers (CCSSO). The CCSSO is a nationwide organization composed of public officials who head departments of elementary and secondary education in the 50 states, the District of Columbia, the Department of Defense Education Activity, and five other state jurisdictions.

According to ISLLC (1997), the new vision for school leaders should include a common core of standards that can be used to inform program instructional content as well as assessment tools for awarding new principal licensure and advanced certification. To this end, ISLLC developed six standards that focus on the knowledge, performance, and disposition of school leaders. Each of these standards has indicators of effectiveness in each of these three areas. A comprehensive review of these standards offers guidance and a shared vision of what school leaders should know and be able to do. They also offer a process of performance accountability, reflecting both the importance and the responsibility of effective school leaders. Table 1.2 contains a listing of the ISLLC Standards; specific indicators of these standards appear in the Appendixes.

The ISLLC Standards and Effective Leadership Practices

Some state agencies believe that prospective school leaders should demonstrate proficiency on the ISLLC Standards prior to receiving a license to practice in a school or school district. In fact, at the time of publication of this text, nine states (Arkansas, Kentucky, Maryland, Mississippi, Missouri, North Carolina, Pennsylvania, Tennessee, and Virginia) and the District of Columbia required prospective school leaders to demonstrate a level of proficiency on a standards-based assessment for licensure.

TABLE 1.2   ISLLC Standards

Standard 1: A school administrator is an educational leader who promotes the success of all students by facilitating the development, articulation, implementation, and stewardship of a vision of learning that is shared and supported by the school community.

Standard 2: A school administrator is an educational leader who promotes the success of all students by advocating, nurturing, and sustaining a school culture and instructional program conducive to student learning and staff professional growth.

Standard 3: A school administrator is an educational leader who promotes the success of all students by ensuring management of the organization, operations, and resources for a safe, efficient, and effective learning environment.

Standard 4: A school administrator is an educational leader who promotes the success of all students by collaborating with families and community members, responding to diverse community interests and needs, and mobilizing community resources.

Standard 5: A school administrator is an educational leader who promotes the success of all students by acting with integrity, fairness, and in an ethical manner.

Standard 6: A school administrator is an educational leader who promotes the success of all students by understanding, responding to, and influencing the larger political, social, economic, legal, and cultural context.

SOURCE: Interstate School Leaders Licensure Consortium of the Council of Chief State School Officers, 1997. Reprinted by permission.

The assessment instrument being used by these states is the School Leadership Series (SLS). The SLS, a program of the Educational Testing Service, offers two standards-based assessments, one for school leaders' licensure and one for the assessment of prospective superintendents. The assessment tools require individuals to respond to a series of scenarios and short vignettes to which a score is awarded (Educational Testing Service, 2001–2002). The type of scenarios and vignettes used will be discussed later in this chapter. Examples of these scenarios and vignettes will be presented and discussed throughout the remaining chapters.

Standards and Leadership Preparation–Program Accreditation

In addition to standards being used to inform effective leadership practices and to make judgments about granting a license to prospective school leaders, some school accreditation agencies use them to judge, influence, and shape the quality of college and university preparation programs. One major player in this arena is NCATE, member of NPBEA.

The Educational Leadership Constituent Council Standards   The Educational Leadership Constituent Council (ELCC) is comprised of

- American Association of School Administrators (AASA)
- Association for Supervision and Curriculum Development (ASCD)
- National Association of Elementary School Principals (NAESP)
- National Association of Secondary School Principals (NASSP)

NPBEA, on behalf of NCATE, fostered the development of a set of standards that they use in their accreditation process.

Members of NPBEA first crafted a set of guidelines to be used by NCATE in their review of school administration preparation programs. A group commissioned by NPBEA then combined these guidelines with the ISLLC Standards. The final product is a set of nationally recognized standards used by NCATE as they review leadership preparation programs.

As a result of the creation and implementation of these standards, "preparation programs are now being assessed on how well graduates of the programs are prepared to perform in the workplace, rather than the number of courses offered or objectives listed in the syllabi of professors" (NPBEA, 2002, p. 6). Subscribing to the belief that performance standards assist individuals in acquiring the skills and attributes necessary to be effective school leaders, NPBEA (2002) advocates that school leaders and the professors who prepare them should strive to meet each of these standards. A listing of these standards appears in Table 1.3.

TABLE 1.3 NPBEA Standards

Standard 1.0: Candidates who complete the program are educational leaders who have the knowledge and ability to promote the success of all students by facilitating the development, articulation, implementation, and stewardship of a school or district vision of learning supported by the school community.

Standard 2.0: Candidates who complete the program are educational leaders who have the knowledge and ability to promote the success of all students by promoting a positive school culture, providing an effective instructional program, applying best practices to student learning, and designing comprehensive professional growth plans for staff.

Standard 3.0: Candidates who complete the program are educational leaders who have the knowledge and ability to promote the success of all students by managing the organization, operations, and resources in a way that promotes a safe, efficient, and effective learning environment.

Standard 4.0: Candidates who complete the program are educational leaders who have the knowledge and ability to promote the success of all students by collaborating with families and other community members, responding to diverse community interests and needs, and mobilizing community resources.

Standard 5.0: Candidates who complete the program are educational leaders who have the knowledge and ability to promote the success of all students by acting with integrity, fairness, and in an ethical manner.

Standard 6.0: Candidates who complete the program are educational leaders who have the knowledge and ability to promote the success of all students by understanding, responding to, and influencing the larger political, social, economic, legal, and cultural context.

Standard 7.0: Internship. The internship provides significant opportunities for candidates to synthesize and apply the knowledge and practice and develop the skills identified in Standards 1–6 through substantial, sustained, standards-based work in real settings, planned and guided cooperatively by the institution and school district personnel for graduate credit.

SOURCE: NPBEA, 2002, p. 20. Reprinted by permission.

The Combined Standards   The two sets of standards are similar in content and inform a contemporary approach to practicing the art of leadership. These standards have clear implications for practicing and aspiring school leaders and are informing leadership behavior on a national level. It is with this acceptance and the belief that we need to understand a new way of defining leadership that we take an in-depth look at the ISLLC Standards.

Unpacking the ISLLC Standards

Accompanying the six ISLLC Standards are 183 indicators. Forty-three indicators describe the knowledge needed by the school leaders; 43 speak to the disposition of school leader, and the remaining 97 address the outcome performance expected of the school leader. Relative to implementing each standard, the school leader's primary purpose is to promote the success of all students. The indicators under each area address an appropriate process that can be used.

Knowledge Indicators

The knowledge indicators identify the minimum knowledge base necessary to accomplish the task described by a specific standard. They describe what the school leader needs to know in order to promote the success of all students. With adequate knowledge, the school leader can identify an appropriate and acceptable process to address the task of the standard. In addition, to select the appropriate process for a given situation, the leader will need knowledge relative to various facets of education.

Disposition Indicators

In the operation of a school, a leader interacts with a variety of individuals and groups in situations in which the leader's disposition is a major determinant of success. The disposition indicators denote an individual's beliefs, values, and type of commitment that tend to be most effective in a school situation.

Performance Indicators

Finally, if the desired outcome is to be achieved in an efficient and effective manner, the leader will have taken steps to ensure that certain actions occur during the various processes used.

The ISLLC Standards and their indicators are presented in the Appendixes.

Moving Standards Into Practice

Considering the fast adoption of the ISLLC Standards, a book of scenarios describing the leader behaviors informed by those standards is one way to move them into practice. For a number of years, in the fields of law, business, and medicine, case studies (scenarios) have proven to be a very effective instructional tool. Today, there is increased enthusiasm for the use of this pedagogical approach in the field of educational administration. In fact, the case/scenario format is becoming a part of a national movement to reform school leadership preparation (CCSSO, 1996). Many institutions of higher education are revising their leadership preparation programs, and some are changing their pedagogical approach to include scenario-type strategies, emphasizing theoretical and clinical knowledge, applied research, and supervised practice (Murphy & Hallinger, 1993).

The Value of Using Scenarios

The value of scenarios and vignettes, as used in this text, is that they provide a method for the reader to relate theory to practice and to identify the relationship that exists between the literature and the ISLLC Standards. Understanding this relationship should endow the new practitioner with a greater appreciation for the complementary connection between theory and practice.

Scenarios can also assist prospective leaders in acquiring skills of critical analysis and problem solving. These skills will foster their capacity to analyze situations, make decisions, and communicate with constituents. They will also equip them to develop, implement, and evaluate action plans and to secure the assistance of others in the process (Ashbaugh & Kasten, 1995; Christensen & Hansen, 1987; Conley, 1997; Fullan, 1999; Merseth, 1997).

A careful review and analysis of the scenarios presented in this text provide an effective approach to placing the standards into practice. Also, the scenarios and vignettes used in the text are similar to those used by the Educational Testing Services for licensure. Therefore, the reader might elect to use the text scenarios and vignettes as practice prior to engaging in that assessment. An in-depth review of the text materials will be helpful in a variety of ways.

CHAPTER SUMMARY

Multiple changes are occurring in society, leading to new challenges for leaders of today's schools. The belief that few school leaders are prepared to address the demands of these challenges is being advanced by many individuals and organizations (NPBEA, 2002). As a result of this perceived void, uniform national standards have been designed and are being used to inform school leadership practices.

As we look to the future of school leadership, it is important to recognize that change in schools is being directly related to the individuals who lead them, and the leadership required is being informed by standards. The standards receiving the most notoriety and leading the reform movement are those developed by the ISLLC and the NPBEA. Therefore, it is advisable for concerned individuals to develop an understanding of and appreciation for these standards and outline procedures and processes to effectively utilize them. Because of their direct relationship to school leaders, national use, and permanence, the ISLLC Standards are incorporated and operationalized in the following chapters.

SUGGESTED READINGS

National Policy Board for Educational Administration. (2002). *Instructions to implement standards for advancement in educational leadership for principals, superintendents, curriculum directors, and supervisors.* Arlington, VA.

Reeves, D. B. (2002). *The leader's guide to standards: A blueprint for educational equity and excellence.* San Francisco: Jossey-Bass.

Riley, R. (2002). Educational reform through standards and partnerships, 1993–2000. *Phi Delta Kappan, 83*(9), 700.

WEBSITES

Interstate School Leaders Licensure Consortium (ISLLC) Standards:
http://www.ccsso.org/content/pdfs/isllcstd.pdf

The National Council for Accreditation of Teacher Education (NCATE):
http://www.ncate.org/

NCATE Standards:
http://www.ncate.org/standard/m_stds.htm

National Association of Secondary School Principals (NASSP):
http://www.nassp.org/

National Association of Elementary School Principals (NAESP):
http://www.naesp.org/

REFERENCES

Ashbaugh, C. R., & Kasten, K. L. (1995). *Educational leadership: Case studies for reflective practice* (2nd ed.). New York: Longman.

Bottoms, G., & O'Neill, K. (2001). *Lending school improvement what research says: A review of the literature.* Atlanta, GA: Southern Regional Education Board.

Christensen, C., & Hansen, A. (1987). *Teaching and the case study method.* Boston: Harvard University School Publishing Division.

Conley, D. T. (1997). *Roadmap to restructuring: Charting the course of change in American education.* Eugene, OR: University of Oregon (ERIC Clearinghouse on Educational Management).

Council of Chief State School Officers. (1996) *Interstate school leaders consortium standards for schools.* Washington, DC: Author.

Educational Testing Service (2001–2002). *Registration bulletin: School leader licensure assessment, school superintendent assessment.* Corporate Headquarters, Princeton, NJ.

Fullan, M. (1999). *Change forces: The sequel.* New York: Farmer Press.

Hess, F. M. (2003). A license to lead. *Education Week, 22*(42), 39–41.

Interstate School Leaders Licensure Consortium of the Council of Chief State School Officers. (1997). *Candidate information bulletin for school leaders assessment.* Princeton, NJ: Educational Testing Service.

Kouzes, J. M., & Posner, B. Z. (2002). *The leadership challenge.* San Francisco: Jossey-Bass.

Lashway, L. (1999). *Preparing school leaders: Research roundup. NASESP, 15*(3), 1–4.

Merseth, K. (1997). *Case studies in educational administration.* New York: Longman.

Murphy, J., & Hallinger, P. (1993). *Restructuring schooling: Learning from ongoing efforts.* Newbury Park, CA: Corwin.

National Policy Board for Educational Administration (NPBEA). (2002). *Instructions to implement standards for advancement in educational leadership for principals, superintendents, curriculum directors, and supervisors.* Arlington, VA.

Reeves, D. B. (2002). *The leader's guide to standards: A blueprint for educational equity and excellence.* San Francisco: Jossey-Bass.

Riley, R. (2002). Educational reform through standards and partnerships, 1993–2000. *Phi Delta Kappan, 83*(9), 700.

2

ESTABLISHING A FRAMEWORK FOR LEADERSHIP

The literature on education is filled with descriptions of the challenging nature of schools. Of all the challenges posed, the one that appears to be most pronounced is providing the type of leadership necessary to assist schools in expanding their traditional boundaries to meet the needs of all children.

As society becomes more complex, schools become equally complex, placing a greater demand on the individuals who lead them. But what is leadership? Do leaders have special personalities and physical traits? Do leaders tell people what to do, closely monitor their performance, and punish them if things are not done as prescribed? Do leaders have a specific set of behaviors that they use in the course of their interactions with others? Do leaders articulate a vision and inspire other members in the organization to share that vision? Or, perhaps leaders are individuals who can cultivate a special type of relationship with people, making each individual feel unique.

In pursuit of answers to these questions and to establish a clear definition of leadership, theorists, researchers, and practitioners have spent over a century researching and analyzing the subject of leadership. Their efforts have generated responses to each of these questions in the affirmative, producing theories on (a) the personal traits or characteristics of leaders, (b) patterns of leader behavior, (c) leaders' approach to decision making, and (d) the way leaders respond to situations to acquire the support of followers.

The purpose of this chapter is to provide the reader with an opportunity to review major theories in each of these areas and explore their implications for leadership in today's schools. In addition, the relationship between these theories, the ISLLC Standards, and contemporary practices for effective leadership in schools is identified. This chapter also includes scenarios that offer the reader an opportunity to analyze the practical aspects of leadership characteristics, styles, and strategies. To assist the reader in relating the ISLLC Standards to the behaviors exhibited in the scenarios, the standards are referenced throughout the chapter and most specifically within the discussion of each scenario.

Leadership Traits, Characteristics, and Behaviors

Traditionally, in an attempt to differentiate between leaders and nonleaders, studies classified traits or characteristics of effective leaders under the heading of capacity, achievement, responsibility, participation, and status (Stogdill, 1948). Leaders were believed to be a select group of individuals who focused their attention on identified tasks. Their primary functions were to tell people what to do, monitor their progress in the workplace, and ensure that organizational rules and regulations were followed. Also, they rewarded excellence performance and penalized poor performance.

In these early studies, the organization was designed in a hierarchical fashion and individuals in leadership roles functioned at or near the top of the hierarchy. The work of the organization was clearly defined, and tasks were broken down into key components. The power of leaders was derived from their position in the organization, and effectiveness was judged by the productivity of the organization. The more productive the organization was in achieving its goals, the more effective the leader. However, results of these studies revealed that a set of traits could not be used to differentiate leaders from nonleaders (Gibbs, 1954).

Many of today's schools are organized and operated in a hierarchical fashion similar to organizations used in early trait studies, and they experience similar results. School leaders develop goals and outline processes to achieve them. Formal policies, procedures, and job descriptions direct these processes and define the roles and responsibilities of faculty and staff. With the pressure of high-stakes testing, the productivity of the school and the effectiveness of school leaders are judged by the performance of students on tests.

The preceding discussion represents an attempt to dispel the concept that traits can be used to separate leaders from nonleaders or that a set of identifiable traits can be used to prepare leaders for today's schools. In fact, the hierarchical top–down perspective of the early period was criticized because it implied that leaders were in a select group. That same criticism exists today. The objective of hierarchical leadership in today's schools might be obtaining organizational efficiency through the establishment of clear goals and objectives, job specialization, and planned supervision, but this type of structure is not well received. Hierarchical leadership minimizes the contributions of followers and perhaps reduces their level of motivation to organizational goal attainment. Further, in today's schools, as the results of early trait studies showed, a single set of characteristics are not likely to prove to be effective in all school situations. Today, a school leader who possesses a specific set of characteristics may be effective in one school situation but ineffective in another. Notwithstanding, there are traits that tend to increase the likelihood of leader success. Therefore, a discussion of those traits follows.

Traits and Leader Effectiveness

In emphasizing the importance of traits, it should be noted that some traits do increase the likelihood of success for leaders. Recent studies reported by Kirkpatrick & Locke (1991) and Bass (1998) identified several traits that are consistently associated with successful leadership. Also, the ISLLC Standards describe a set of traits for effective school leadership. Both sets of traits appear in Table 2.1.

Effective leaders, inside and outside the field of education, exhibit these traits. One such leader is the late Sam Walton, founder of Wal-Mart. According to Walton and Huey (1992), Sam had passion and vision, was an effective communicator, empowered followers, and motivated them to share his vision. Through his vision, he was able to influence and motivate others by empowering them and creating a feeling of ownership and responsibility. Walton communicated his passion and vision to

Table 2.1 Traits of Effective Leaders

TRAITS FROM RECENT LEADERSHIP STUDIES	TRAITS FROM THE ISLLC STANDARDS
Ambition and energy	Vision
The desire to lead	Knowledge
Honesty and integrity	Effective communication skills
Self-confidence	Fairness
Intelligence	Dignity
Job-related knowledge	Respect
Vision	Risk taking
Passion	Trustworthiness
Courage	Acceptance of responsibility
	Ethics
	Caring
	Acceptance of consequences
	Collaboration
	Effective consensus building

SOURCE: Compiled from the works of Kirkpatrick & Locke (1991), Bass (1998), and Council Of Chief State School Officers, *Interstate School Leaders Licensure Consortium Standards for School Leaders*, November 2, 1996, Washington, DC.

his followers through words and actions. These traits are among those advocated for
school leaders by the ISLLC Standards and are being modeled by many effective
school leaders.

Another leader exhibiting these traits is Myra Whitney, principal of Crump Elementary School in Memphis, Tennessee. Ms. Whitney is a charismatic person with
tremendous energy, is highly intelligent, has self-confidence, and draws people to
her through a feeling of caring and concern. Ms. Whitney leads Crump with integrity and "walks the talk." She is honest and displays equity and fairness in all of
her actions. Her display of fairness, honesty, and equity motivates commitment from
the faculty. She is also flexible and demonstrates this flexibility through her willingness to try some innovative ideas if they are well planned. Local newspaper articles
during the period from 1999 to 2003 describe how she used these traits to transform a school with some unreceptive faculty members and some nonsupportive
parents into a productive learning environment wherein the faculty is committed to
educating all children, and parents are supportive of the school's programs.

It is important for today's school leaders to attach a high priority to characteristics and traits that influence school effectiveness. The ISLLC Standards (Standard 5
in particular) identify characteristics that are common among effective school leaders. The standards tend to reflect the personal qualities of the leader and reference
the type of disposition necessary for effectiveness. They speak of vision, knowledge,
effective communication, fairness, dignity, respect, risk taking, trustworthiness, accepting responsibility, being ethical, caring, accepting consequences, collaborating,
and being a consensus builder. The characteristics in Table 2.1 and their effectiveness are demonstrated in scenarios throughout the text. In analyzing these scenarios, readers may find it beneficial to compare them with their own personal
characteristics.

Studies of Leader Behavior

With the decline of interest in the study of traits, a series of leadership theories
emerged from the study of specific behaviors exhibited by leaders. Whereas the concern had previously been the identification of traits of effective leaders, the question
became What type of behaviors do effective leaders display? In search of an answer to
this question, researchers studied the *different patterns of behavior used by leaders* to complete organizational tasks. They focused on the manner in which goals were established, how roles and task requirements were clarified, and how leaders motivated
followers in the direction of goal attainment. From these studies, the concept of leadership style emerged and was recognized as the characteristic manner in which an individual exhibited behavior in interactions with others in the organization.

Of the many behavior studies conducted, three have provided great insight into the
behavior of school leaders: those conducted at the University of Iowa, The Ohio State
University, and the University of Michigan. These studies identify several critical factors

regarding leader behavior and provide a theoretical explanation for many of the leadership principles embraced by the ISLLC Standards.

Styles of Leader Behavior

At the University of Iowa, three styles or patterns of leader behavior were studied: autocratic, democratic, and laissez-faire (Lewin, Lippitt, & White, 1939). Leaders with the autocratic style were very direct, and decision making and power were centralized in the role of the leader. Leaders with this style allowed little or no participation in the decision-making process and tended to take full responsibility from the initiation of a task to its completion. When a leader used a democratic style, emphasis was placed on shared decision making and viewing followers as equals. Group discussion and decisions were encouraged. The leaders with a laissez-faire style gave complete freedom to the group and displayed little concern for completing a job. Followers were left to make decisions on their own.

In various instances, different styles had different effects on followers. However, the results of the studies showed that the democratic style was considered to be most effective and most preferred by followers. The laissez-faire style was next, and the authoritarian style was the least preferred by followers (Lewin et al., 1939).

In a general sense, ISLLC Standards 3 and 4 encompass the findings of the Iowa studies. These standards discourage the hierarchical autocratic style of leadership and support leader behavior that offers direction and is highly inclusive, allowing followers a voice in decisions that affect them. Conversely, the standards discourage the use of a style that tends to be direct and highly task oriented, allowing members of the faculty and staff little or no participation in the decision-making process. The type of leader behavior that offers little or no direction and allows followers complete freedom is also discouraged. Such a style is not likely to be effective in today's schools or preferred by followers.

It is strongly advocated that to be effective in today's schools, the leader must be democratic, driving fear out of the workplace and fostering a community of learners who collaborate on all major issues. Such a style is a positive factor in shaping the school culture into one that enhances the teaching and learning process (Deal & Peterson, 1999; Ryan & Oestreich, 1991).

Dimensions of Leader Behavior

At The Ohio State University, researchers (Stogdill & Coons, 1957) defined leadership as the behavior an individual displays when directing a group toward goal attainment. Their characterization of leader behavior consisted of two dimensions: initiating structure and consideration.

The *initiating structure* dimension (task-oriented leader behaviors) consisted of behaviors that related to the degree to which leaders defined their behavior and the behavior of followers for the completion of tasks within an organization. The focus was on the manner the leader used in establishing well-defined patterns of organization, channels of communication, methods, and procedures. Such behaviors as maintaining performance standards, enforcing work deadlines, and scheduling were included.

The second dimension, *consideration* (people-oriented leader behaviors), consisted of behaviors that related to the degree to which the leader expressed a concern for the welfare of other individuals in the organization. Such behaviors as being approachable, exhibiting warmth, trust, respect, and a willingness to consult with followers before making decisions were included.

Using the Leader Behavior Description Questionnaire (LBDQ) to assess the behavior of individuals relative to the two dimensions, the researchers determined that the two factors seemed to be separate and distinct. Thus, four quadrants of leadership could be formed (see Figure 2.1):

- Quadrant 1: high consideration/low structure
- Quadrant 2: high structure/high consideration
- Quadrant 3: low structure/low consideration
- Quadrant 4: high structure/low consideration

From these studies, it was concluded that the combination of high structure/high consideration leads to higher satisfaction and performance among leaders than do any of the other three combinations. However, there were enough variations in these conclusions to suggest that in certain situations, various combinations might be effective (Halpin, 1966).

In summary, the results of these studies are articulated to leaders of today's schools through ISLLC Standards 2 and 3. Standard 2 directs the leader to be highly considerate of the values and needs of individuals inside and outside of the schoolhouse, and Standard 3 recommends that leaders ensure a safe, efficient, and effective learning environment. In schools, there are times when use of various combinations of the dimensions will be appropriate. For example, if the leader is simply focused on initiating structure for task completion, many of the school goals may be accomplished, leaving the needs of individuals unattended.

FIGURE 2.1   Four Quadrants of Leadership

Quadrant 1 High Consideration/Low Structure	Quadrant 2 High Structure/High Consideration
Quadrant 3 Low Structure/Low Consideration	Quadrant 4 High Structure/Low Consideration

Conversely, if the leader is highly considerate of individuals and groups but indifferent to the goals of the school, the needs of individuals and groups may be met, but the goals of the school are not likely to be achieved. The challenge for the school leader is matching the appropriate combination in a manner that will produce a win-win situation.

Organizational Dimensions

Using an explanation of organizations theorized by Getzel and Guba (1957), one can acquire a deeper understanding of the two dimensions described in the preceding section. They advise that the school is an organization consisting of two independent and interacting dimensions, the normative and the idiographic. As an organization, the school has a role to play, and there are expectations concerning that role (normative dimension). To fulfill established goals and meet the expectations of stakeholders, individuals are employed to work in the school (idiographic dimension). These individuals have personalities and needs that must be met. The challenge for the school leader is to engage in leadership behavior that results in a balance of emphasis being placed on the performance of the role requirements of the school and the expression of personal needs by individuals and groups affiliated with the school (Getzel, Lipham, & Campbell, 1968). While establishing this balance, the leader must also motivate followers to expend the necessary efforts to reach the school goals and reward them according to their accomplishments (Bass & Bruce, 1994). This is not an easy assignment; however, the leaders acquire an understanding of various situations and develops rapport with faculty members and individuals served by the school, they are likely to meet the challenges (Zuker, 1991). This theory was briefly discussed here and will be revisited in Chapter 3.

Tasks, Relationships, and Participative Leader Behavior

At the University of Michigan, researchers conducted additional studies on the behavior of leaders. The Michigan research focused on the identification of relationships among leader behavior, group processes, and measures of group performance using Likert's (1961, 1967) theory of organization. The initial and subsequent studies revealed that three types of leader behaviors differentiate leader effectiveness from ineffectiveness: task-oriented behavior, relationship-oriented behavior, and participative leadership behavior. These behaviors were described in the following manner:

1. *Task-oriented behavior.* Effective leaders focused on followers, set work standards that were high but obtainable, carefully organized tasks, identified the methods to be used in carrying them out, and closely supervised the work of followers. The task-oriented behaviors found to be important in these studies

were quite similar to the initiating structure behaviors found to be important in the Ohio State studies.

2. *Relationship-oriented behavior.* Effective leaders who displayed relationship-oriented behavior emphasized the development of interpersonal relations, while focusing on the personal needs of followers and the development of the kind of relationships that would motivate followers to set and achieve high performance goals. The relationship-oriented behaviors found to be important were similar to the consideration behaviors found to be important in the Ohio State studies.

3. *Participative leadership:* The third factor, participative leadership, involved extensive use of group supervision, rather than the separate supervision of each follower. In their experiments, the Michigan researchers placed considerable emphasis on the use of groups. Likert proposed that the role of leaders in group meetings should be to enhance follower participation in decision making, communication, cooperation, and resolving conflict. During group meetings, the leader took on the role of being directive, constructive, and supportive, allowing some degree of autonomy regarding group work. Researchers concluded that when followers participate in making decisions, they tend to reach a higher level of satisfaction and performance (Likert, 1967).

An analysis of leader behaviors described in the Michigan studies revealed that effective leaders were generally task oriented, set high performance goals, and focused on such administrative functions as planning, coordinating, and facilitating work. It was also found that effective leaders gave consideration to good interpersonal relations, allowing followers some degree of autonomy in deciding how to conduct their work and at what pace. Leaders who were relationship oriented, rather than task oriented, tended to have the most productive work group. High morale, in some instances, did not result in high productivity. However, as leaders used the kind of practices that resulted in high productivity, the results were often high morale (Likert, 1967).

From the University of Michigan studies and others that followed, a strong assumption regarding shared leadership emerged. A keen focus was placed on leadership that involves allowing followers to participate in procedures (i.e., site-based management) that influence leaders' decisions. The participatory movement emerged and is alive in today's schools in the form of power sharing, decentralization, democratic management, and shared decision making. The ISLLC Standards, Standard 4 in particular, support participatory decision making and indicate that it is essential for the school leader to respect diversity, trust people and their judgment, and collaborate with stakeholders, families, and community members, involving them in the management processes of the school.

Contemporary works also support this line of reasoning, indicating that in addition to being concerned with task completion, effective school leaders express a concern for people, as these leaders have come to realize that one cannot mandate what matters (Fullan, 1993). Consequently, leadership effectiveness lies in the balance between the desired results and the leader's ability to produce the desired results (Bowers, 1977; Covey, 1989; Halpin, 1966). To that end, principals are providing avenues for teachers, students, parents, and other stakeholders to feel a sense of personal dignity and purpose regarding their involvement with the school. Teams that foster strong interpersonal relationships are being established, and individuals are bonding to solve problems at the lowest organizational level. As a result of this involvement, individuals can experience confidence and fulfillment and remain committed to the organizational process. A review of Blake and Mouton's (1985) Managerial Grid offers additional insight into this type of leadership style, adding strength to the belief that it positively influences the behavior of followers.

Blake and Mouton

Blake and Mouton (1985) identify two dimensions of leader orientation: *concern for production (task)* and *concern for people (relationship)*. Using these two concepts, five leadership styles are portrayed on their managerial grid:

1. *Country club management*: Even if production is less than desired, the leader places major emphasis on developing good relations among colleagues and faculty members.
2. *Authority obedience*: Power, authority, and control are used to maximize production.
3. *Impoverished management*: The leader completes the minimum requirements necessary to remain employed.
4. *Organization nonmanagement*: The leader maintains the status quo and displays an attitude of go-along-to-get-along.
5. *Team management*: The leader emphasizes a high concern for both task completion and maintenance of positive interpersonal relationships (Blake & Mouton, 1985).

Of the five styles portrayed, the team management style (which allegedly is equally effective and equally applicable in all situations) is identified as the one that is superior to all other styles.

The positions of the theorists described in this section have contributed greatly to leadership principles informing practices in today's schools. With these principles in mind, we now turn to another group of theorists who advocate contingency and situational leadership behavior.

Contingency and Situational Leadership Theories

In the late 1970s, a group of theorists began to explore a set of variables believed to influence the relationship between leadership styles and follower responses to those styles. This definitive approach attempted to determine how behavior influences outcomes differently from situation to situation. These studies resulted in a series of situational theories. According to Yukl (1989), "a situational theory is more complete if it includes intervening variables to explain why the effect of behavior on outcomes varies across situations" (p. 98). In the following section, a brief description of three widely discussed situational theories is presented. In presenting these theories, the author attempts to raise the reader's awareness of the benefits that can be derived from having knowledge of followers, the situation in question, and allowing that knowledge to influence behavior.

Vroom and Yetton Normative Model

Vroom and Yetton (1973) analyzed the effects of leader behavior on decision quality and follower acceptance of the decision. They theorized that decision quality and follower acceptance are intervening variables that work collectively to affect group performance. They further theorized that aspects of the situation moderate the relationship between decision procedures and the intervening variables of quality and acceptance. These two important factors are defined in the following manner:

1. Decision acceptance is the degree of follower commitment to implement a decision effectively.
2. Decision quality refers to the objective aspect of the decision that affects group performance aside from any effects mediated by decision acceptance.

A basic assumption of the model is that participation increases decision acceptance if it is not already high. Also, the more influence followers have, the more they will be motivated to implement a decision (Yukl, 1989, p.113).

The researchers reasoned that a follower who is not consulted regarding a decision might not understand either the decision or the reason for it. As a result, followers may believe the decision to be detrimental to their interests. Also, if a decision is made in an autocratic manner, followers may resent not being involved and refuse to accept the decision. Therefore, group decision making is likely to result in greater decision acceptance.

A leader should be concerned with decision quality when a variety of alternatives exist and the alternative selected holds important consequences for the performance of the group. When the best alternative is selected, a decision is of high quality. The Vroom-Yetton model offers that follower participation will result in higher-quality decisions when followers possess relevant information and are willing to participate in the decision-making process. The model outlines five aspects on which decision effectiveness can depend in a given situation. Those aspects are listed in Table 2.2.

TABLE 2.2   Aspects on Which Decision Effectiveness Depends as Outlined in the Vroom-Yetton Model

The Vroom-Yetton model offers that decision effectiveness in a given situation can depend on:
1. The amount of relevant information the leader and the follower possess.
2. The amount of disagreement among followers regarding the desired alternative.
3. The extent to which the decision/problem is structured or unstructured and the extent to which creativity is needed.
4. The likelihood followers will cooperate, if allowed to participate.
5. The likelihood followers will be receptive to an autocratic decision.

Source: Yukl, 1989, p. 113.

The model also provides a list of seven rules that a leader can apply in conjunction with these assumptions. The rules are listed in Table 2.3.

Vroom and Jago Revision Model

A later model developed by Vroom and Jago (1988) offered revisions to the original model. The revised model denotes actions that the leader should not take, but refrains

TABLE 2.3   Rules That Guide a Leader in Determining the Type of Leader Behavior to Use in Decision Making

1. Autocratic decisions are not appropriate when followers have important relevant information lacked by the leader. In such an instance, the leader would make decisions with inadequate or incomplete data.
2. Group decisions are not appropriate if decision quality is important and followers do not share the leader's concern for task goals. Group involvement gives too much influence to possibly uncooperative or hostile individuals.
3. When the quality of a decision is important, if the leader lacks the information and expertise necessary to address the problem and the problem is unstructured, interaction should occur among people who have the relevant information to make the decision.
4. When decision acceptance is important and followers are not likely to accept an autocratic decision, then an autocratic decision should not be made by the leader. Followers may not effectively implement such a decision.
5. Autocratic decision procedures and individual consultations are not recommended when decision acceptance is important and there is likely disagreement among followers relative to the best alternative. Such action is not likely to resolve the differences that exist among followers and between followers and the leader.
6. When decision acceptance is critical and unlikely to result from an autocratic decision and if decision quality is not in question, the only appropriate procedure is a group decision. In such instances, acceptance is maximized without risking quality.
7. When decision acceptance is important but is not likely to occur from an autocratic decision and if followers share the leader's task objective, followers should be given equal partnership in the decision process; then acceptance is maximized without risking quality.

Source: Yukl, 1989.

from advising actions to take. It also contains features that enable the leader to prior-
itize the different criteria, thus reducing the feasible set used in the original model to
a single procedure. To describe a situation in the revised model, leaders are required
to differentiate between five choices (no, probably no, maybe, probably yes, yes). In
addition, the Vroom-Jago model takes into account time constraints, geographical
dispersion of followers, and amount of follower information, whereas the Vroom-
Yetton model uses only two outcome criteria in reaching the decision rule, decision
acceptance and decision quality.

The Vroom-Yetton model has been tested by a number of studies, and a number
of weaknesses have been identified. Nevertheless, of the situational leadership theories, it is probably the best supported. The model places the focus on specific aspects
of behavior, addresses meaningful intervening variables, and identifies factors about
the situation that allow the relationship between behavior and outcomes to be
moderated.

Path-Goal Theory

R. J. House (1971) theorized that the behavior of leaders has an effect on the performance and satisfaction levels of followers. House took the position that the
motivational function of the leader is to clarify the routes followers must travel to
reach work-goal attainment and remove any roadblocks or pitfalls that may exist.
He offered that this type of leader behavior improves the work performance and
increases the opportunity for followers to receive personal satisfaction en route to
work-goal attainment.

He further theorized that the type of behavior displayed by the leader to motivate
and bring satisfaction to followers is dependent on the situation, adding another dimension to the equation. Such factors as the ability and personality of followers,
characteristics of the work environment, and work group preferences contribute to
the satisfaction and motivational level of followers and must be given consideration.
Using the principles of this theory, House (1971) suggested that there are four categories of behavior from which leaders may choose, depending on the situation. The
four categories suggested by House appear in Table 2.4.

This theory holds many implications for the effective administration of a school.
Assessing the ability of the faculty and staff, understanding individual personalities,
and identifying factors in the environment that influence the transformation process
of the school can prove to be of considerable benefit to the school leader in achieving established goals.

Hersey and Blanchard's Theory of Situational Leadership

Another theory that has applications for educational leaders is Paul Hersey and
Kenneth Blanchard's (1977, 1982) situational leadership theory. These researchers

TABLE 2.4 House's Categories of Leader Behavior

▶ Supportive Leadership: A supportive leader is approachable, maintains a pleasant work environment, is considerate, and shows concern for the needs and well-being of followers.

▶ Leadership: A directive leader sets performance standards, lets followers know what is expected of them, schedules the work, and establishes specific directions.

▶ Participative Leadership: A participative leader consults with followers concerning work-related matters and takes their opinion into consideration when making decisions.

▶ Achievement-Oriented Leadership: An achievement-oriented leader stresses excellence in performance, sets goals that are challenging, and shows confidence in the ability of followers to achieve challenging performance standards.

SOURCE: House, 1971.

attempted to provide some understanding of the relationship between effective leadership styles and the maturity level of followers by adding the variable of level of maturity to Fiedler's (1967) contingency factors. They argued that to be effective, the leader must take into account the followers' maturity level. In their research, maturity level was defined as the extent to which a follower demonstrates the ability to perform a task (job maturity) and willingness to accept responsibility (motivational level) for its completion.

Using a similar design, as was the case in the Ohio State studies, Hersey and Blanchard (1977) developed a leadership effectiveness model consisting of two dimensions of leader behavior—task and relationship. The two variables were defined in the following manner:

- *Task behavior:* the extent to which the leader engages in one-way communication by explaining what is to be done, how it is to be done, and when it is to be completed
- *Relationship behavior:* the extent to which the leader engages in two-way communication to provide supportive and facilitative behaviors

Using the possible combinations of the two dimensions, leadership behaviors were aligned in four quadrants (see Figure 2.2):

- Q1: High task and low relationship
- Q2: High task and high relationship
- Q3: High relationship and low task
- Q4: Low relationship and low task

Depending on the condition of the relationships among the leader, the follower, and the situation, the leader may elect to use one of four styles: directing, coaching, supporting, or delegating. The following is the suggested leader behavior for each style:

- When leaders choose to use a directing style, they provide the follower with specific instructions regarding the completion of a task and closely supervise

FIGURE 2.2 Leadership Behaviors

Quadrant 1 High Task/Low Relationship	Quadrant 2 High Task/High Relationship
Quadrant 3 High Relationship/Low Task	Quadrant 4 Low Relationship/Low Task

the performance of the follower throughout the process (high task, low relationship).

- If leaders choose to use a coaching style, they give specific directions, closely supervise the task, explain directions, solicit suggestions, and support the progress toward task completion (high task, high relationship).
- When the supportive style is chosen, leaders facilitate and support the efforts of followers toward task accomplishment and share responsibility for decision making with them (low task, high relationship).
- Leaders may find it acceptable to turn over the responsibility for decision making and problem solving to followers. In such instances, the leader behavior is referred to as delegating (low task, low relationship).

In a continuous search for the right approach to influence the desired outcome behavior, many theorists have focused on the situation and characteristics of the situation that would be effective. However, like the theorists who probed traits and leader behavior, the results remain inconclusive; leadership effectiveness may occur for any number of reasons. The major factor to be considered in achieving success with situational leadership theory is selecting the leadership style that is appropriate for the specific situation and the individuals of the group involved (Hanson, 1996). In making that determination, the leader is wise to give consideration to the source and use of power.

Power and Authority

Power and its source are important factors in leadership effectiveness. The nature and use of power, influence, and authority often determine the effectiveness of the leader. John French (1993) presented four sources from which a leader might acquire power. Quite clearly, one source is the position held (legitimate or position power). A leader has legal power that is vested in the position, or role, in the organizational hierarchy. The reader will be able observe this type of power being used by Dr. Sterling in Scenario 1 beginning on page 32.

Another source of power is derived from the personality of the leader (referent or personality power). Many leaders are able to influence followers from the strength of their personality. This type of power is also referred to as charismatic power. President John Kennedy and Dr. Martin Luther King, Jr. are examples of leaders who possessed such power.

A third source of leader power is known as coercive power. Using this source of power, leaders control, administer punishment to followers for noncompliance with the leader's directives, or reward selected behavior. Principal Joe Clark in the movie *Lean on Me* displayed such power.

A fourth source of leader power is expert power, which is derived from the special ability and/or knowledge possessed by the leader and needed by followers. In Scenario 2 beginning on page 38, "Changing the Way We Teach Science," Principal Johnson displayed this type of power.

Regardless of the source of power, the manner in which a leader exerts power and authority determines the leader's effectiveness. Based on the manner in which it is used, followers in the organization solidify and grant additional power to the leader (by shared agreement) as they accept the leader's influence and directions. Also, individuals in a higher position solidify and grant power to the leader as they assign tasks and share responsibility. These two sources build on one another. As one gets stronger, the other is likely to get stronger. Conversely, as one gets weaker, so does the other.

Over the years, there has been extensive research into behaviors of effective leaders and the use of power. Recent literature based on structured observations of leader behavior shows that effective school leaders use a combination of legitimate and referent power (Fullan, 1993; Newstrom & Davis, 1993). They use a transformational approach to inspire followers to transcend their own interests for the good of the organization (Bass, 1985).

Bridging the Past and the Present

As noted earlier in this chapter, the theories on leadership previously presented are long-standing and have provided and continue to provide tremendous insight into practices that inform effective leadership in today's schools. From a review of Table 2.5, the reader can begin to connect these theories, behaviors, and practices to those that are suggested for leaders of today's schools.

Findings from these early studies hold many practical implications for today's school leaders. The knowledge acquired about task completion, leader behavior, and the behavior of followers when a particular leadership style is used is very informative. They underpin what current writers and researchers characterize as participatory governance, servant leadership, site-based management, collaborative leadership,

TABLE 2.5 Leadership Studies and Theories

THEORIES	AUTHORS OF STUDIES AND MODELS	MAJOR FOCUS	BASIC ASSUMPTION	IMPLICATIONS FOR LEADERSHIP IN SCHOOLS
Early Trait Theories	Ralph M. Stogdill (1948)	Identification of specific characteristics that contribute to an individual's ability to perform in a leadership role	Relative to their effectiveness, leaders have specific characteristics and/or traits that differentiate them from the people they lead	Traits of leaders do not necessarily contribute highly to their performance. An individual does not become a leader because of the possession of some combination of traits.
Recent Studies	Gary Yukl (1989)			Leaders have vigor and use persistence in their pursuit of goals. They have self-confidence, sense of personal identity, and the ability to influence others.
Behavior Theories	Ohio State Studies, Univ. of Michigan Studies, Iowa Studies, managerial grid (Blake and Mouton, 1964)	Leader patterns of activities and categories of behavior: What do leaders do? How do effective leaders behave?	Leader behavior has an influence on the performance of the group. One behavior style of leadership can be developed and applied across all situations.	
Contingency Theories	House's Path-goal Theory	The importance of situational factors on task accomplishment and psychological state of followers and processes	Leader behavior is shaped and constrained by situational factors	When the traits of the leader match the situation, the leader is likely to be effective in achieving organizational goals. There must be a good fit between the leader's personality and the favorableness of the situation that produces leader effectiveness.
	Vroom and Yetton Normative Model	Decision and procedures	Participation increases decision acceptance	Followers are likely to be receptive to decision outcomes when they are involved
Situational Theories	Hersey and Blanchard (1982)	Relationship between effective leadership styles and the maturity level of followers	Leader effectiveness depends on a match between the leader's behavior and the follower's maturity level	Leadership behavior that changes with the maturity level of the individual or group should produce leader effectiveness
Power Theories	John French and Bertrom Raven (1968, p. 259–269, cited in Cartwright & Zander), Yukl (1981), Henry Mintzberg (1983)	How effective leaders use power: source, amount, and leader use of power over followers	Leaders influence followers through power acquired from various sources. The behavior of the leader and the leader's influence on followers are determined by the source of power and its use.	A combination of referent and expert power should lead to greater follower satisfaction and performance

teaming, empowerment, learning communities, and shared governance. To complete the connection, the following section draws the reader's attention to some key approaches appearing in the literature that incorporate these concepts into contemporary practice. Because it is assumed that individuals using this text have previously addressed these approaches in an in-depth manner, they will be presented in a brief summary format.

Contemporary Approaches to School Leadership

Building on the works of early theorists, current literature (Bennis & Nanus, 1985; Covey, 1989; Fullan, 1999; Gardner, 1990; Lundy, 1986; Manz & Sims, 1989; Senge, 1990; Smith, 1997) offers that today's leaders should create a learning environment that fosters the development of a shared vision and the pursuit of that vision through various forms of participatory decision making. After spending a number of years studying leadership, Bennis (1995) suggests that leaders should concern themselves with doing the right thing, whereas managers emphasize doing things right. Doing things right includes such activities as planning, organizing, and monitoring. Individuals who are concerned with doing the right thing manage the four areas of attention, meaning, trust, and self (p. 396).

According to Bennis (1995), the leader manages attention by being highly committed to a vision that is compelling. He suggests that leaders manage meaning when they use words and symbols to make ideas seem real and tangible to others. Leaders manage trust by demonstrating that they are reliable, congruent, and consistent in their beliefs. Regarding the fourth area, which is self, leaders know their skills and use them effectively. They learn from mistakes and focus on success, rather than failure (p. 397).

A Shift in the Leadership Paradigm

The leadership paradigm is shifting; in schools today, it is no longer effective to threaten people into compliance. Our society, through its laws and practices, is emphasizing the worth of the individual. To address this shift, rather than directing and assigning, today's leaders are coaching, influencing, and assisting followers in fulfilling individual, as well as organizational, goals. Responsibility for addressing organizational challenges is shared, and leaders are identifying problems that fall within the realm of followers and empowering them to share in the decision-making process (Blanchard, Oncken, & Burrows, 1989).

Today, leadership involves working with individuals to establish teams and motivating them to focus on the vision of the school to share leadership responsibility. To accomplish this, the leader must use the power of influence that can best be displayed through the use of motivation (Gardner, 1990). The prime motivators for achievement are the inner forces that drive an individual's expectations and beliefs (Smith, 1997). Therefore, leaders must establish a climate in which relationships that influence a desire within followers to achieve school goals are built. Priorities are set, and individuals understand the mission of the school, buy into that mission, have a personal vision, feel empowered to participate in the decision-making process, and communicate the benefits that will be derived from mission attainment (Covey, 1989).

Leaders are establishing this type of productive work environment, and it is occurring because they define the roles of followers, build trust, and participate in humanistic interaction that allows them to know constituents on a personal level. They recognize the value of stakeholder involvement and consider cooperative working relationships essential to organizational effectiveness.

The Moral Dimension of Leadership

There are a number of writers who argue that the leader must be prepared to address moral dilemmas that will occur in schools (Fullan, 1999; Goodlad, 1994; Sergiovanni, 1992; Strike, Haller, & Soltis, 1988). These writers argue that objective ethical reasoning is possible and should be used by leaders of today's schools. They further argue that the leader should be a moral agent who applies the principles of equal respect and benefit maximization.

The principle of equal respect requires that human beings be regarded as having intrinsic worth and should be treated accordingly. "The principle of benefit maximization holds that whenever we are faced with a choice, the best and most just decision is the one that results in the most good or the greatest benefit for the most people" (Strike et al., 1988, p. 16). The challenges faced by leaders of today's schools appear to warrant the use of these two principles.

Moral Principals

In espousing moral leadership, leaders take into account the best interest of all children, teachers, parents, and themselves. Sergiovanni (1992) writes that leaders have a moral responsibility to make people feel welcome, wanted, and a part of the school with which they are affiliated. Individuals in schools have a common purpose, a shared vision, and seek mutual goals. People are drawn to leaders who first have a vision to serve others and a willingness, when necessary, to experience personal sacrifices in order to promote their ideas (Greenleaf, 1977). They reflect what Sergiovanni describes as the heart, head, and hand of leadership.

In adhering to the concepts of moral leadership, the leader must assist individuals in understanding and adjusting to the environment of the school. Ineffective patterns of behaviors that inhibit progress must be replaced by behaviors that aid in the process of managing change, and the leader's behavior must seek the delicate balance between completing organizational tasks and building relationships with stakeholders. Above all, it is the leader's beliefs about schools, teachers, children, parents, and the community that form the foundation upon which leadership for school improvement is based. Constructs characterizing the disposition of effective leadership appearing most frequently in the literature are listed in Table 2.6. Readers might review this list to identify those that hold meaning for them. The moral aspect of leader behavior will be explored in greater depth in later chapters.

Leadership for Today's Schools

In today's schools, the principal is being asked to be the instructional leader. This chapter has outlined concepts the prospective or practicing leader can use to develop a style that will enhance quality instructional programs. From a rational perspective, a leader must find the balance between task and relationship, power and influence, reward and punishment, and autocratic and participatory decision making. Fear must be removed from the workplace, and the challenges of the school must be addressed from within (Barth, 1990; Ryan & Oestreich, 1991). Teachers will necessarily have to share the vision of the school, conduct inquiries into the teaching and learning process, take risks, explore new methods of doing things, and expand their role outside of the classroom to include activities and programs that affect the entire school (Conley, 1997). This means redistributing power, establishing effective committee structures, and engaging in comprehensive planning.

In addition to the concept of moral leadership and the other leadership approaches mentioned, there are a number of other contemporary theories and postulates that offer explanations concerning the qualities and attributes of effective leaders, a list that is much too extensive to include in a text of this nature. *Practicing*

TABLE 2.6 Leadership Constructs That Comprise the Disposition of Effective Leaders

compassion	integrity	trust	communication
persuasion	character	knowledge	tact
insight	fortitude	vision	diplomacy
sensitivity	passion	management	predictability
respect	commitment	dignity	courage
creativity	intelligence	consistency	decisiveness
rapport	ethics	fairness	equity
credibility	charisma	diversity	honesty
organization	tenacity	planning	openness
morality	humility	timeliness	adaptability
support	imagination	accountability	
reasoning	accuracy	judgment	
reliability	influence	logic	

SOURCE: Compiled from various writings and studies on leadership

the Art of Leadership: A Problem-based Approach to Implementing the ISLLC Standards adopts the view that a leader is an individual who has the capacity to influence others to use their skills and expertise to move the organization toward established goals. In this process, the leader must assist individuals in understanding and adjusting to the environment of the organization. Ineffective patterns of behaviors that inhibit progress must be replaced by behaviors that aid in the process of managing change, and the delicate balance between task and relationship must be achieved.

The scenarios that follow will allow readers an opportunity to explore their disposition and apply some of the constructs, as well as the theoretical principles previously discussed. Supporting variables, which appear in Chapter 3, help to further establish a foundation for selected constructs and other organizational influences that affect leadership.

The Scenarios

In Scenario 1, the leader makes several adjustments in her style to fit changes in faculty attitude. Adult motivation, the effects of school culture and climate, and leadership behaviors that are effective in working cooperatively with a faculty entrenched in tradition are exhibited. Also, the scenario illustrates what can happen if the leader gets too far ahead of followers.

In Scenario 2, Principal Johnson makes a major change in the science program and acquires the cooperation of the entire faculty. The leadership style and strategies she uses are visionary and reflective of those advocated by Standard 1.

As a result of working through these scenarios, the reader will have an opportunity to compare and contrast two different leadership styles and analyze the indicators of ISLLC Standards 1, 2, and 3 being used in practical situations.

SCENARIO 1
THE NEW PRINCIPAL AT FROST

STANDARD 1

A school administrator is an educational leader who promotes the success of all students by facilitating the development, articulation, implementation, and stewardship of a vision of learning that is shared and supported by the school community.

STANDARD 2

A school administrator is an educational leader who promotes the success of all students by advocating, nurturing, and sustaining a school culture and instructional program conducive to student learning and staff professional growth.

STANDARD 3

A school administrator is an educational leader who promotes the success of all students by ensuring management of the organization, operations, and resources for a safe, efficient, and effective learning environment.

Frost Elementary School, with a population of 1,100 students, prekindergarten through sixth grade, is located in the inner city of a large southern, metropolitan area. The ethnic/socioeconomic makeup of the school is African-American and poor. The faculty composition is 45% Caucasian and 55% African-American. Although the school district has been desegregated for a number of years, Frost's enrollment remains totally African-American.

Scores on achievement tests, which are used to measure student progress and serve as a means of comparison with students in other parts of the city and state, are at an all-time low. They have been some of the lowest scores in the district for a number of years. Mr. Shaw, who served as principal of the school for 15 years, was considered by most faculty members to be an individual who loved children and had their best interests at heart. He was always in the community conveying to parents his interest in the children, the school, and the community. Mr. Shaw was quite knowledgeable and worked diligently with the faculty to enhance the school's instructional program. However, in spite of his efforts, achievement scores remained low and incidents of discipline high. During the last 5 years of his tenure, the average daily attendance of students fluctuated between 84 and 86%. Nevertheless, his traditional instructional program was highly supported by the faculty and staff. In addition, the school was several thousand dollars in debt, and fund-raising was virtually nonexistent.

With the appointment of a new superintendent and a push for educational reform and restructuring, Mr. Shaw retired, and Dr. Sterling was appointed principal. Upon her appointment, she received directions to improve student achievement at Frost using some form of site-based management. During the first week of her assignment, she sent the following memorandum to the faculty and staff:

Frost Elementary School
MEMORANDUM TO FACULTY AND STAFF

From: Dr. Patricia Sterling, Principal
Re: Task Force for School Improvement
Date: August 21, 2003

I would like to request volunteers to serve on a task force to develop a plan of action to bring about improvements in the instructional program here at Frost. One of the responsibilities of the task force will be to survey the entire faculty and staff for the purpose of ascertaining their ideas, suggestions, and recommendations for program improvements. The work of the task force will be very time consuming; however, the results should propel us into the 21st century and beyond.

Please notify my secretary by September 1, 2003, if you are available to serve. Thank you for your cooperation in this matter.

On September 1, Dr. Sterling asked her secretary for the list of volunteers; there were no responses. The word on the grapevine was, "The new principal has considerable work in mind for the faculty, and the faculty is already totally consumed with just maintaining discipline."

SELECTING THE TASK FORCE

Having received no volunteers, the principal invited (selected) one teacher from each grade level to serve on the task force. The individuals selected were not thrilled about being drafted; however, they accepted the principal's invitation and attended the first meeting on September 5, 2003. All subsequent meetings were held once a week (between Principal Sterling and the task force) until the plan was ready for partial implementation on Oct 2, 2003.

Developing the Plan

The task force met for approximately 40 hours developing the plan. Having read Bradley's *Total Quality Management for Schools,* the principal introduced the task force to the Affinity, Fishbone, and Pareto designs. They used the Affinity Diagram to brainstorm and define the issues that needed to be addressed. The Affinity Diagram allowed her to organize output from the brainstorming session of the task force. Using this design, all of the information could be consolidated. The Fishbone Diagram (cause and effect) was used to get an overall picture of how to move from current reality to the established goals. Using this design, elements that may have been contributing to the problem and their cause-and-effect relationships could be identified. The Pareto Diagram (a simple bar chart) was utilized to identify the pros and cons of various challenging school issues (ranking the problems separating the major ones from the trivial ones) and to ensure that the programs selected for implementation would be effective. Reports were provided to the faculty and staff who, in turn, provided feedback to the task force on their work. Of the issues identified, the most pressing was student discipline. Thus, the task force made the recommendation to the principal that improving schoolwide discipline should be the first issue addressed. Principal Sterling accepted the recommendation, and discipline became the order of the day.

Implementing the Plan

Realizing that the faculty would need professional development to effectively implement new programs in the area of discipline, Principal Sterling again turned to the task force for an assessment of the professional development program needs of the faculty. By a large majority, the faculty voted to be trained in various methods of assertive discipline, discipline with dignity, and discipline techniques for today's children. In addition, the faculty requested that Principal Sterling formally develop a schoolwide discipline plan and schedule workshops during faculty meetings so teachers could begin to implement various techniques in their classrooms. They also requested that Dr. Sterling actively recruit men teachers to provide students with male role models. In concluding their work, the task force clearly stated, "For the new programs to be successful, it will be necessary for all faculty and staff to be involved; there can be no exceptions."

In subsequent meetings with the task force, a decision was reached to open the lines of communication between the home and the school so that parents would not feel isolated from the process. Principal Sterling announced an open-door policy and instituted school conferences to inform parents about appropriate and inappropriate behaviors. Communication to homes included phone calls, notes from teachers, and monthly informational calendars. An automated phone system was installed to keep parents informed of all school activities and events.

Results of the Plan

During the first year, discipline was hard and fast; 80 out-of-school suspensions were issued to students. Parents were extremely upset and stated they never had this problem with the previous principal. However, the administration, faculty, and staff held firm. Parent workshops were conducted on parenting skills and the fair, firm, and consistent policies used by the administration, faculty, and staff. The following year, out-of-school suspensions dropped to 10. Discipline was under control, and the faculty was able to focus on the instructional program.

After improvement in discipline began to occur, Principal Sterling turned to the second item on the list generated by the faculty: "curriculum, instruction, and evaluation." Again, she asked for individuals to serve on a committee, and this time the response was quite different; 16 individuals volunteered to serve. In her businesslike manner, Principal Sterling accepted all 16, and the committee went to work. After 3 weeks of discussion, the committee determined that the school had to change and change drastically. Student regression (failure to retain information from the previous year) over the summer nullified any achievement gains the students had made the previous year. Year-round education was determined to be the educational direction for the school to pursue.

Remaining on the Fast Track

To continue to make improvements at Frost, subcommittees were formed for various initiatives; frequent fund-raising events were held; teachers were in the community visiting with parents, and instructional planning meetings were continuous. With the planning and implementation of year-round education, Frost became the talk of the educational community. Professors from the local university took an interest in the school and often asked to be allowed to help implement programs. Visitors from other schools in the city, state, and nation frequented the school, and Principal Sterling received and accepted invitations to participate in a variety of local, state, and national conferences. At the end of Principal Sterling's fourth year, discipline had improved, the year-round school concept had been implemented, and most of the faculty were supporting the site-based management concept. However, teacher turnover was above 10%. Some of the turnover appeared to be initiated by the principal, and some was teacher initiated.

REFLECTIVE THINKING

The ISLLC Standards

1: Principles of developing strategic plans are used; communication, consensus-building, and negotiation skills are effectively utilized, and there is continuous school improvement.
2: Applied motivational theories are used; knowledge of the change process for systems, organizations, and individuals is evident; leader behavior indicates that student learning

is the fundamental purpose of schooling, and the culture of the school is recognized as a factor in the change process.

5: The ideal of the common good is illustrated; the interest of the principal is subordinated for the good of the school community; the principal uses her office constructively and productively in the service of all students and their families, and a caring school community is developed.

Reflective Questions and Scenario Analysis

1. How would you describe Dr. Sterling's vision for Frost, and how would you evaluate her effectiveness in articulating that vision to the faculty?
2. To what extent did Dr. Sterling's leadership traits and characteristics align with the requirements of Standards 1 and 2?
3. What specific traits and characteristics can you identify as being most beneficial in her plight to enhance instruction at Frost?
4. Upon entering Frost as principal, giving consideration to the requirements of Standard 1, what type of leader behavior would you have used? How would you justify the use of that behavior?
5. As principal, if you wanted to maximize ownership and accountability for the attainment of school improvement, would you reword the initial memo? If so, how would it read?
6. Was Dr. Sterling within her rights to assign members of the faculty to the task force? Is that not a display of authoritarian behavior, and is that kind of behavior acceptable in today's schools?

ADDRESSING THE CRITICAL ISSUES

In practicing the art of leadership at Frost Elementary School, the critical issues are (a) the type of leadership style used by the principal, (b) the maturity and readiness level of the faculty, and (c) the principal's approach to decision making.

Leadership Style of Principal Sterling

Principal Sterling entered Frost and attempted to establish a positive and supportive relationship with the faculty. She invited them to become a part of a task force that was being developed to address the needs and challenges of the faculty, staff, students, and community. However, the faculty was unresponsive. In order to fulfill the directive of the superintendent, she altered her style to one that was directive. She drafted faculty members to serve on the task force, provided them with specific directions, and closely supervised their performance. After achieving a degree of success and acquiring the confidence, trust, and support of the faculty, she changed her style again, this time to one of a participative nature.

Hersey and Blanchard (1982) would describe Dr. Sterling's behavior as situational; she took into account the maturity level of the faculty and adjusted her behavior to their level of maturity. As the maturity and motivation levels of the faculty changed, she changed her leadership behavior accordingly.

Faculty Maturity Level

The major factor to be considered in achieving success with situational leadership is selecting the leadership style that is appropriate for the situation and the individuals of the group involved (Hanson, 1996). Entering a school as principal, as was the case with Dr. Sterling, assessment of the faculty's maturity level is critical. Without such an assessment, task completion becomes extremely difficult.

Standard 1 stipulates that a school leader should facilitate processes and engage in activities that ensure the development and implementation of a plan that clearly articulates objectives and strategies to achieve the vision and goals. In order to meet this standard, the leader needs to have knowledge of what is to be accomplished (the situation) and the area of expertise (maturity level) of individual faculty members. With this information, individuals can be assigned to select tasks. When the leader assesses the ability of the faculty and staff, understands individual personalities, and identifies environmental factors that influence the teaching and learning process, the leader is implementing the principles of House's path-goal theory, and thus the potential of achieving the desired goals is enhanced.

Principal Sterling followed the principles of this theory, and her behavior had a positive effect on the performance and satisfaction level of the faculty. She took the necessary action to motivate the faculty, clarifying tasks and removing roadblocks to goal attainment.

Readiness Level of the Faculty

When Principal Sterling arrived at Frost, the faculty was not ready to actively participate in a major change process. A critical factor to be considered prior to implementing a major reform effort is characteristics of the work environment. The work environment often will suggest the faculty's readiness level for change (Conley, 1997).

The Frost faculty had just experienced the loss of a very supportive principal. Although (under his leadership) the conditions of the school were less than favorable, the faculty had trust and confidence in him. To say the least, he was a known entity. Principal Sterling was an unknown entity. A new principal, under the best of circumstances, is likely to raise the anxiety level of the faculty, making relationship building necessary. When entering a new assignment, it is beneficial for the leader to spend time acquiring an understanding of the situation and building relationships. Building relationships with faculty members, individually and collectively, enhances the probability of the leader achieving a match between the skills and attributes of the faculty and tasks to be completed.

Approach to Decision Making

Initially, Principal Sterling's decision to implement a process that would address the problematic situation existing at Frost was autocratic. Her decision may have been good, but it was not accepted by the faculty, which was demonstrated by their lack of response to her first memorandum. The lack of volunteers from the faculty was possibly precipitated by their lack of understanding and involvement. To her credit, she initiated structure, appointed a task force, gave the task force specific directions, and established lines of communication with the faculty, the task force, and her office. She also received reports from the task force, which enabled her to evaluate their work.

Decision Acceptance

At Frost, acceptance of the change process was enhanced when members of the faculty became actively involved in the change process. It was further enhanced (faculty participation increased) when the principal accepted their ideas and put them into practice. By accepting the initial request of the task force, Dr. Sterling demonstrated confidence in the faculty's ability, respect for their judgment, support for their recommendations, and interest in their welfare.

From the outset, Principal Sterling was highly structured in her approach to making changes at Frost. However, she was also highly considerate of the faculty, their expertise, and the contributions that they could make to the improvement process. Her behavior generated a level of satisfaction among the faculty. Considering the faculty's receptivity to the discipline plan and their willingness to serve on the second task force, her actions were successful. Principals are often successful when using an approach that is high in structure and high in consideration (Hoy & Miskel, 1991). To fully appreciate what occurred at Frost and to underscore the importance of the type of leader behavior necessary to achieve decision acceptance, it is suggested that the reader review the disposition indicators of Standard 5.

SCENARIO 2
CHANGING THE WAY WE TEACH SCIENCE

STANDARD 1

A school administrator is an educational leader who promotes the success of all students by facilitating the development, articulation, implementation, and stewardship of a vision of learning that is shared and supported by the school community.

At the first faculty meeting of the school year, Principal Shirley Johnson informed her faculty that in order to prepare the students for the science competency test that would be given at the end of the next school year, consideration should be given to using a different process of teaching science. She suggested using a hands-on, inquiry-based method. Principal Johnson was very persuasive in communicating a need for this type of curriculum. She stated that her goal was to assist all students at Walton Elementary in becoming scientifically literate. She praised the faculty on a job well done in implementing manipulatives into the mathematics curriculum over the past two years and spoke of the dedication and strengths of the Walton faculty. Principal Johnson informed the faculty that moving toward the new science goal would give Walton the opportunity to be in the forefront of changes in science education. In addition, she advised, "The concerns you have expressed in the past will be addressed, and your frequently mentioned desires regarding our teaching and learning process will be fulfilled." She also advised that teachers would be provided professional development, and the district would pay for substitutes.

After sharing her vision of Walton's future in becoming a leader in the new methods of teaching science, she asked the faculty for their ideas on how to make the change work.

Comments and questions from the faculty were addressed in detail. Principal Johnson listened to all the concerns and jotted them down on chart paper. Faculty members were given the opportunity to assist in addressing the concerns.

Committees of teachers were formed to discuss the concept and develop instructional plans and implementation strategies. Having gained insight into the readiness level of the faculty to implement the new science program, a date (two weeks later) was set for the committees to report, share ideas, and form advisory groups on science topics. Many members of the faculty were enthusiastic about the concept, but not all. Some voiced that it could not be done in a year. As the meeting ended, Principal Johnson carefully noted members of the faculty who appeared uncomfortable with the new concept.

The next day, Principal Johnson invited those teachers into her office individually. After listening to the individual concerns, she gave each teacher several articles to read and assigned each a specific task that complemented that teacher's strengths. Then, she invited members of the faculty who were already teaching science using the hands-on approach into her office and asked them for their assistance in developing the concept.

During the next two weeks, Principal Johnson visited classrooms and left numerous positive comments. She put short articles and actual lessons that she had found to be helpful to teachers on managing change in their mailboxes. At the end of the two-week period, she waited anxiously to see what the committees would report.

Two weeks later, the second faculty meeting of the year was convened at 2:30 p.m. The agenda for the meeting had been disseminated several days earlier, and the New Science Curriculum was the only item on the agenda. When Principal Johnson entered the room, she could feel the excitement. Every member of the faculty was present, and chairs of committees had their reports ready to be distributed. Teachers were chatting among themselves, and she could tell that they were raising questions and discussing possibilities about the new program in science. Before calling the meeting to order, Principal Johnson walked around the room politely speaking to individuals and making comments about various school and personal activities. After a short period, having greeted everyone, she called the meeting to order.

In her opening remarks, she thanked everyone for the cooperation she had received over the past two weeks, carefully noting that all individuals had cooperated by participating in meetings and sharing their expertise and experience in the area of science. She then asked for reports from the various committees.

Committee chairs conveyed their reports with enthusiasm and excitement. One report contained information and recommendations about the needs in the internal environment; another contained information about the possibility of establishing partnerships in the external environment, and still another addressed the professional development needs of the faculty. In every instance, it was evident that each committee had met, discussed the key issues, and prepared recommendations. After hearing all the reports, in a very charismatic manner, Principal Johnson advised the faculty that she would take the lead in categorizing the recommendations, seeking the required approvals, acquiring the necessary financial resources, and developing a time-task calendar for the design of the new program. However, she advised, "I would like members of the faculty to form a task force to work with me."

The meeting ended with members of the faculty expressing a desire to serve on the task force.

REFLECTIVE THINKING

The ISLLC Standards

1: A school vision of high standards of learning is shared; action is taken to ensure that students have the knowledge, skills, and values needed to become successful adults, and the work required for high levels of personal and organizational performance is identified.

3: People and their judgments are trusted, risk is taken to improve the school, and stakeholders are involved in management processes.

Reflective Questions and Scenario Analysis

1. How would you characterize the approach Principal Johnson used in presenting her vision to the faculty? What particular leadership behaviors appeared to be most beneficial in fostering her success?

2. How would you describe Principal Johnson's source of power? Cite passages from the scenario to support your response.

3. Describe the actions taken by Principal Johnson to identify, clarify, and address barriers that would prevent her from achieving her vision?

4. Based on your knowledge of faculty members' resistance to change and the need for positive interpersonal relations between school leaders and their faculty, how would you characterize the factors that contributed to the lack of faculty resistance experienced by Principal Johnson? Explain your response.

ADDRESSING THE CRITICAL ISSUES

One of the pivotal leadership activities of a principal is to engage constantly in the dynamic process of sharing with the faculty, staff, students, parents, and the community-at-large a vision of things to come (Owens, 1991) and getting them to buy into that vision through genuine acts of caring. Leaders who are effective are results oriented and can persuade others to share their vision in a manner that causes them to commit their resources and energies to making that vision a reality (Nanus, 1992). An example of this type of leadership is observable in the behavior of Principal Johnson.

In practicing the art of leadership at Walton Elementary School, the critical issues are (a) the leadership characteristics of the principal, (b) the approach used to articulate a vision of learning, and (c) the principal's approach to motivating faculty commitment.

The Leadership Characteristics of Principal Johnson

Principal Johnson is a highly skilled, proactive principal and an example of an educational leader who adheres to ISLLC Standard 1. Her behavior exhibited concern for production and people. She had a keen vision of the future in science education, and she used a proactive model in presenting that vision to the faculty. Having carefully planned her presentation, Principal Johnson presented it to the faculty and remained flexible, diagnosing the needs of the faculty at each phase of the process. The lines of communication were always open, generating a high comfort level between her and the faculty. Her knowledge of the subject area and her personal skills of informing, influencing, and listening enhanced her presentation.

Articulating a Vision

In presenting her vision to the faculty and facilitating its implementation, Principal Johnson used what Lethwood (1992) classifies as a transformational approach. She conveyed high performance expectations, provided appropriate models, and demonstrated knowledge of the new project and its effectiveness. A principal can have a vision of what is necessary for students to reach the established standards. However, to be effectively implemented, the faculty, staff, students, parents, and community-at-large must share that vision. "In short, for leadership to succeed, it needs both form and function, both process and purpose, and that all starts with a clearly articulated vision of the future of the organization" (Nanus, 1992, p. 15).

Sharing the Vision

Perhaps you have not given consideration to the approach you would utilize to facilitate the development, articulation, implementation, and stewardship of a vision of learning that would be shared and supported by a school community. If this is the case, you should begin thinking of the approach you would use and the influence that approach would have on your followers.

The type of behavior exhibited by Principal Johnson embraces House's Path-Goal Theory (House, 1971). She influenced the Walton faculty to accept and assist in the achievement of her vision by removing all roadblocks. She let her faculty know what was to be done, conveyed the benefits they would receive, communicated expectations, and then scheduled and coordinated the work. These are characteristic of directive leadership behavior (House, 1971). This is not to suggest that directive behavior is the most appropriate to use in articulating and implementing a vision, but rather, that there are times when a visionary principal might be directive in presenting ideas to the faculty.

Principal Johnson's situation at Walton was different from that of Dr. Sterling at Frost. Therefore, the leadership approach used was different. Principal Johnson's behavior motivated and brought satisfaction to followers. She gave consideration to the ability and personality of faculty members, characteristics of the work environment, and work group preferences. The behavior of Principal Johnson proved to be of considerable benefit to her success in facilitating the development, articulation, and implementation of a vision for the school.

Motivating the Walton Faculty

Initially, some members of the Walton faculty were reluctant to take on the new approach to teaching science. The question to be addressed is: How does a leader motivate faculty members to share a vision and assume new roles, responsibilities, and challenges? For present purposes, in responding to this concern, the leader must give consideration to the change process for systems, organizations, and individuals (Standard 2) and use the principles of "Expectancy Theory" to inform that process.

Expectancy theory advises that the motivational level of a school faculty member will depend on the individual's mental expectations about his or her ability to (a) successfully complete a task assigned by the principal, (b) achieve the desired level of performance, and (c) receive a reward as a result of completing that task (Vroom, 1969). Members of a faculty are likely to work harder to complete a task if the reward they anticipate is one that is valued highly, and they believe that putting forth the effort will produce the desired level of performance. However, if faculty members think they are not likely to succeed in earning that reward because of the lack of the ability to complete the task, the time frame not being adequate to the task, or the reward not being meaningful, the motivation to try is not likely to be as great. The theory advocates a connection between the effort of the individual, the possibility of a high level of performance, and the desirability of the reward resulting from a task completed at a highly successful level (Vroom, 1969).

To develop a deeper understanding of the principles of this theory and how the behavior of a leader can motivate an unresponsive school faculty to accept new responsibility, the reader might compare and contrast the various reactions of faculty members to the requests made by the principals of Frost and Walton. In each instance, faculty members responded positively when the assignment or request was within their realm of expertise; they were comfortable with the time frame, and the reward was meaningful. When these circumstances were not evidenced, faculty motivation was not as high.

CHAPTER SUMMARY

In an attempt to establish a theoretical framework for the understanding of leadership over the past century, hundreds of studies have been conducted. Although none of these studies provided a clear definition of leadership or offered a definitive destination between leaders and nonleaders, several have deepened our understanding of the concept.

From the study of leadership traits, we understand that no one specific set of traits can be used to single out leaders from nonleaders. Also, we came to the realization that the top-down perspective of leadership is not a popular one. Equally important, although there is no single set of traits that can be used to identify effective leaders, we accept the premise that there are some leadership traits that are well received by followers. However, the benefit of any trait appears to be its positive influence on followers.

Other studies on leadership conducted at the University of Iowa, The Ohio State University, and the University of Michigan suggest that leaders tend to be most successful when they exhibit democratic principles, initiate structure, are considerate of followers, and allow them to participate in the decision-making process when appropriate. Building on the foundation laid by these studies, other writers and researchers have identified various cause-and-effect relationships and variables that influence leader behavior. Taken collectively, these studies offer two basic elements concerning effective leadership—concern for people and concern for task completion. Finding the delicate balance between these two elements appears to be the leadership challenge.

Also, studies have addressed power and its use. Four major types of power have been identified: legitimate, referent, reward, and expert (French, 1993). Though power is often misunderstood and misused, it is a necessary variable in the mix of influencing and persuading individuals to achieve organizational goals. In using power, a combination of legitimate and referent powers has proven to be most effective (Fullan, 1993).

Finally, contemporary researchers and writers offer that leaders should create learning communities (Barth, 1990; Fullan, 1999; Goodlad, 1994; Senge, 1990; Sergiovanni, 1992). In such communities, they proffer that individuals should have a shared vision and work collaboratively to acquire that vision. The process should be sensitive to the need for open lines of communication, diversity in the workplace, the values of all individuals, and the need to establish trusting relationships. Writers and researchers who advocate such a process argue that objective ethical reasoning is possible and should be used by leaders of today's schools.

In searching for the characteristics of the most effective leaders of today's schools, one might, in summary, turn to Bennis (1995), who offers that leaders should have four competencies—management of meaning, trust, attention, and self. They can then use these competencies to ensure that the organization has purpose and structure, offering a sufficient amount of freedom to followers. It is this combination that allows people to experience success (Sergiovanni, 1984).

MOVING INTO PRACTICE

Review the scenarios in Chapter 2. Using the pros and cons of the various situations, identify several approaches that you would use to address the following school-related issues. Project yourself into the role of the principal and take care to formulate a rationale for your selected behavior.

◆ Conduct a comparative analysis of the behavior of Principal Sterling and Principal Johnson and identify similarities and differences. Cite instances where the differences are justified.

◆ You have served as principal of a large urban high school for 8 months. The superintendent advised you when you accepted the job that he expected you to implement a form of block scheduling during your first year. The daily challenges of administering the school have not allowed you to make much progress toward implementing the concept. However, the superintendent is expecting a status report during your annual review, which will occur in 4 months. Describe your actions over the next 4 months.

◆ Write a description of your leadership style, taking care to make sure it reflects your belief system. From this description, identify various characteristics contained therein and provide a supportive rationale for each.

◆ Devise a set of strategies for use in organizing an effective school program.

◆ Make a list of 10 school situations in which you would delegate the responsibility of completing a task to faculty, staff, or others.

◆ Identify the steps you would use to convince a faculty to accept one of your innovative ideas.

◆ Outline a process you would use to align the strengths of a prospective faculty member with school program needs.

ACQUIRING AN UNDERSTANDING OF SELF

◆ What are three strengths that you have and can use effectively at all times?

◆ What is the philosophical basis for your style of leadership, and how was it formulated?

◆ Draw a line down the center of a sheet of paper. On one side of the sheet identify challenges that you experience in addressing leadership issues. On the other side, identify the ISLLC Standards Indicators that would be most beneficial in reducing each challenge.

DEEPENING YOUR UNDERSTANDING

Now that you have read this chapter, visit the Companion Website for this book at **www.prenhall.com/green** *and take the Self-Assessment Inventory for this chapter.*

Completing this inventory will give you an indication of how familiar you are with the ISLLC standards knowledge indicators that relate to this chapter.

SUGGESTED READINGS

Bass, B. M. (1998). *Transformational leadership: Industrial, military, and educational impact.* Mahwah, NJ: Lawrence Erlbaum.

Daft, R. L. (1999). *Theory and practices.* Ft. Worth, TX: Harcourt Brace.

Manz, C. C., & Sims, H. P. (2001). Superleadership: Beyond myth of heroic leadership. In J. Osland, D. Kolb, & I. Rubin (Eds.), *The organizational behavior reader* (7th ed., Rev. pp. 383–384). Upper Saddle River, NJ: Prentice Hall.

Marion, R. (2002). Leadership in education: Organizational theory for the practitioner. Upper Saddle River, NJ: Prentice Hall.

McEwan, E. K. (2003). Ten traits of highly effective principals: From good to great perform-ance. Thousand Oaks, CA: Corwin Press.

Ramsey, R. D. (2003). School leadership from A to Z: Practical lessons from successful schools and businesses. Thousand Oaks, CA: Corwin Press.

Sergiovanni, T. J. (2000). Leadership as stewardship. In *The Jossey-Bass reader on educational leadership*. San Francisco: Jossey-Bass.

AVAILABLE POWERPOINT PRESENTATIONS

 After completing this chapter, log on to the Companion Website for this book at **www.prenhall.com/green** *and click on the PowerPoint module.*

- Leadership Defined
- Condition Requisites for Leadership
- The Nature of Leadership Part I
- The Nature of Leadership Part II
- The Social System

WEBSITES

Southwest Educational Development Laboratory: Leadership Characteristics that Facilitate School Change
http://www.sedl.org/change/leadership/history.html

Classical Leadership
http://www.infed.org/leadership/traditional_leadership.htm

Principal Leadership Resources
http://www.bestpracticescenter.org/publ/wtel-res.html

PRACTICE ISLLC EXAMS

 After reading this chapter, log on the Companion Website for this book at **www.prenhall.com/green** *to take the practice ISLLC exams.*

REFERENCES

Barth, R. S. (1990). *Improving school from within: Teachers, parents, and principals can make the dif-ference*. San Francisco: Jossey-Bass.

Bass, B. M. (1985). *Leadership and performance beyond expectations*. New York: Free Press.

Bass, B. M. (1998). *Transformational leadership: Industrial, military, and educational impact*. Mah-wah, NJ: Lawrence Erlbaum.

Bass, B., & Bruce, J. (1994). *Improving organizational effectiveness through transformational leader-ship*. Thousand Oaks, CA: Sage.

Bennis, W. (1995). The 4 competencies of leadership. In D. Kolb, J. S. Osland, & I. M. Rubin (Eds.), *The organizational behavior reader* (pp. 395–401). Upper Saddle River, NJ: Prentice Hall.

Bennis, W., & Biederman, P. (1997). *Organizing genius*. Reading, MA: Addison Wesley Longman.

Bennis, W., & Nanus, B. (1985). *Leaders: The strategies for taking charge*. New York: Harper & Row.

Blake, R. R., & Mouton, J. S. (1985). *The managerial grid III*. Houston, TX: Gulf.

Blanchard, K., Oncken, W., & Burrows, H. (1989). *The one minute manager meets the monkey*. New York: William Morrow.

Bowers, D. G. (1977). *Systems of organization: Management of human resources*. Ann Arbor: University of Michigan Press.

Cartwright, D. & Zander, A. (1968). *Group dynamics: Research and Theory* (3rd ed.). New York: Harper & Row.

Conley, D. T. (1997). *Roadmap to restructuring: Charting the course of change in American education*. Eugene: University of Oregon (ERIC Clearinghouse on Educational Management).

Covey, S. R. (1989). *The 7 habits of highly effective people*. New York: Simon & Schuster.

Deal, T. E., & Peterson, K. D. (1998). How leaders influence the culture of schools. *Educational Leadership 56*(1) (Sept. '98), 28–30.

Fiedler, F. E. (1967). *A theory of leadership effectiveness*. New York: McGraw-Hill.

French, J. R. (1993). *A formal theory of social power*. New York: Irvington.

French & Reven, B. (1968). *The bases of social power*. chapter 20, pp. 259–269 as cited in Group Dynamics: Research and Theory, 3rd. ed., edited by D. Cartwright and A. Zander, NY: Harper and Row.

Fullan, M. G. (1993). *Change forces*. New York: Falmer.

Fullan, M. G. (1999). *Change forces: The sequel*. New York: Falmer.

Gardner, J. W. (1990). *On leadership*. New York: Free Press.

Getzel, J. W., & Guba, E. G. (1957). Social behavior and the administrative process. *School Review, 65*, 423–441.

Getzel, J. W., Lipham, J. M., & Campbell, R. F. (1968). *Educational administration as a social process*. New York: Harper & Row.

Gibb, C. A. (1954). Leadership. In G. Lindzey (Ed.) *Hand-book of social psychology*, Vol. II (pp. 877–920) Reading, MA: Addison-Wesley.

Goodlad, J. I. (1994). *Educational renewal: Better teachers, better schools*. San Francisco: Jossey-Bass.

Greenleaf, R. K. (1977). *Servant leadership: A journey into the nature of legitimate power and greatness*. New York: Paulist Press.

Halpin, A. W. (1966). *Theory and research in administration*. New York: Macmillan.

Hanson, M. E. (1996). *Educational administration and organization behavior* (4th ed.). Needham Heights, MA: Allyn & Bacon.

Hersey, P., & Blanchard, K. H. (1977). *Management of organizational behavior: Utilizing human resources* (3rd ed.). Upper Saddle River, NJ: Prentice Hall.

Hersey, P., & Blanchard, K. H. (1982). *Management of organizational behavior: Utilizing human resources* (4th ed.). Upper Saddle River, NJ: Prentice Hall.

House, R. J. (1971). A path-goal theory of leader effectiveness. *Administrative Science Quarterly, 16*, 331–333.

Hoy, W. K., & Miskel, C. G. (1991). *Educational administration: Theory, research and practice* (4th ed.). New York: McGraw-Hill.

Kirkpatrick, S. A., & Locke, E. A. (1991) Leadership: Do traits matter? *Academy of Management Executive, May*, 48–60.

Lewin, K., Lippitt, R., & White, R. K. (1939). Patterns of aggressive behavior in experimentally created "social climates." *Journal of Science Psychology, 10*, 271–299.

Likert, R. (1961). *New patterns of management.* New York: McGraw-Hill.

Likert, R. (1967). *The human organization: Its management and value.* New York: McGraw-Hill.

Lundy, J. L. (1986). *Lead, follow, or get out of the way.* New York: Berkley.

Lunenburg, F. C., & Ornstein, A. C. (1996). *Educational administration: Concepts and practices* (2nd ed.). Belmont, CA: Wadsworth.

Manz, C. C., & Sims, H. P., Jr. (1989). *Superleadership.* New York: Berkley.

Mintzberg, H. (1983). *The structuring of organizations.* Upper Saddle River, NJ: Prentice Hall.

Nanus, B. (1992). *Visionary leadership: creating a compelling sense of direction for your organization.* San Francisco: Jossey-Bass.

Newstrom, J. W., & Davis, K. (1993). *Organizational behavior: Human behavior at work* (9th ed.). New York: McGraw-Hill.

Owens, R. G. (1991). *Organizational behavior in education.* Boston: Allyn & Bacon.

Ryan, K. D., & Oestreich, D. K. (1991). *Driving fear out of the workplace: How to overcome the invisible barriers to quality, productivity, and innovation.* San Francisco: Jossey-Bass.

Senge, P. M. (1990). *The fifth discipline: The art and practice of the learning organization.* New York: Doubleday.

Sergiovanni, T. J. (1984). Leadership and excellence in schooling. *Educational Leadership, 41*(5), 4–14.

Sergiovanni, T. J. (1992). *Moral leadership: Getting to the heart of school improvement.* San Francisco: Jossey-Bass.

Smith, D. M. (1997). *Motivating people* (2nd ed.). Hauppauge, NY: Barron's Series.

Stogdill, R. M. (1948). Personal factors associated with leadership: A survey of the literature. *Journal of Psychology, 25*, 35–71.

Stogdill, R. M., & Coons, A. E. (1957). *Leader behavior: Its description and measurement.* Columbus: Bureau of Business Research, The Ohio State University.

Strike, K. A., Haller, J., & Soltis, J. F. (1988). *The ethics of school administration.* New York: Teachers College Press, Columbia University.

Vroom, V. H. (1969). Industrial Social Psychology. In *The handbook of social psychology*, Vol. 5 (2nd ed. pp. 196–268), G. Lindzey & E. Aronson (Eds.). Reading, MA: Addison-Wesley.

Vroom, V. H., & Jago, A. G. (1988). *The new leadership: Managing participation in organizations.* Upper Saddle River, NJ: Prentice Hall.

Vroom, V. H., & Yetton, P. W. (1973). *Leadership and decision making.* Pittsburgh, PA: University of Pittsburgh Press.

Walton, S., & Huey, J. (1992). *Sam Walton: Made in America.* New York: Doubleday.

Yukl, G. A. (1989). *Leadership in organizations* (2nd ed.). Upper Saddle River, NJ: Prentice Hall.

Yukl, G. A. (1994). *Leadership in organizations* (3rd ed.). Upper Saddle River, NJ: Prentice Hall.

Zuker, E. (1991). *The seven secrets of influence.* New York: McGraw-Hill.

DEVELOPING A COLLABORATIVE CULTURE
IN SCHOOLS

In today's schools, it is important for the leader to develop and maintain a school culture that promotes the success of all students, is conducive to staff professional growth, and is accepted by the community (Standards 2 and 4). Although schools appear to be similar, they represent unique differences in size, structure, availability of human and material resources, and the composition of the communities they serve. Also, the constituent group served has specific expectations for individuals who lead them. Therefore, an individual assigned the challenge of leading a particular school must acquire an understanding of the complex nature of its internal functions, as well as the needs, values, and expectations of the individuals to be served. As a result of this understanding, leaders can utilize an effective style and apply approaches and strategies necessary for leadership effectiveness.

The purpose of this chapter is to discuss how forces in the external and internal environment of the schoolhouse affect the culture of the school and influence the behavior of leaders, swaying them to select a particular style or use one strategy as opposed to another. Attention is also given to staff and student motivation, organizational relationships, and other factors that influence behavior in schools. These organizational influences are summarized in Figure 3.1.

To achieve the purpose of the chapter, we define the school as an organization, explore four organizational theories that influence the culture of schools, and illustrate through scenarios the principles that inform the type of culture that must exist in schools if ISLLC Standards 2, 3, and 4 are to be met. Interacting with these scenarios, the reader will be exposed to various approaches a leader might use to understand self, other individuals, and groups inside and outside of the schoolhouse. In addition, attributes needed by leaders to establish a trust-based school culture, build organizational capacity, and positively influence followers are explored.

FIGURE 3.1   Organizational Influences on Leadership

A Definition of Organization

An organization can be defined in a number of ways. Schein (1970) defined an organization as "the rational coordination of the activities of a number of people for the achievement of some common goal, through division of labor and function, and through a hierarchy of authority and responsibility" (p. 9). Katz and Kahn (1978) defined an organization as an open social system that receives resources (input) from its external environment, transforms that input through an internal system (throughput), and returns it to the external environment (output). From another perspective, Hersey, Blanchard, and Johnson (1996) offer that an organization is a social system consisting of many interrelated subsystems (administrative, economic/technological, informational/decision making, human/social), which interact with the external environment. From still another perspective, Scott (2003) defined an organization as a social structure created by individuals to support the collaborative pursuit of specified goals.

The common strand running through these definitions is the reference they make to organizations having structure and consisting of parts that are interdependent and interrelated. The parts interact with one another to achieve organizational goals, and the structure governs that interaction, offering a sense of predictability regarding the functions and behavior of the parts. While all these definitions adequately define an organization and will be referenced throughout the chapter, the definition offered by Katz and Kahn (1978) best aligns with the purpose of this text and, therefore, is the basic premise for the discussion that follows.

Schools as Organizations

Schools are complex organizational systems that are both social and technical. The technical aspect refers to the types of inputs (resources acquired from the external environment), the nature of the internal transformation process (teaching and learning), and outputs (service to the community). This aspect requires the leader to focus on schools from the managerial perspective of (a) identifying the task, (b) determining proper work assignments, (c) implementing forms of supervision, and (d) considering the interrelationships among the people affiliated with the organization. The social aspect addresses the use of technologies by humans. This aspect requires leaders to be able to determine how well the technologies are used (interaction between and among participants) and make appropriate alterations when necessary (Gorton & Schneider, 1991).

To acquire an appreciation for these areas and meet Standard 3, which requires school leaders to develop and maintain a school organization that promotes the success of all students in a safe, efficient, and effective learning environment, leaders need an in-depth understanding of organizational structures and factors that influence the behavior of individuals and groups. To acquire information that will provide that understanding, we turn to four noted organizational theories.

Traditional Theories Influencing Contemporary Practice

Many early theories offering reasons for behavior in organizations have laid the foundation for contemporary ideas about how organizations should be structured and how leaders should function in the different structures. Of the many theories and postulates that address the subject, Classical Organizational Theory, Social Systems Theory, Open System Theory, and the Learning Organization are noted for providing a guiding framework for understanding factors relative to leader behavior in today's schools (Owens, 1995). Several principles advanced by these theories were presented in Chapter 2. However, in an attempt to demonstrate the relationship between the structure and culture of schools and to present a rationale for the importance of indicators of Standards 2, 3, and 4, these theories are explored in greater detail in the following sections.

Classical Theorists

The classical theorists believe that an organization can be most efficient and effective by employing a set of fixed "principles," two of which are establishing a bureaucratic structure and implementing various systems of organizational control. The activities of management and workers are identified, and guidelines are established to control organizational operations. The focus is on structuring the organization for effectiveness and organizing the work of individuals for task completion. (Owens, 1995).

Scientific Management   Classical Theory is often viewed from the perspective of scientific and administrative management. Frederick Taylor (1911), the father of scientific management, theorized that organizations could become efficient by identifying the "one best way" of performing a task. He theorized that through a careful analysis of jobs in the organization, utilizing scientific principles, this "one best way" of performing a job could be identified. After identifying the best approach, the next step is the selection and training of personnel to specifically perform the job. In the third step, management coordination, Taylor suggested that management should coordinate the work to provide assurance that the work is done as prescribed. Finally, he suggested that the work assignments should be divided among managers and workers, with managers having the responsibility of planning, organizing, and decision making, while workers perform assigned tasks.

Administrative Management   A second perspective of Classical Organization Theory, administrative management, focused on the concept of managing the entire organization. Henri Fayol, Lyndall Urwick, Luther Gulick, and Max Weber were major contributors to this perspective (Hanson, 1996). Their work addressed the principles of specialization, delegation of responsibility, span of control, and authority. The following section addresses some of the contributions of these individuals.

Fayol advocated that all managers perform five basic functions: planning, organizing, commanding, coordinating, and controlling. In addition, he characterized management as a continuous process by emphasizing the chain of command, equity, efficiency, stability, and the allocation of authority through the design of 14 principles of management. His theory was that efficiency and effectiveness could be achieved in an organization when these 14 principles were employed (Fayol, 1949). Of these principles, those noteworthy for school leaders are division of labor, authority, discipline, unity of command, order, and equity. Gulick and Urwick heightened the work of Fayol and expanded on his functions, identifying seven: budgeting, planning, reporting, organizing, coordinating, directing, and staffing (Lunenburg & Ornstein, 1996).

The Bureaucratic Structure   Max Weber (1947) built on the work of these individuals and in so doing became one of the major contributors in creating a foundation for organizational theory as we view it today. Weber described the concepts of the bureaucratic structure; his work focused on fixed division of labor, hierarchy of positions, rules to govern performance, terms of employment, technical qualities for seeking personnel, and the separation of the personal rights and property of the worker from those of the organization (Scott, 2003). He theorized that the bureaucratic model was the best structure to use to acquire efficiency in large organizations that are complex in nature. His contention was that use of such a model would influence the behavior of individuals in an effective and efficient manner, enhancing the achievement of organizational goals (Scott, 2003).

A Leader with a Classical Perspective   Classical Theory has a powerful influence on the organization of today's schools, as well as their leadership. Most school districts currently use some form of the classical model (Gorton & Schneider, 1991). When classical leadership is employed, structure is the order of the day, and strict rules and regulations govern the operation of the school and/or school system. The focus is on task completion; little attention is given to the individual or group in the workplace, and the leader is considered to have ultimate authority and responsibility over everything in the system. Experts are employed to function in specialized areas and are grouped according to task specialization. The key concepts are structure, rules, regulations and procedures, organizational control, and efficiency (Gorton, 1987).

A leader who administers a school from a classical perspective would talk about "going by the book" or "running a tight ship" and would assume to have ultimate authority and responsibility over everything that goes on in the school (Hanson, 1991, p. 10). The leader would be specific in actions and very direct, many times displaying autocratic behavior. Problems are not likely to be solved through people, as such leaders view themselves as the problem solvers. Stakeholders may be involved in decisions that affect the school, but such involvement would not be a focus of the leadership, nor would trusting people and respecting their judgment be a primary concern.

Whereas the efficient operation of schools may be attainable using the practices described in the previous section, the ISLLC Standards advocate a more inclusive practice of school leadership. They offer that school organizations should be structured in a manner that reflects the culture of the community served; the disposition of the leader should be one that respects that culture, and the performance of the school should maximize opportunities for successful learning by all students.

Social Systems Theory   Another approach that has proven very useful in understanding the behavior of individuals and groups in schools is the study of the theory that explains the organization as a social system. Social Systems Theory has developed over a period of time, building on a number of theoretical principles. It is defined as a set of interrelated elements that function in a particular manner to achieve a specific purpose. Social Systems Theory provides a way of viewing the organization as a whole, taking into consideration the interrelationships among its parts and its inter-action with its internal and external environments (Hanson, 1996).

The Makeup of the Social System   As was previously noted, within the frame-work of Classical Theory, the needs of the organization and the needs of the work-er were perceived to coincide; if the company prospered, the worker prospered. Quite different from that line of reasoning, social systems theorists believe that a basic difference exists between the needs of the organization and the needs of the worker.

The focus necessarily must be on the whole (the faculty), parts of the whole (members of the faculty), and the relationship among the parts (relationships among faculty members). Hanson (1991) presents his argument in this manner: "If the leader is considerate, uses democratic procedures whenever possible, and maintains open lines of communication, management and workers can talk over their respec-tive problems and resolve them in a friendly, congenial way" (p. 7).

The common strand among organizational definitions previously presented suggests that a structure that governs the individuals and groups functioning therein is formulated. It also offers a sense of predictability regarding their activi-ties and behaviors. Given the implication of this compilation, it seems appropriate at this point to entertain a discussion regarding the leader's need to recognize the power and influence of individuals and groups that function in organizations.

The Power and Influence of Individuals and Groups   Several individuals and groups make up the social system. Within the framework of the system, each in-dividual and/or group has the capability of formulating a power base and using it to influence teaching and learning to a considerable degree, independent of the de-mands of the leader (Hanson, 1991, p. 7). These individuals and groups function in both the external and internal environments of the schoolhouse. Therefore, school leaders should give consideration to both groups and develop cohesiveness between them. Because of the effect these individuals and groups have on the teaching and learning process, a few examples of their influence on leader behavior are pointed out in the next section.

Forces from the External Environment   Because forces in the external envi-ronment of the school influence its internal teaching and learning process, the leader must remain flexible and be willing and able to continually make adjustments to the internal operations of the school. For example, if the State Board of Educa-tion enacts a policy requiring end-of-course examinations, in order to address this new policy, it may be necessary for the leader to work with the faculty to change the school's curriculum and/or instructional approaches. The change will affect a large number of people and may require modifications in their work assignments. Whereas the leader has no control over the enactment of the policy, the leader must respond to that policy in a manner that enhances the teaching and learning process.

Forces in the external environment of the school warrant the constant attention of the school leader. The needs and desires of citizens, changing demographics, new laws, and other factors must always be part of the planning process, and the community must be involved in that process. Because individuals have different opinions about the practices the leader uses or should use, they often form groups and participate in activities to influence the leader's behavior in a direction they favor. Therefore, the leader has to understand, respond to, and influence the larger political, social, economic, legal, and cultural context of the school (Standard 6). Given the power and influence that groups are capable of acquiring and the impact they can have on teaching and learning, meeting Standard 6 can be a challenge that requires some highly developed leadership skills and attributes.

Forces from the Internal Environment

Individuals in schools function as members of the faculty (the formal group), as well as members of subgroups (informal groups) that exist within the faculty. No two individuals functioning as members of the faculty bring the same style or personality to their role. The personalities are different because they are influenced by various factors which are unique to a particular time frame (era) in our history (Boyatzis & Skelly, 1995). A school faculty is likely to consist of a variety of individuals from eras that span as many as 50 years, and individuals from each era are likely to have a different perspective on how the school should operate.

Boyatzis and Skelly (1995) contend that an individual's capability, or competencies, will have significant influence on the effectiveness of that individual's job performance. The beliefs, values, and behaviors an individual brings into the schoolhouse also have that potential and are influenced by the era that individual represents. These individuals make up the faculty and are expected to play major roles in school goal attainment. Thus, it seems reasonable to assume that if leaders are to make management decisions that require trusting people and their judgment and if these decisions support the enhancement of all individuals in the organization, they must develop an understanding of the beliefs, ideas, and values of all faculty members and the effect that their behavior has on members individually and collectively. Without such an understanding, the development of informal groups is likely to be perpetuated. Table 3.1 contains a representation of individuals who are likely to comprise a school faculty and offers a rationale for the position they are likely to take on school-related issues. Because individuals are likely to form groups to foster their issues, it is important to briefly discuss informal groups and why they are formed in schools.

TABLE 3.1 Individuals Functioning in the Social System

PEOPLE	ERA	ETHIC	VALUE	DOMINANT BELIEF	BEHAVIOR
Prebaby-boomer, 49–75 years old 1940–1960	Economic growth	Self-denial, allegiance to family	Hard work, upward mobility, commitment to the organization	If you work hard and have patience, you will get your turn. Single leadership	Expected obedience and loyalty as repayment of effort on someone's behalf
Early baby boomers, 39–48 years old 1960s–1970s	Social fix-it agenda, professional management	Self-fulfillment, people-oriented, protection of the environment	Focus on self and worker happiness	Pluralistic models of how to "beat the system," bottom-up planning, loyalty to one's field, family demands important	Self replaced the organization, did not respond to authority with any automatic respect
Late baby-boomers, 29–38 years old 1970s–1980s	Competitive pragmatism	Self-fulfillment, I want mine, get my share	Winning, not losing, self-knowledge, competitiveness	Identifying with an organization through shared beliefs, cost-effectiveness	Cynical of authority, not a team player, get my share
The X generation, 20 years old 1990s	Social pragmatism	Empowerment	Personal blended agenda, autonomy and independence, less stressful lifestyle	Belief in technology, personal agenda, health and fitness	Strategic positioning, home-type activities

SOURCE: Developed from: Richard E. Boyatzis and Florence R. Skelly (1995). "The impact of changing values on organizational life." In D .A. Kolb, Joyce S. Osland and Irwin M. Rubin (eds.), *The Organizational Behavior Reader* (6th ed.), (pp. 1–17). Upper Saddle River, NJ: Prentice Hall.

Informal Groups

In a social system, individual faculty members become members of subgroups because of common values, shared interests, and a desire to acquire support to achieve individual goals that may be different from the goals being sought by the formal organization (Hanson, 1991). Because of their makeup, these subgroups are often very powerful. Therefore, in order to achieve the most productivity from the faculty, school leaders must be very astute in understanding the patterns of behavior of individuals within these groups. This knowledge is extremely helpful to the leader in determining the manner in which these groups are likely to use their power and influence. The leader is not likely to be able to eliminate these groups; nor should elimination be a primary concern. The critical factor for school leaders is an awareness of their existence, knowledge of their desires, and their source of power. To elaborate on and emphasize the importance of these groups to school goal attainment, we summarize the dimensions of the social system in the following section.

Dimensions of the Social System

As was indicated in the section above, in many instances, the goals and special interests of individuals and subgroups in schools conflict with the functional goals of the formal school organization. Jacob Getzels and Egon Guba (1957) theorize that the social system has two independent and interactive dimensions. The distinction they draw is between the organization and the individuals functioning in the organization. They refer to the organization as the nomothetic or institutional dimension and the individual as the personal or idiographic dimension. The institutional dimension depicts the roles and expectations of the formal organization and the way in which individuals in the organization are expected to behave as they pursue established goals. In a school, such roles are outlined through teaching assignments, job descriptions, special duty requirements, and expectations established through various forms of performance standards.

The second dimension, personal, refers to the nature and personality of the individual, as well as the individual's needs disposition. No two individuals are alike; they react differently to other individuals and to various situations. These differences can be analyzed in terms of the individual's personality because, to some extent, an individual's personality is determined by beliefs, values, and needs. Thus, the personality of an individual predisposes that individual to behave in a certain way in a given situation (Getzels & Guba, 1957).

Commitment to Organizational Goal Attainment

In schools, the values held by individuals, to a large extent, determine their willingness to accept an assignment and the amount of effort they will exert to be effective in completing that assignment (Boyatzis & Skelly, 1995). The individuals' values set forth their commitment to the organization and affect their relationships with colleagues and people receiving services from the organization. In essence, the compatibility between the values of the individual in the organization and the inherent values of the culture of the organization is the basis for an individual establishing a social or psychological contract with the organization (Boyatzis & Skelly, 1995). This social or psychological contract reflects an individual's beliefs, expectations, and assumptions about work and life in the organization and establishes the parameters by which the individual functions.

For example, in a school, a high school science teacher occupies a given role and is expected to meet certain established standards. However, that teacher has needs to fulfill and expectations regarding the role the school should play in providing assistance. These are personal needs and expectations and may be quite different from the expectations and requirements of the school or the science department. Nevertheless, any differences in expectations may negatively influence the teacher's performance. Conversely, if there is compatibility relative to expectations, the teacher's performance is likely to be positively influenced (Getzels & Guba, 1957). It is ideal when the needs of the individual and the goals of the organization are compatible; however, this is not always the case, and when it is not, conflict between the individual and the organization is heightened (Getzels & Guba, 1957).

A Leader with a Social Systems Perspective

A school leader with a Social Systems perspective seeks to employ individuals with a need disposition compatible with the mission and goals of the school, making use of such strategies as compromising, bargaining, retreating, and changing. In both the school and community, the leader strives to maximize the productivity of subgroups that are sometimes hostile and conflicting. The vision of the school is communicated, and clear directions are given without creating hostility. The leader is not an empire builder; rather, the primary concern is for the growth of the organization and the people in the organization. Problems are solved through people, as the leader is sensitive to the feelings of others. The leader listens to the ideas and suggestions of others, appreciates their actions, and expresses that appreciation to them.

Open Social Systems Theory

An organization functioning as an open social system has a set of interrelated parts that interact with its environment and, as a result, is capable of self-maintenance. The system receives input from the external environment and transforms that input into a product (output) that goes into the external environment and eventually returns as input. This throughput is essential to the system's viability (Buckley, 1967). The system is closely connected to the characteristics of its external environment, and its complexity and differential structure are determined by the throughput. By acquiring inputs of greater complexity than outputs, the system can alter its practices or completely change its structure (Pondy & Mitroff, 1979).

Schools Functioning as Open Social Systems   Schools do not operate as separate entities; they function as part of a larger system and, as a result, they must respond to a variety of external forces that affect the internal teaching and learning process. Therefore, to effectively administer the school's program, responding to diverse interests and needs and mobilizing community resources, the leader has to collaborate with individuals and groups inside and outside of the schoolhouse (Standard 6). The effectiveness of this interaction is influenced by such factors as (a) the structure of the organization, (b) the behavior of the leader, (c) the behavior of members of the organization functioning individually and as members of formal and informal groups, (d) the manner in which various actions are perceived, (e) individual motivational levels, (f) the manner in which power is distributed, and (g) the needs of the organization. These factors affect the culture and climate of the school and often offer challenges for the leader that warrant a modification of the school structure; yet they are a part of the leadership equation (ISLLC, 1997). These factors are summarized in Figure 3.2.

The preceding theories have a rich history and have withstood the test of time. The principles of these theories provide a guiding framework for understanding and predicting many of the behaviors in today's schools, and they are the foundation upon which contemporary ideas that currently appear in leadership literature are built.

FIGURE 3.2   Major Elements Impacting the Operation of Schools

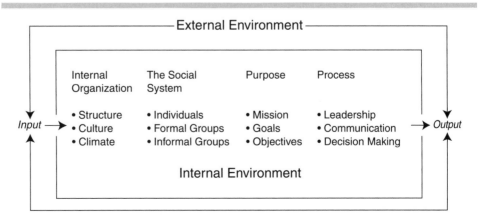

Contemporary Postulates Informing Leadership in Schools

In recent years, a number of theoreticians, researchers, and writers have addressed the behavior of individuals in organizations from an all-inclusive perspective (Garvin, 1995; Hanson, 1996; Manz & Sims, 1989; Senge 1995). They argue that a school or school district is not administered by a single center of power and authority. Rather, it is administered by a number of power centers that function with semi-autonomous power and contribute significantly to the direction the school or district is taking. These theorists suggest that all individuals have value and can make a significant contribution to the growth of the organization. Senge (1995) suggests that leaders are responsible for helping individuals expand their capacity to shape their future; in essence, leaders are responsible for followers learning. He states, "The old model, 'the top thinks, and the local acts' must now give way to integrating thinking and acting at all levels" (p. 76).

It is also advocated that leaders of today's schools spend time encouraging individuals and groups and helping them to keep up with the changes and demands of the organization, so they might understand the benefits to be derived from achieving the school's vision (Manz & Sims, 1989). In addition, the leader must provide members of the organization with opportunities to learn from failure, and it is critical that when failure occurs, individuals are approached without repercussions. When there are repercussions, barriers to quality work develop and individuals withdraw, leaving the organization void of their creativity (Ryan & Oestreich, 1991). Organizations that function in the manner described above have been defined in a number of ways; however, they are most commonly referred to as learning organizations.

Learning Organizations Defined

"Learning organizations are places where people continually expand their capacity to create the results they truly desire, where new and expansive patterns of thinking are nurtured, where collective aspiration is set free, and where people are continually learning how to learn together" (Senge, 1990, p. 3). In a learning organization, the climate and culture are such that individuals feel valued, respected, and appreciated. The leader facilitates team learning, and the communication process fosters full participation, with everyone feeling a sense of importance about making a contribution to organizational growth. The leader seeks a shared vision and serves as a designer, teacher, and steward. The leader utilizes these qualities to ensure that individuals in the organization understand current reality, recognize creative tension, and seek the vision that members of the organization hold.

Creative tension exists when members of the organization have a clear understanding of the current state of the organization, as well as the vision. The gap between the two creates a natural tension (Senge, 1990). Creative tension can be reduced by moving the vision toward current reality or by moving current reality toward the vision. However, having developed an understanding of the internal organization, the interaction of individuals and groups in the social system, and the influences of the external environment, the effective leader selects a process to use in moving current reality toward the vision (see Figure 3.3).

Schools as Learning Organizations

The research and writings of Bennis and Biederman (1997), Covey (1989), Senge (1990), Sergiovanni (1994), and others indicate that schools can become learning organizations. However, it will be necessary for the leader to devote time and attention to the structure of the school, the individuals who serve the school, and their relationships with students, as well as with each other. Schools that are becoming learning organizations have taken these actions. Green (1997) identified 13 characteristics that exist in such schools. These characteristics cluster into four themes that are consistent with those advocated for a learning organization (see Table 3.2). In a later study (Green, 1998), it was shown that the magnitude of the existence of these themes may, in some schools, have had a positive effect on student achievement, attendance, and behavior.

Cypress (2003) determined that a significant difference existed in the instructional program of some schools when the characteristics of those schools were different. Characteristics, such as a shared vision, a learning community, a positive and safe school culture, effective collaborative leadership, effective use of resources, using data to drive reform, and the involvement of parents and community, were more salient in schools where students were meeting established standards than in those that were not.

FIGURE 3.3 Creative Tension in Schools

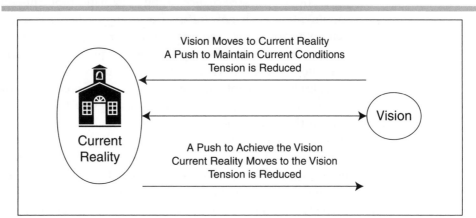

SOURCE: Designed from Peter Senge's definition of creative tension

TABLE 3.2   Thirteen Characteristics of Nurturing Schools

Theme A—Student-teacher relationships
- There is mutual trust and positive interaction between teachers and students.
- Teachers have an in-depth knowledge of students' in-school and out-of-school lives.
- Teachers model caring attitudes for students.

Theme B—Professionalism among administration, faculty, and staff
- There is a sense of caring among individuals and a collective sense of responsibility for student success.
- The need for self-actualization is respected and encouraged.
- Teachers demonstrate a love for their subject matter and continuously search for competence.

Theme C—Environment of the school and classroom
- A sense of community and a sense of family exist in the school, and there is collaboration among professionals.
- Everyone values individual differences, and the self one brings into the environment is respected and nurtured.
- There is recognition of a wide range of talent and the need for the empowerment of all individuals.
- The school draws in the values of the community and involves the community in the education of children.

Theme D—Students' feelings about themselves
- Students feel a sense of self-worth and acceptance.
- Students feel safe and involved in their education.
- Students value themselves and others.

SOURCE: Reginald Leon Green, Ed.D. © Copyright 1996. Educational Services Plus. All rights reserved.

Garvin (1995) also described characteristics of schools that are learning organizations. He offered that school leaders who have created learning organizations are fostering participatory governance, using systematic problem-solving techniques, and experimenting with new instructional approaches. Leaders are also learning from their own experiences and past history, learning from the experiences and best practices of others and transferring knowledge quickly and efficiently throughout the organization. In the schools described and others that have become learning organizations, leaders are implementing the concept of site-based management, opening lines of communication, and allowing all stakeholders an opportunity to participate in the governance of the school. There is openness to the degree that people feel free to express their views and are willing to give and take. There is consistency in words and actions; the message given out is acted upon, and people have developed a sincere belief that they are valued and respected. Everyone receives equal treatment, and the goal of the school is to advance the welfare of the community (Etheridge & Green, 1998). The ISLLC Standards propose to support the position that school leaders of today should hold firm to the proposition that all students can learn, view student learning as the fundamental purpose of schooling, and understand diversity and its meaning for educational programs. Leaders should give consideration to the needs and expertise of every individual in the school and the influence that structure will have on the internal and external culture of the school. However, before this can occur, the leader must develop an understanding of self and his or her perceptions about people. It is this understanding that will allow the leader to act with integrity, fairness, and in an ethical manner, valuing diversity and being sensitive to the needs of individuals and groups inside the schoolhouse and in the community (Standards 2 and 5). In the following section, we provide a rationale for this line of reasoning.

Understanding Self

Before leaders can really develop a clear understanding of the organization and people affiliated with the organization, they must first develop an understanding of themselves. What one values, what one thinks of oneself, what one believes about people, what one believes about children, and what one believes to be the purpose of schools comprise one's disposition, and one's disposition influences leadership behavior. Therefore, knowledge of self helps individuals understand their own dispositions and enables them to acquire deeper understandings of how to respond to people and challenges in the organization (DuBrin, 1996).

The Public and Private Self

Often a distinction is made between the self of the leader that individuals affiliated with the organization observe (the public self) and the inner self (private self) of the leader. The public self is what an individual displays to the outside world and the perception others have of that individual. The private self is what the person is in actuality (Snyder, 1988). Knowledge of both the public and private self is an important factor in building relationships necessary to lead an organization. Having knowledge of both enables leaders to determine the level of agreement between their beliefs and values and the internal and external culture of the school. Leaders may not be able to circumvent the influence of their values, but being aware of them will enable the monitoring of their ethical nature and the formulation of a course of action that will demonstrate that the leader is sensitive to the needs and concerns of others and is committed to building and sustaining a school culture and instructional program that challenge all individuals to reach their full potential.

Failure to Understand Self

Leaders who do not acquire an understanding of self and how their behavior affects others are subject to continuous error (Brewer, Ainsworth, & Wynne, 1984). This claim is based on the premise that the success of the leader depends on support from followers. The leader does not function in isolation; a leader's ability to obtain information and acquire resources sufficient to achieve organizational goals is influenced by the type of relationships that exist between the leader and members of the organization, as well as many other environmental factors (Brewer et al., 1984). Then, it seems important for the leader to realize that the actions of people in the organization, functioning as individuals and as members of formal and informal groups, can be positively and negatively influenced by the leader's behavior. In some instances, leader perception may be influencing that behavior. To best appreciate leader perception and its influence on the human condition in schools, we examine McGregor's Theory X and Theory Y.

Leader Perception

Douglas McGregor (1960), the formulator of Theory X and Theory Y, believes that administrative behavior is influenced by two basic assumptions about the nature of people. Following are the main characteristics of this theory:

THEORY X

1. The average human being has an inherent dislike for work and will avoid it when possible.
2. Because of this human characteristic of dislike of work, most people must be coerced, controlled, directed, and threatened with punishment to get them to put forth adequate effort toward achievement of organizational goals.
3. The average human being prefers to be directed, wishes to avoid responsibility, has relatively little ambition, and wants security above all.

THEORY Y

1. External control and the threat of punishment are not the only means for bringing about effort toward organizational objectives. People will exercise self-direction and self-control in the service of objectives to which they are committed.
2. The average human being learns, under proper conditions, not only to accept, but also to seek responsibility. Avoidance of responsibility, lack of ambition, and emphasis on security are generally consequences of experience, not inherent human characteristics.
3. The capacity to exercise a relatively high degree of imagination, ingenuity, and creativity in the solution of organizational problems is widely, not narrowly, distributed in the population (McGregor, 1960).

It has been found that when leaders differ relative to Theory X and Theory Y, the difference is likely to occur in their attitudes toward people. These attitudinal differences are most pronounced when leaders make a determination regarding the manner in which they will interact with followers and the extent to which they will involve followers in decision making (Owens, 1995).

A Theory X leader would likely emphasize policies and procedures, give directions in a blunt and to the point manner, and demand action with the overt threat of punishment. If an error occurs in leader behavior, it is likely to be on the side of task completion.

A Theory Y leader would likely function as a facilitator, an individual who is as interested in the process as the product. Decisions would likely be made through people, creating an environment conducive to self-direction and intrinsic motivation. If an error occurs in leader behavior, it is likely to be on the side of consideration and relationship building. The behaviors advocated by ISLLC Standard 2 are most noted in leaders who exhibit Y characteristics.

Leadership for Today's Scholar

The theories, postulates, and practices presented here and in Chapter 2 support many of the principles that inform leaders' behavior necessary to meet this standard. The scenarios that follow will allow readers an opportunity to use these theories, postulates, and practices, as well as others, to assess their leadership dispositions and provide a rationale for the behavior of individuals functioning in schools.

Many writers and researches use concepts and terms to suggest the behavior that leaders should exhibit in today's schools. In one way or another, most of these suggestions relate to the concepts that are advocated by individuals who subscribe to the creation of learning organizations. ISLLC Standard 3, which advocates that school leaders are administrators who manage the school organization, operations, and resources to ensure a safe, efficient, and effective learning environment, also supports these concepts.

The Scenarios

In Scenario 3, the superintendent of schools has requested that Principal Harris complete two tasks during the school year: development of a school improvement plan and establishment of a site-based management team. After allowing the year to elapse without making very much progress toward the completion of either task, Principal Harris takes action to complete both tasks within the requested time frame. The reader will want to pay attention to the effects of leader behavior on the environment of the school and followers functioning in that environment.

In Scenario 4, the principal addresses an issue involving teachers from different eras. The issue poses a threat to relationships in the environment and could deprive students of a valuable learning experience. The key factor in this scenario is the ability of the leader to influence a change in the attitude of a follower.

Scenario 5 addresses two standards, with collaboration and management being the focus. From the scenario, the reader should be able to discern how leadership behavior, the climate and culture of a school district, and influences of the external environment can create a situation that threatens the entire teaching and learning process. In working through these scenarios, the reader will have an opportunity to review indicators of ISLLC Standards 2, 3, and 4 in practical situations.

SCENARIO 3
UNDERSTANDING AND PREDICTING INDIVIDUAL AND GROUP BEHAVIOR IN SCHOOLS

STANDARD 3

A school administrator is an educational leader who promotes the success of all students by ensuring management of the organization, operations, and resources for a safe, efficient, and effective learning environment.

After Principal Harris's appointment to Washington High School, Superintendent Glover advised him that the districtwide strategic plan required the administration, faculty, staff, and parents of each school to develop a site-based management team and implement a plan for instructional improvement that would be aligned with the district's strategic goals. Superintendent Glover then gave him a copy of the district's strategic plan and advised him that he should establish the site-based management team, develop a local school improvement plan, and have that plan in operation within the first two years of his tenure.

As Principal Harris entered the school year and began to carry out his duties, he often thought about the charge he had received from the superintendent and how he would collaborate with the faculty, staff, and community in designing a plan that would be most appropriate for the school. However, the pressures of getting adjusted to a new job and operating a large school were all-consuming, and there never seemed to be time to develop the site-based management team or discuss a new instructional design for the school. He rarely left his office because he was so saturated with paperwork.

As Principal Harris approached the end of his first year, it became clear that unless he took immediate action, the year would end, and the school would not have a site-based management team or a school improvement plan. Therefore, he convened a meeting with his two assistant principals, Alice Harmon and William Johnson. He reviewed the tasks with them, asking Mr. Johnson to research and formulate a plan that could be used to establish a site-based management team and requesting that Mrs. Harmon formulate the framework for a school improvement plan.

While Mr. Johnson sat silently accepting the assignment, Mrs. Harmon vehemently opposed the assignment. She advised Principal Harris that the time frame was much too short to accomplish the task with any degree of quality, as most of the faculty would not have adequate time to research ideas for program changes this late in the school year. She also spoke against the establishment of a site-based management team, offering that prior to his appointment, many members of the faculty had expressed that unless there was extra pay and/or a reallocation of instructional time, they would prefer not to be engaged in any additional committee work.

Principal Harris voiced regrets that so much had to be done in such a short period; then he advised his assistants to move forward with the assignments as expeditiously as possible. Mrs. Harmon left the office in a state of anger, voicing the reasons for her resistance to Mr. Johnson's directions. "We will just see what occurs," she stated. Mr. Johnson made no comments but returned to his office and began to ponder the assignment.

At the next faculty meeting, Principal Harris advised the faculty that the school staff would be implementing a site-based management model and that Mr. Johnson would be providing the leadership for its development. He also advised the faculty that the leadership for the design of a school improvement plan was being provided by Mrs. Harmon. He went on to say that he was sure that the faculty would appreciate the need for these two new initiatives, as they were part of a districtwide effort to improve student achievement. He asked for the support of the faculty and assured them that they would in turn have the support of his office.

Two weeks later at the regularly scheduled monthly meeting of the subject area department chairs, Mrs. Harmon reviewed the request made by the principal with the group. She then asked if anyone had suggestions on how to begin the task. At least three individuals (department chairs of English, mathematics, and science) spoke to the time frame and a need to wait until the fall to start any new program initiatives. The social studies department chair stated that he believed that if the effort got underway before the end of the school year, the summer could be spent researching and collecting data on new programs. Mrs. Harmon gave a quaint chuckle and asked the question, "Anyone for summer work without pay?" The music department chair then spoke up and said, "There are several closing-of-school band activities scheduled, but I can find time to attend a few meetings." "Well, that settles it," replied Mrs. Harmon, "I'll report to Principal Harris that it is the consensus of the department chairs that we delay this activity until the fall." Hearing no opposition, the meeting was adjourned.

Two days later, Mrs. Harmon wrote a memo to Principal Harris, advising him that she had met with the department chairs and that they had expressed a strong desire to postpone any new curriculum efforts until the fall.

During the three weeks that elapsed after the meeting with Principal Harris, Mr. Johnson conducted an extensive literature review on site-based management models. From his review, he developed a list of the pros and cons of various models operating in large urban school districts. He then began to talk with faculty members individually and in small groups. He spoke with the president of the Parent Teacher Organization, as well as a number of parents and community leaders. After several meetings in which he collected the ideas and opinions of many individuals, he formulated a set of recommendations on site-based management for review by Principal Harris.

At the next faculty meeting, Mr. Johnson presented his report and recommendations to the faculty. After he passed out his report, he described the process he had used to collect data, explained the content, and provided a rationale for his recommendations. Then he gave the faculty time to review the report and raise questions. The faculty appeared stunned at the request but reviewed the material and began to comment among themselves. At once, Mrs. Harmon spoke to the plan, "Why are there so many parents on the team? Parents outnumber teachers." Frances Jones, a senior English instructor, noted "Yes, I see a parent is slated to chair the committee, but why can't a teacher chair the committee?" The chair of the mathematics department then spoke, "I believe we should all be involved in determining the committee structure." Mrs. Harmon replied, "Yes, isn't that what site-based management is all about?" The English Department's Chair, followed by the Science Department's Chair, voiced negative comments. Many other faculty members appeared to want to speak but could not get the attention of Mr. Johnson, who was stunned by the strong resistance to his report. He had spoken to all these individuals and whereas they did not voice any strong support for the concept of site-based management, they did not express any concern with his recommendations. In fact, some teachers had spoken very positively about the concept. Why didn't these individuals speak up earlier? Then he remembered that several teachers had met with Mrs. Harmon to discuss the concept and its merits.

Principal Harris then intervened. He thanked Mr. Johnson for his hard work, complimented him on his recommendations, and told the faculty that some additional work was needed and the plan would be discussed further in a later meeting. He completed the remaining items on the agenda and adjourned the meeting.

REFLECTIVE THINKING

The ISLLC Standards

The following are indicators of the ISLLC Standards addressed in the scenario:

3: Human resources were not developed and managed; management decisions that enhance learning and teaching were not made; people were trusted, but good judgment was not always employed; responsibility for assigned tasks was not accepted by some individuals; stakeholders were not involved in management processes; operational plans and procedures to achieve the vision and goals of the school were not put in place; time was not managed to maximize attainment of organizational goals; potential problems and opportunities were not effectively identified, and problems were not confronted and resolved in a timely manner.

4: Community relations and marketing strategies and processes were not evident; families and other stakeholders did not participate in the decision-making processes; collaboration and communication with families occurred, and opportunities for staff to develop collaborative skills were provided.

Reflective Questions and Scenario Analysis

1. Characterize Principal Harris's major problems.
2. What are some possible explanations for the behavior of Mrs. Harmon?
3. What factors in the internal environment of the school might be influencing the type of behavior exhibited by the faculty?
4. Outline the approach you would use to complete the original tasks assigned by Principal Harris.
5. Analyze the last faculty meeting, then briefly describe the management decisions you would make. What potential problems and opportunities can you identify?

ADDRESSING THE CRITICAL ISSUES

Practicing the Art of Leadership at Washington High School

Effective school leaders structure the organization for success and manage it using leadership skills, strategies, and techniques that influence human behavior toward goal attainment. This process requires the leader to have knowledge and understanding of how people behave as individuals and members of groups. Equally important is the need for the leader to understand the influence of forces in the internal and external environments of the school. Forces, such as the culture and climate of the school, its structure, and staff and student motivation, influence the behavior of both the leader and followers.

In practicing the art of leadership at Washington High School, the following questions are critical: (a) What is the nature of the culture and climate of the school? (b) How effective are the leadership approaches utilized by Principal Harris? (c) What is the quality of the interpersonal relationships in the school? (d) To what extent do informal groups exist, and how much influence do they have? We will now offer a response to each of these questions.

The Culture of Washington High

School culture is the interwoven pattern of beliefs, values, practices, and artifacts that specify for faculty members, students, parents, and stakeholders who they are and how they are to function (Bolman & Deal, 1997). It is learned behavior that shapes the processes members of the school family use in responding to their problems of survival in the external environment and their problems of internal integration (Schein, 1992). Sometimes in schools, as well as other organizations, this behavior is not overt and observable. In such instances, a set of hidden assumptions drives the behavior of individuals and groups (Schein, 1984). These assumptions shape the thinking of the faculty and drive their sense of identity relative to their work, the manner in which they relate to their colleagues, and the mission of role groups.

Culture creates reality for individuals, and at Washington High School, that reality allowed Mrs. Harmon to view task completion in a distinctive way. The pattern of behavior in the school provided a basis for her actions and supported her approach to personal goal attainment. She had background knowledge of the faculty and was aware of the possible reaction her behavior would cause. Having knowledge of previous organizational activities and the behavior of individuals relative to those activities allows one to determine group norms and craft a pattern of behavior that will be accepted.

The Washington High Faculty

Principal Harris was appointed principal of a faculty that was well established and entrenched in a well-developed culture, and the climate of the school reflected that culture. The school was not organized for success, and Principal Harris did not put in place operational procedures that took into consideration the power and influence of faculty members functioning individually and as members of formal and informal groups. Without operational procedures, the faculty remained highly fragmented and divided into groups that viewed decision making from a perspective of power. This view of power and control became the norm. It is the way things are done at Washington.

Sustaining a school culture conducive to student learning and staff professional growth is a responsibility of the principal (Standard 2). The principal's behavior should influence a culture of high expectations for self, students, and staff performance, and that culture should be assessed on a regular basis. Principal Harris's behavior did not positively influence that type of culture, nor did he establish a vision for the school that was shared by the faculty. In fact, his behavior contributed to the lack of organizational effectiveness. To effect change, the leader has to understand the existing culture, work within that culture, and carefully make modifications in a manner that will motivate high expectations for self, students, and staff performance. A change in the existing culture of Washington High School is not likely to occur without the leader articulating a new vision or making a change in the operational procedures and/or structure of the school.

The Climate of Washington High

Climate is a measure of the quality of the school's environment. Indications of the type of climate that exists in a school are the appearance of the building, the mannerisms of the people, and the feelings individuals have about visiting the school and transacting business there (Halpin & Croft, 1963). The climate of a school may be warm and pleasant, or it may be hostile and unpleasant. Teachers, students, parents, and others may be treated with dignity and respected as individuals, or they may be disrespected and experience remarks that are in poor taste.

Standard 5 emphasizes the type of climate that should exist in schools. The standard requires people to be treated fairly, equitably, and with dignity and respect. Also, it stipulates that leaders are to consider the impact their behavior has on others. Mrs. Harmon's leadership behavior did not adhere to Standard 5, and the climate of the school was negatively impacted by her behavior. The climate of Washington High School did not embrace the characteristics advocated by Standard 5.

The Quality of Interpersonal Relations

At Washington High School, there was no central focus around which the faculty could unite. In essence, Principal Harris failed to manage what Bennis (1995) refers to as management of self and attention, thereby causing a breakdown in the relationship between himself and members of his staff. He failed to manage the attention of Mrs. Harmon, in particular, and the faculty in general. There was a void in terms of effective interpersonal relationships between the principals and teachers. Of all the relationships that exist within a school, none has a greater effect on quality of life than the relationship between teachers and principal (Barth, 1990).

When leaders enter a new assignment, they should take action to draw individuals to them. This can be accomplished by managing attention and establishing a compelling vision (Bennis, 1995). Principal Harris took no action that communicated commitment, nor did he provide a thrust around which the faculty could unite. More importantly, his procrastination and lack of planning negatively affected the school climate.

Principal Harris also failed to manage self. He did not realize the influence his behavior had on the behavior of his assistants or the faculty. When entering a new school situation, it is wise for the leader to assess the culture and climate, examine the existing structure, and determine the attitude of the faculty, individually and collectively. After such an examination, the leader can move forward, building relationships and establishing a climate wherein principles and practices of trust, caring, and collaboration can exist. It is imperative that school leaders model the type of behavior they seek from followers.

Having failed to model the type of behavior he desired from the faculty (intentionally or unintentionally) or to establish the capacity for change, he was forced to resort to actions that challenged existing values, ideas, and past behaviors of the faculty.

> The ultimate in disrespect of individuals is to attempt to impose one's will on them without regard for what they want or need and without consulting them. Thus, treating people with respect is what moral leadership is about, and nothing could be harder. But when there is organizational or social necessity for change, nothing is more practical. (O'Toole, 1995, p. 12)

The Existence of Informal Groups

Mrs. Harmon used power derived from participation in informal groups to influence actions and behaviors in the formal arena, thereby fostering her individual goals at the expense of the goals established by Principal Harris. She appears to have built a power base in some of the school's subunits, as well as among several informal groups that exist within the faculty, and in each, her power base appears to be very strong. As a result of her power in these settings, she was able to divert the faculty from the goal it was attempting to achieve. Examples of such behavior were evident in her meeting with the department chairs and were reflected in the manner in which she directed the behavior of the group. Although some members were reasonably receptive to the task and wanted to work toward its completion, she managed to direct the group's final decision in a manner that was in line with her personal way of thinking. The operational procedures of the school did not offset her behavior, nor did Principal Harris employ effective conflict-resolution skills. Some of the conflict resolution skills he could have used will be discussed in a later chapter.

In summary, Principal Harris met with challenges only after he failed to plan and organize his responsibilities in a manner that would allow tasks to be completed effectively in a timely manner. New challenges surfaced when he delegated assignments to his assistant principals and failed to consider organizational influences that could negatively affect goal attainment. He took too narrow a view of his responsibilities and did not manage attention or self. In addition, he did not acknowledge the culture of the school in which the faculty functioned or the influence of informal groups in the school.

SCENARIO 4
ADDRESSING DYSFUNCTIONAL THINKING

STANDARD 2

A school administrator is an educational leader who promotes the success of all students by advocating, nurturing, and sustaining a school culture and instructional program conducive to student learning and staff professional growth.

Oakview High School is located in a large urban city with a student population that reflects its community. Until this year, the faculty of the school was composed of veteran teachers who had spent 5 to 10 years at Oakview. In the fall of 2004, a large number of new faculty members were assigned to the school. Many of them were first-year teachers who were anxious to practice their newly learned techniques and eager to make a difference in the lives of their students. However, the veteran faculty members were somewhat defensive and resistant to new faculty, often labeling them as inexperienced and refusing to offer assistance or camaraderie. In fact, there was talk that central administration was attempting to save money by pushing veteran teachers out and employing faculty with less experience.

For the first time this year, Oakview has been chosen to participate in the citywide annual Wordsmith contest, a prestigious competition among honor students in English. The contest attracts community support, and one company traditionally awards $10,000 for computer equipment to the winning school. Ms. Farmington, a new faculty member, is experienced in Wordsmith competition and has demonstrated her ability to work well with the students, as well as her competence in English and literature. Nevertheless, Mrs. Douglas, a veteran teacher at Oakview, is opposed to appointing a "neophyte" to chair such an important event. Although she is not desirous of working with the Wordsmith competition, Mrs. Douglas feels that an experienced faculty member could supervise the students more effectively and get assistance from teachers who have previously participated in Wordsmith events.

Mrs. Douglas is a "faculty favorite." She chairs the homecoming program and shares after-school tutoring duties with other faculty members. She also meets regularly with several faculty members who are affiliated with her sorority. Discussion in each of these arenas often centers on school events and activities.

The principal, Gerald Carroll, feels that Ms. Farmington would make an excellent chair for Wordsmith. However, he is aware of Mrs. Douglas's concerns, and she has requested a meeting with him to discuss the assignment.

REFLECTIVE THINKING

The ISLLC Standards

The following are indicators of the ISLLC Standards addressed in the scenario:

2: Student learning is not seen as the fundamental purpose of schooling; the benefit that diversity brings to the school is not appreciated; the learning environment is not supportive; all individuals are not treated with dignity and respect, and the contributions of all individuals are not acknowledged.

3: Human resources have to be managed and developed; a management decision has to be made that will enhance teaching and learning; risk has to be taken to improve the school; potential problems and opportunities have to be identified, and effective conflict resolution skills have to be used.

4: Diversity has to be recognized and valued; there is an opportunity for staff to develop collaborative skills, and there is an opportunity for the school and community to serve one another as resources.

Reflective Questions and Scenario Analysis

1. Why is the leadership of Principal Carroll so important in this situation?
2. What climate and cultural factors might be influencing the divisiveness that exists among faculty members?
3. What is likely to be the difference between the needs disposition of Ms. Farmington and Mrs. Douglas?
4. What professional development activities might be recommended to Mrs. Douglas? Explain your position.
5. In order to sustain a school culture conducive to student learning, what characteristics have to be reflected in the leadership style of Principal Carroll?

ADDRESSING THE CRITICAL ISSUES

Practicing the Art of Leadership at Oakview High School

In practicing the art of leadership at Oakview High School, the following questions are critical: (a) What approach should Principal Carroll take in addressing this situation? (b) How should the principal respond to Mrs. Douglas? (c) In selecting a course of action, what long-term concerns should the principal factor into his decision?

Responding to Dysfunctional Behavior

School leaders must work with their faculties to promote the success of all students. They must sustain a school culture and instructional program conducive to student learning and professional growth. In the process, all individuals must recognize that student learning is the fundamental purpose of school (Standard 2). Therefore, Principal Carroll must acknowledge and utilize the expertise of Ms. Farmington without diminishing the support of Mrs. Douglas.

He would be well advised to take the human relations approach, listen to the ideas of both individuals, and express an appreciation for their positions. To further understand an approach to addressing such issues, the reader might consult the group decision-making techniques discussed in Chapter 6.

Displaying high consideration behavior, Principal Carroll would demonstrate that all individuals have value and are needed for the school to effectively address the needs of all students. This premise must be emphasized, as the interpersonal relationships of Mrs. Douglas and Ms. Farmington are of paramount importance to the school climate and future school projects. Also, Principal Carroll must understand diversity and how it affects the development of learning experiences. Using effective group-process and consensus-building skills, he can advocate nurturing and sustain a school culture that will foster student learning and professional growth of both faculty members. Such actions will maximize the motivational level of both Ms. Farmington and Mrs. Douglas.

The Meeting with Mrs. Douglas

In the meeting with Mrs. Douglas, Principal Carroll is likely to be most successful by taking a compromising approach to obtaining a solution to the issue. First, he could talk with each of the teachers individually, providing them with a rationale for his position. Then he could proceed to acquire the opinion of each teacher as to an acceptable solution and conclude with a persuasive argument that would foster the involvement of both teachers. Also, he might invite the two teachers to be partners in this and other school activities. Perhaps Mrs. Douglas could serve as a mentor to Ms. Farmington or even co-chair the activity. Regardless of the approach taken by Principal Carroll, each teacher must leave this situation feeling that she has been treated professionally and her talents and attributes are respected.

Selecting a Course of Action

In selecting a course of action regarding the behavior of faculty members, school leaders have to consider several motivational factors. Two theories informing the behavior of Mrs. Douglas and Ms. Farmington are Maslow's Needs Hierarchy and Herzberg's Motivational-Hygiene Theory.

Abraham Maslow (1970) theorized that people are influenced by a series of needs that are grouped into five basic categories. The categories begin with the most basic needs of an individual and extend through a hierarchy to self-actualization. Individuals are first driven by the most basic needs; however, once one's basic needs are satisfied, another need will become the priority for satisfactorily moving up the hierarchy. Maslow grouped the needs in the following five categories:

1. Physiological needs are viewed as a need for food, shelter, and health.
2. Safety needs are viewed as a desire for protection from danger, attacks, and threats.
3. Social needs are expressed through a desire for belonging and the establishment of relationships.
4. Esteem needs are viewed as being expressed through a desire to feel valued and to value oneself.
5. Self-actualization needs are expressed through an individual's desire to reach his or her full potential.

While addressing the attainment of the goals and objectives of the organization, it is helpful when the leader is aware of the needs individuals are seeking to satisfy. For example, if a veteran teacher has the desire to chair the English Department and teach the Advanced Placement classes, the principal might be sensitive to those needs and not assign such responsibility to a first-year teacher. The first-year teacher is likely to be appreciative, as that teacher's primary concern is likely getting adjusted and becoming familiar with the school's overall program. The effective leader gives careful consideration to the comfort level of individuals who function in the organization, removing any impediments to the satisfaction of their needs.

At Oakview High School, Mrs. Douglas is likely seeking self-esteem, whereas Ms. Farmington is likely seeking a sense of belonging. The environment of the school must foster success for both. For this to occur, the leader must acquire knowledge of the values, desires, and aspirations of both individuals. In doing so, he develops positive interpersonal relationships and influences and sustains a positive school climate—one that is conducive to teaching and learning.

In summary, relationships in schools are very important, and leaders should influence positive relationships between and among all individuals and groups affiliated with the school. People have to work with each other, and the work environment must be one that allows individuals to have their needs met and acquire personal desires and goals. When the leader has an understanding of the needs and concerns of each individual, motivational and learning theories that foster the desired organizational climate can be applied. Therefore, the leader must be creative, using the leadership position to open the lines of communication so people will bond, embrace the culture of the school, share ideas, provide assistance to one another, and take pride in being a part of a team that successfully achieves its goals.

SCENARIO 5
ONE OF THE BUS CONTRACTS HAS BEEN CANCELED

STANDARD 3

A school administrator is an educational leader who promotes the success of all students by ensuring management of the organization, operations, and resources for a safe, efficient, and effective learning environment.

STANDARD 4

A school administrator is an educational leader who promotes the success of all students by collaborating with families and community members, responding to diverse community interest and needs, and mobilizing community resources.

On July 1, 2003, Alice Wallace became superintendent of the Arrowhead School District. She began her tenure by establishing a good relationship with the entire community, her administrative staff, and the teachers in the district. Her opening presentation to district administrators was received with a thunderous standing ovation. She followed that meeting with a visit to each school. During her visit to the schools, she engaged in dialogue with the principal, PTA members, and other individuals who were available. Then she held town meetings in each section of the community, met with the leadership of each bargaining unit, and hosted a luncheon for political, religious, and business leaders of the larger community. Everyone expressed great expectations for her as the new superintendent. In fact, one could sense that people throughout the district were charged with newfound positive energy.

The new school year was fast approaching, and she had planned well. Everything was in order. The media had indicated that the district was poised for a successful opening. Then, on August 3, just four weeks before the first day of the 2003–04 school year, the director of transportation advised Superintendent Wallace that a bus-contracting agency that serviced 27 bus routes had canceled their contract. The bus routes in question provided service to students from the areas of the district where people felt they never received equitable treatment. At once, Superintendent Wallace took charge of the situation. She advised the Arrowhead Board of Education of the problem and assured them that a new contract would be obtained prior to the opening of school. A similar announcement was made to the community.

Superintendent Wallace then contacted the contracting agency in question and asked them to reconsider, but to no avail. She contacted other contracting agencies and attempted to enter into a contractual agreement with them, but because of the late notice, they were unable to offer the district bus services. Contacts with the State Department of Education and other districts in the state yielded no positive results. Over the next three weeks, she held several meetings in the community, assuring parents that a solution was being sought and that the problem would be resolved before the first day of school. However, as the first day of school approached with no solution in sight, the community meetings grew increasingly hostile. Even though the director of transportation was very knowledgeable about transportation issues and had served the district for a number of years, he had very little involvement in the community meetings. Principals of affected schools also attended the meetings; however, they were not invited to participate in the discussions.

Often the superintendent held meetings with the director of transportation to obtain status reports, and the results were always the same, "We are working on getting additional buses, and we will have them by opening day." Weekly the superintendent made a similar report to the board and community.

After three weeks passed with no additional buses being secured, the superintendent developed an alternate plan. The plan required a double schedule for some buses to return middle school students to their homes as late as 5:30 P. M. This was an acceptable practice until the fall ended, and students were reaching their homes after dark. Parents throughout the district, even those not affected, demanded a change in the bus schedule. The newspaper reported that the district was returning to its past practices.

REFLECTIVE THINKING

The ISLLC Standards

The following are indicators of the ISLLC Standards addressed in the scenario:

   3: Stakeholders are involved in decisions affecting their schools, but principles and issues relating to fiscal operations of school management are not adequate; people are not trusted, and their judgment is not respected; the superintendent does not share responsibility with stakeholders; and potential problems and opportunities are not identified.

4: The school system is operated as an integral part of the larger community; collaboration and communication occurs with families; the public is kept informed, but media relations are not effectively developed.

Reflective Questions and Scenario Analysis

1. What are the major leadership issues facing Superintendent Wallace? Relate your response to the leadership skills and attributes presented in this chapter, as well as in Chapter 2.
2. What, if anything, was flawed in the statement Superintendent Wallace made to the board and community? What statement(s) would you have made?
3. What are the leadership issues pertaining to Superintendent Wallace's involvement (micromanagement) in the day-to-day operations of the district?
4. What are some of the emerging issues that could potentially impact the total school community? Provide a rationale for your response.
5. How important are community relations strategies and practices in a situation of this nature? Explain your response.
6. What roles should principals and central office administrators play in resolving an issue of this nature?

ADDRESSING THE CRITICAL ISSUES

Practicing the art of leadership in Arrowhead, Superintendent Wallace should be concerned with (a) her leadership behavior, (b) effectively utilizing staff talent, (c) responding to environmental influences, and (d) maintaining positive energy in the district.

The Leadership Behavior of Superintendent Wallace

Superintendent Wallace is a school leader with considerable confidence in herself. In seeking a solution to the transportation challenge, she was highly structured in her approach and not very considerate of her staff. She personally handled the situation from beginning to end, only collaborating with her staff when necessary.

It is obvious that she deemed the issue to be very important, as she immediately took charge of the situation and sought a solution to the problem. Her first action was to call the President of the Board of Education and advise him of the matter. Then she directed the staff to schedule a meeting with parents in the affected community. She met frequently with the director of transportation and kept all members of the board informed of progress being made. Nevertheless, her focus was on the needs of the organization and task completion, giving little consideration to individuals on her staff. This type of behavior likely influenced other problems and challenges.

Effectively Utilizing Staff Talent

Although the superintendent should have been very concerned with finding a solution to this problem, her approach should have been one of working cooperatively with the staff to find a solution, rather than getting directly involved. By taking charge of the situation, Superintendent Wallace failed to give her staff the opportunity to perform their assigned tasks. She was unable to benefit from the talents of members of her leadership team.

The director of transportation was very knowledgeable about transportation issues and had served in the district for years, but he was not charged with the responsibility of finding a solution to the problem. Principals of affected schools attended the community meetings, but they were not invited to participate in the discussions. The behavior of the superintendent could have been perceived in a very negative manner by her staff. They could have perceived that she did not trust their ability and/or that she was the only one who knew how to resolve the problem.

In a learning community, all individuals participate in the decision-making process, and there is a sense of shared responsibility for the success of the organization. Leaders can develop this type of community when they are high on both initiating structure and consideration (Halpin, 1956).

Responding to Environmental Influences

Giving assurance to the board and community that the bus problem would be resolved by the first day of school was problematic. Superintendent Wallace projected a solution to a problem issue in which there were unknown variables over which she had no control. She promised something that she could not deliver. When addressing a situation of this nature, internal and external organizational influences must be considered, and information should be provided to supervisors and the press based on facts, not assumptions or hopes.

Actions of the superintendent failed to take into account the culture of the district or the state. Not fully aware of the culture of the district or the state, she was unable to accurately assess the actions of others. At best, she could only apply practices that had worked well in the past and trust that people would do the right thing. Unfortunately, the approaches utilized were not effective, and the influences in the external environment prevailed.

In summary, it is important that school leaders make decisions that will positively affect both the organization and the people the organization serves. In order to do this, they must be aware of cultural influences and be able to predict the behavior of people. This is extremely difficult for any leader, but particularly difficult for one who is new to a district.

The central issue of concern is the fact that Superintendent Wallace took too active a role in resolving the busing situation. She made the right contacts with her staff and the public, but she failed to factor the human side of the equation into her efforts. The results were community meetings from which the public left angered and without a solution. The staff, namely school principals, felt they did not have a voice; therefore, they did not actively work toward the goal. Also, the skills of the director of transportation were ineffectively utilized.

CHAPTER SUMMARY

The school is an organizational system in which people function to achieve established goals. The effective leader manages this system in ways that allow the organization to achieve its goals while the needs of employees are being met. However, in schools, there are many factors that influence the manner in which individuals and groups behave and the extent to which they are willing to commit to working to achieve the established goals. Among these are leader behavior, environmental influences, and the beliefs, values, and needs of individuals and groups. In order to provide effective leadership, the leader needs to acquire knowledge and understanding of these factors and influences. To some extent, a leader can obtain this knowledge and understanding from theories. The principles embedded in the theories presented in this chapter have laid much of the groundwork for understanding leadership practices that are advocated for leaders of today's schools.

These practices require leaders to operate with a shared vision and a compelling mission, acting on the accepted concept that collaboration is essential to their success and the success of the school. Time and attention are devoted to establishing and building relationships with teachers, students, parents, other professionals, and members of the community. The disposition of the leader illustrates a belief that student learning is the fundamental purpose of schools, professional development an integral part of school improvement, and collaborative relationships with all stakeholders essential to organizational effectiveness. Leaders of today's schools must have knowledge and understanding of the influences that impact organizational behavior and be able to apply the leadership principles described.

MOVING INTO PRACTICE

Review the scenarios in Chapter 3. Using the pros and cons of the various situations, identify several approaches that you would use to address the following school-related issues in an actual situation. Project yourself into the role of the principal and take care to formulate a rationale for your selected behavior.

◆ Describe the process you would use to formulate a set of goals with individual faculty members, an entire faculty, and/or members of various community groups.

◆ Describe the approach you would use to acquire the support necessary to resolve an issue similar to the bus contract cancellation in Arrowhead.

◆ Formulate a list of school characteristics that are negatively impacting the teaching and learning process in a school where you are principal and identify an organizational structure that you would advocate for that school. Take care to provide a theoretical base for your selection of the organizational structure.

◆ Cite four ways in which the school and community serve one another as resources.

◆ Describe a school environment where you would feel pleased to serve as principal.

◆ Describe the issues from the cases that offer you the best opportunity to utilize your leadership skills and attributes.

ACQUIRING AN UNDERSTANDING OF SELF

◆ What do you believe about schools?

◆ What do you believe about children?

◆ How do you behave in your current role? How does that behavior compare with the expectations individuals hold for the role?

DEEPENING YOUR UNDERSTANDING

Now that you have read this chapter, visit the Companion Website for this book at **www.prenhall.com/green** *and take the Self-Assessment Inventory for this chapter.*

Completing this inventory will give you an indication of how familiar you are with the ISLLC Standards knowledge indicators that relate to this chapter.

SUGGESTED READINGS

Barth, R. S. (1990). *Improving schools from within: Teachers, parents, and principals can make a difference.* San Francisco: Jossey-Bass.

Bennis, W., & Biederman, P. (1997). *Organizing genius.* Reading, MA: Addison Wesley Longman.

Greenberg, J. (1996). *Managing behavior in organizations.* Upper Saddle River, NJ: Prentice Hall.

Hord, S. M. (2004). Learning together, leading together. New York: Teachers College Press.

Roberts, S. M. and Pruitt, E. Z. (2003). Schools as professional learning communities. Thousand Oaks, CA: Corwin Press.

Senge, P. M. (2001). Schools that learn: A fifth discipline field book for educators, parents, and everyone who cares about education. New York: Doubleday.

Senge, P. M. (1990). *The fifth discipline.* New York: Doubleday.

Sergiovanni, T. J. (1994). *Building community in schools.* San Francisco: Jossey-Bass.

Short, P., & Greer, J. (1997). *Leadership in empowered schools: Themes from innovative efforts.* Upper Saddle River, NJ: Merrill/Prentice Hall.

AVAILABLE POWERPOINT PRESENTATIONS

After completing this chapter, log on to the Companion Website for this book at **www.prenhall.com/green** *and click on the PowerPoint module.*

- Theories Informing Leadership
- Leader Behavior in Organizations
- Defining Culture and Climate in Schools

WEBSITES

Leadership and Organizational Vitality
http://www.nwrel.org/scpd/re-engineering/keyissues/leadership.shtml

Schools as Learning Organizations
http://www.ascd.org/publications/books/1998brandt/chapter3.html

Educational Leadership Theorists
http://cw.mariancollege.edu/bstucky/DOC/theory.doc

PRACTICE ISLLC EXAMS

After reading this chapter, log on the Companion Website for this book at **www.prenhall.com/green** *to take the practice ISLLC exams.*

REFERENCES

Barth, R. S. (1990). *Improving schools from within: Teachers, parents, and principals can make the difference.* San Francisco: Jossey-Bass.

Bennis, W. (1995). The 4 competencies of leadership. In D. A. Kolb, J. S. Osland, & I. M. Rubin (Eds.), *The organizational behavior reader* (pp. 395–401). Upper Saddle River, NJ: Prentice Hall.

Bennis, W., & Biederman, P. (1997). *Organizing genius.* Reading, MA: Addison Wesley Longman.

Bolman, L. G., & Deal, T. E. (1997). *Reframing organizations: Artistry, choice, and leadership* (2nd ed.). San Francisco: Jossey-Bass.

Boyatzis, R. E., & Skelly, F. R. (1995). The impact of changing values on organizational life: The latest update. In D. A. Kolb, J. S. Osland, & I. M. Rubin (Eds.), *The organizational behavior reader* (pp. 1–17). Upper Saddle River, NJ: Prentice Hall.

Brewer, J. H., Ainsworth, J. M., & Wynne, G. E. (1984). *Power management: A three-step program for successful leadership.* Upper Saddle River, NJ: Prentice Hall.

Buckley, W. (1967). *Sociology and modern systems theory.* Upper Saddle River, NJ: Prentice Hall.

Covey, S. R. (1989). *The 7 habits of highly effective people.* New York: Simon & Schuster.

Cypress, S. (2003). *A comparative analysis of the characteristics of probationary and non-probationary title I schools and the instructional analysis used by those principals.* Unpublished dissertation, University of Memphis.

DuBrin, A. J. (1996). *Human relations for career and personal success* (4th ed.). Upper Saddle River, NJ: Prentice Hall.

Etheridge, C. P., & Green, R. (1998). *Union district collaboration and other processes related to school district restructuring for establishing standards and accountability measures* (technical report for the 21st Century Project). Washington, DC: National Educational Association.

Fayol, H. (1949). *General and industrial management.* London: Pitman (first published in 1919).

Garvin, D. A. (1995). Building a learning organization. In D. A. Kolb, J. S. Osland, & I. M. Rubin (Eds.), *The organizational behavior reader* (pp. 96–109). Upper Saddle River, NJ: Prentice Hall.

Getzels, J. W., & Guba, E. (1957). Social behavior and the administrative process. *School Review, 65,* 423–441.

Gorton, R. A. (1987). *School leadership and administration: Important concepts, case studies, and simulations* (3rd ed.). Dubuque, IA: McGraw-Hill.

Gorton, R. A., & Schneider, G. T. (1991). *School-based challenges and opportunities* (3rd ed.). Dubuque, IA: McGraw-Hill.

Green, R. L. (1997). In search of nurturing schools: Creating effective learning conditions. *NASSP Bulletin, 81*(589), 17–26.

Green, R. L. (1998). Nurturing characteristics in schools related to discipline, attendance, and eighth grade proficiency test scores. *American Secondary Education, 26*(4), 7–14.

Halpin, A. (1956). *The leader behavior of schools.* Columbus: The Ohio State University.

Halpin, A. W., & Croft, D. B. (1963). *The organizational climate of schools.* Chicago: University of Chicago Press.

Hanson, M. E. (1991). *Educational administration and organization behavior* (3rd ed.). Needham Heights, MA: Allyn & Bacon.

Hanson, M. E. (1996). *Educational administration and organization behavior* (4th ed.). Needham Heights, MA: Allyn & Bacon.

Hersey, P., Blanchard, K. H., & Johnson, D. E. (1996). *Management of organizational behavior: Utilizing human resources* (7th ed.). Upper Saddle River, NJ: Prentice Hall.

Interstate School Leaders Licensure Consortium of the Council of Chief State School Officers. (1997). *Candidate information bulletin for school leaders assessment.* Princeton, NJ: Educational Testing Service.

Katz, D., & Kahn, R. L. (1978). *The social psychology of organizations* (2nd ed.). New York: Wiley.

Lunenburg, F. C., & Ornstein, A. C. (1996). *Educational administration: Concepts and practices* (2nd ed.). Belmont, CA: Wadsworth.

Manz, C. C., & Sims, H. P., Jr. (1989). *Superleadership.* New York: Berkley.

Maslow, A. (1970). *Motivation and personality* (Rev. ed.). New York: Harper & Row.

McGregor, D. (1960). *The human side of the enterprise.* New York: McGraw-Hill.

O'Toole, J. (1995). *Leading change: Overcoming the ideology of comfort and the tyranny of custom.* San Francisco: Jossey-Bass.

Owens, R. G. (1995). *Organizational behavior in education* (5th ed.). Boston: Allyn & Bacon.

Pondy, L. R., and Mitroff, I. I. (1979). Beyond open system models of organization. In B. M. Staw (Ed.), *Research in organizational behavior,* Vol. 1, (pp. 3–39). Greenwich, CT: JAI Press.

Ryan, K. D., & Oestreich, D. K. (1991). *Driving fear out of the workplace: How to overcome the invisible barriers to quality, productivity, and innovation.* San Francisco: Jossey-Bass.

Schein, E. H. (1992). Facing the complexities of culture change: A case study. In E. H. Schein (ed.), *Organizational Culture and Leadership* (2nd ed, pp. 334–359). San Francisco: Jossey-Bass.

Schein, E. H. (1984). *Coming to a new awareness of organizational culture,* Sloan Management Review, 25, 3–16.

Schein, E. H. (1970). *Organizational psychology* (2nd ed.). Upper Saddle River, NJ: Prentice Hall.

Scott, W. (2003). *Organizations: Rational, natural, and open systems* (5th ed.). Upper Saddle River, NJ: Prentice Hall.

Senge, P. M. (1990). *The fifth discipline: The art and practice of the learning organization.* New York: Doubleday.

Senge, P. M. (1995). The leader's new work: Building learning organizations. In D. A Kolb, J. S. Osland, & I. M. Rubin (Eds.), *The organizational behavior reader* (pp. 76–96). Upper Saddle River, NJ: Prentice Hall.

Sergiovanni, T. J. (1994). *Building community in schools.* San Francisco: Jossey-Bass.

Snyder, C. R. (1988, January). So many selves. *Contemporary Psychology,* vol. 77. American Psychological Association.

Taylor, F. W. (1911). *Principles of scientific management.* New York: Harper.

Weber, M. (1947). *The theory of social and economic organization* (T. Parsons & A. M. Henderson, Trans.). New York: Oxford University Press.

4

ENHANCING LEADERSHIP EFFECTIVENESS THROUGH COMMUNICATION

The importance of communication practices in today's schools cannot be overemphasized. "In the area of leadership, there is no talent more essential than one's ability to communicate" (Guarino, 1974, p. 1). "Communication is the lifeblood of the school; it is a process that links the individual, the group, and the organization" (Lunenburg & Ornstein, 1996, p. 176). Through effective communication, relationships are built, trust is established, and respect is gained.

The purpose of this chapter is to emphasize the importance of communication in schools and the need for school leaders to be effective communicators. In so doing, the communication process will be described and removing barriers to effective communication will be discussed. The ethics of conversation will be explored, and the relationship of communication to select ISLLC Standards will be demonstrated.

The scenarios in the chapter, which characterize ISLLC Standards 1 and 2, serve a twofold purpose: (1) They offer examples of how communication effectiveness can enhance the progress of schools, moving them toward their vision and mission, and (2) they emphasize how the lack of communication can prove to be problematic. Analyzing these scenarios, the reader will be able to experience, through practical school situations, the importance of communication in terms of both the content of a message and the feelings being conveyed by the sender of the message.

The Importance of Effective Communication

In a school, as is the case in any organization, the efforts of individuals and groups must be coordinated, and communication is a powerful tool in that process. In fact, communication plays an important role in every facet of the school's operation and is considered one of the major proficiencies of an effective school leader (NAESP, 2001). It is the essence of the organization—the glue that holds it together (Lunenburg & Ornstein, 1996). The latter statement is made clear by the ISLLC Standards, as the standards require the school leader to facilitate, advocate, ensure, collaborate, promote, and influence stakeholders. To meet any of the aforementioned requirements, the leader must have mastered various communication strategies.

Although all of the standards require skills in communication, it is important to acknowledge that Standard 1 has perhaps the most profound communication focus. This standard requires school leaders to be able to develop, articulate, implement, and provide stewardship of a vision of learning that is shared and supported by the school community (Standard 1). It is significant because the vision establishes a sense of direction for the school and serves as a road map for stakeholders to follow. In order to persuade stakeholders to share the vision and assist in its attainment, leaders must be proficient in various forms of communication.

In addition, leaders transmit messages to advocate, nurture, delegate responsibility, and assist followers in developing their potential. They also transmit messages to ensure that the school culture and instructional program are conducive to student learning and staff professional growth (Standard 2).

Transmitting messages is a major function of school leadership. However, in the daily operation of schools, leaders not only communicate by transmitting messages, they also receive, monitor, and seek them. Studies indicate that school leaders spend up to 80% of their time communicating with parents, members of the community, and other members of the organization (Kmetz & Willower, 1982; Sobel & Ornstein, 1996). Consequently, the leader's ability to communicate with people is tantamount to the school operating in an efficient and effective manner. Leaders who are sensitive and use a reliable network of communication patterns with which stakeholders are familiar and comfortable are not only likely to be effective, but they can also transform the school into a pleasant place to work. When school leaders are effective communicators, their potential for meeting the ISLLC Standards is tremendously enhanced.

The Communication Process

The communication process involves transmitting information from a person (the sender) to another person or group(s) (the receivers) and may occur verbally or nonverbally. When a message is transmitted using spoken language, verbal communication is occurring. This type of communication may be spoken face-to-face, over a public address system, in a telephone conversation, or it may be written in a letter, a memo, or electronically.

When a message is transmitted without the use of words, the form of communication is considered nonverbal. Nonverbal behaviors are very important to the communication process, for more than half of what is communicated is not conveyed by words, but by body language (Sobel & Ornstein, 1996). The manner in which the leader hesitates in speech and the tone of voice can reveal much about how the leader is feeling about a situation. Certain ideas may be expressed in a loud tone, whereas others may be expressed in a mumbled tone. Hand movements, eye movements, and facial expressions are all actions that help to convey a message. The leader is never in a position where communication is not occurring. Any activity that conveys a message between individuals (and all activities do) is considered communication (Myers & Myers, 1982). Figure 4.1 graphically depicts the communication process.

Communication in Schools

When you think of people in schools communicating with one another, a typical situation might involve the principal providing a faculty member with directions. Another situation might be the exchange of curriculum information between faculty members or a faculty member providing a parent with a student progress report. In each of these instances, the individuals receiving the message will interpret the meaning of the message and base their subsequent actions on those interpretations. Therefore, understanding is a fundamental aspect of communication.

When effective communication occurs, there is a mutual sharing of ideas and feelings out of which understanding develops and action is taken. Words and gestures being sent out does not necessarily mean communication has occurred, and certainly one cannot assume that it has occurred in a manner that will generate the desired results. Consequently, the sender of the message must develop a variety of communication

FIGURE 4.1 The Communication Process

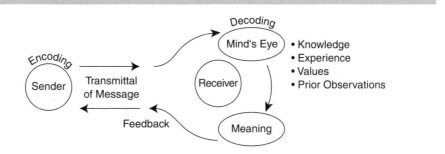

skills and apply them appropriately in a manner that enhances understanding. To accentuate this point, we turn to a discussion of the transmittal process.

The Transmittal Process

In transmitting messages, the leader must realize that meaning is not in the words of the sender, but rather in the mind of the receiver. Meaning is not transmitted; the receiver gives the message meaning. The receiver gives meaning to the message based on background, knowledge, experience, values, and prior observations. In some instances, because of differences in these areas, the same words hold different meanings for different people, causing a problem in semantics or a lack of understanding. Considering this factor, the sender must strive to encode and transmit the message, using symbols that will be most familiar to the receiver. The greater the agreement regarding the meaning of the symbols, the greater the probability that understanding will exist between the two parties when the receiver decodes the message (Gibson, Ivancevich, & Donnelly, 1976).

Agreement on the Meaning

The agreement on the meaning of the message can be enhanced through two-way interactive forms of communication and repetitiveness. Such is the case with face-to-face meetings where both verbal and nonverbal clues are a part of the transmittal process. Television presentations, videotape presentations, and telephone conversations also allow the type of interaction that enhances the possibility that the receiver will give the message the meaning that is intended by the sender. Letters, memoranda, and other one-way forms of communication do not allow verbal and nonverbal clues to assist in the transmittal process, and therefore, the message is subject to interpretation. It is advisable in most school situations to use multiple forms of communication, as repetitiveness improves effectiveness.

The Skilled Communicator

A leader who is truly a skilled communicator will perfect the communication process and deliver messages using techniques or strategies that are appropriate to the requirements of the situation. A number of researchers and writers have offered suggestions concerning such a process. Two worthy of note are Rogers and Farson (1995). They suggest that the leader must be available, approachable, and able to listen intelligently and carefully to others, conveying the feeling that the leader is as concerned about them as the situation that is being addressed. Further, they suggest that the leader must be attentive to both the content of the message and the feelings of the sender. The feedback given the sender must make clear that the message was appreciated in terms of both its meaning and the feelings with which it was conveyed. More specifically, they advise that to be an effective communicator, the leader must be an active listener. In doing so, the leader acquires the total meaning of the message and observes the underlying feelings of the message, while noting and being sensitive to all verbal and nonverbal clues displayed by the sender.

One way for the leader to become an active listener is to view communication as a people process, rather than a language process (Gibbs, 1995), and develop a clear understanding of the networks used in a social system to transmit messages. To provide a deeper understanding of the need for the leader to be an active listener and to assist in that process, some active listening skills are summarized in Table 4.1. More will be said about active listening later in the chapter. First, we discuss the flow of communication in schools.

TABLE 4.1   The Active Listener

OBJECTIVE OF THE LISTENER	ACTIVITY PERFORMED	IMPLICATIONS OR END RESULT
Understand the message	Grasp the facts and feelings	The sender of the message is assisted in presenting the message.
Demonstrate respect for the potential worth of the speaker	Demonstrate a positive attitude toward the sender of the message and for its content	The sender is less defensive, more democratic, less authoritarian, and more open to experiences.
Listen with sensitivity	Demonstrate the willingness to change	Information is acquired about people; positive relations are built, and attitudes are constructively altered.
Reduce any threat that might exist	Create a climate that is not critical, evaluative, or demoralizing	Defensiveness is reduced, and the individual feels safe enough to address new values and experiences.
View the issue in an objective manner	Refrain from being directive and influencing a position	One can listen with understanding and be open to change.
Listen for total meaning and remain sensitive	Seek to understand the content of the message and the feeling underlying the message, noting the nonverbal actions or cues of the speaker	Positive relationships are enhanced, and the climate is supportive.
Convey interest in the speaker, respect for his/her position, and the fact that it is valid from his/her perspective	Demonstrate respect for the speaker through behavior	A tone is set for positive interaction to occur.
See the world from the speaker's perspective	Reflect on what the speaker seems to mean by his/her words	The climate is less emotional.

SOURCE: Constructed from the readings of Carl Rogers and Richard E. Farson's "Active Listening" in David A. Kolb, Joyce S. Osland, and Irwin M. Rubin, *The Organizational Behavior Reader,* pp. 203–214.

The Flow of Communication in Schools

Information in schools (open social systems) is transmitted through formal and informal networks. Formal networks are the means of transmitting messages sanctioned by the organization in accordance with its hierarchy. Informal networks emerge as individuals in the organization interact with each other in ways that do not reflect the organization's hierarchy. Such an approach is likely to be taken by the informal groups discussed in Chapter 3. The leader must be knowledgeable of both networks and recognize that the network being used to transmit information is essential to goal attainment. The following are examples of how these networks function in school settings.

If the principal holds a faculty meeting and shares information regarding the new reading program, the formal communication network is being used. The formal network is also being used when the principal receives a message from the superintendent and passes the message to teachers who, in turn, pass it to students. However, members of the faculty interacting personally may use the informal network. If Jackie (a science teacher at Weaver High School) advises her friend Betty (the school's reading coordinator) that a new reading program is going to be announced by the principal and Betty shares the information with James (who teaches reading), the informal network is in use.

Both networks have their place in the organization and, if effectively utilized, can enhance communication. However, the informal network, often referred to as the grapevine, does have some negative features, of which the most noted are distortion and rumors (unsubstantiated information). When the needs of faculty and staff are not met, rumors tend to spread and may signify that the leader is not meeting the informational needs of the faculty and staff. Although it is somewhat difficult and may be virtually impossible for a leader to eliminate all rumors, knowledge of them can be very beneficial.

The positive aspects of the grapevine are flexibility and speed in disseminating information. If used in a positive manner, the grapevine can help keep followers informed, give administrators insight into followers' attitudes, and provide a test arena for new ideas. Nevertheless, in a school system, the objective of the communication process is to provide a means for the flow of information so that activities regarding goal attainment can be coordinated, fostering a climate of trust and respect. Therefore, the formal network should be as effective as possible. To further illustrate the importance of the transmittal process, we present a discussion of the flow of communication in schools and school districts.

The Direction of Communication in Schools

Communication in schools or school districts flows in several directions: downward, upward, horizontally, and diagonally. Downward communication often involves sending messages down the chain of command of the hierarchical structure. It is not atypical for school district personnel to use downward communication to keep employees informed, provide a sense of mission, impart information to followers regarding their performance, and orient new employees to the system. Information flowing down the chain of command passes through several filters (different individuals) and therefore, it is helpful when the leader uses several forms of verification to ensure the accuracy and understanding of information.

Upward communication occurs when individuals in the role of followers send messages up the chain to their leaders. Such communication is often in response to messages that have come down the chain of command. The receiver is providing feedback to individuals at a higher level. Upward communication is perhaps the form of communication that is most prone to filtering (sharing only select portions of a message). Sometimes out of fear of the outcome, teachers resist providing principals with unpopular or negative information. Lewis (1980) offers that this reluctance stems from three interpersonal factors: (a) teachers not wanting to take the risk of making suggestions that could possibly result in additional work, (b) teachers fearing that the principal will negatively impact future promotions, and (c) teachers being uncertain of the manner in which the principal will receive the information and how the principal will use his or her power in the future. In such instances, there is a breakdown in communication as the message is modified, and the leader is only provided information that followers believe will be well received (Barge, 1994).

When individuals communicate with other individuals of the same status in the organization, horizontal communication is occurring. If individuals at one level in the organization communicate with individuals at another level in a different division or department, then the communication flow is considered diagonal. Communication in an organization can also be described as vertical. The term *vertical* is not used here to refer to the direction of the communication; rather, it describes a pattern that focuses on combining upward and downward communication, making leaders more visible through face-to-face contact. It is the effective flow of communication in schools that provides task coordination and furnishes emotional and social support among peers. The direction of the communication flow in a typical school district appears in Figure 4.2.

Each of these directions provides a means of effectively transmitting a message of a specific nature. Therefore, if breakdowns in communication are to be avoided, it is important for the leader to clearly understand which direction is most appropriate for use in any given situation and the medium of communication that will be most effective.

The Participation of Individuals in the Network

In a social system, individuals have various means of exchanging information. Another pattern of communication flow in schools is the communication network

FIGURE 4.2 The Flow of Communication in a Typical School District

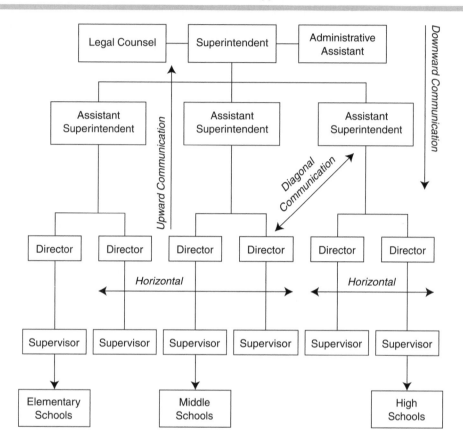

connecting senders and receivers. The network system consists of five patterns, de-scribed as star, wheel, chain, circle, and Y, that illustrate degrees of centralization and structure that can occur between senders and receivers (Lewis, 1987). This network is graphically depicted in Figure 4.3.

The most structured and centralized of the patterns is the wheel network. The wheel structure would allow the principal to discuss a curriculum issue with each teacher on the fourth-grade curriculum team.

The chain network, the second most restrictive, characterizes two people who communicate with each other and then with one other person. For example, if the principal gets a directive from the superintendent regarding the curriculum issue previously discussed with members of the fourth-grade curriculum team and com-municates that directive to the department chair of the fourth grade, then the chain network is operable.

FIGURE 4.3   Communication Network

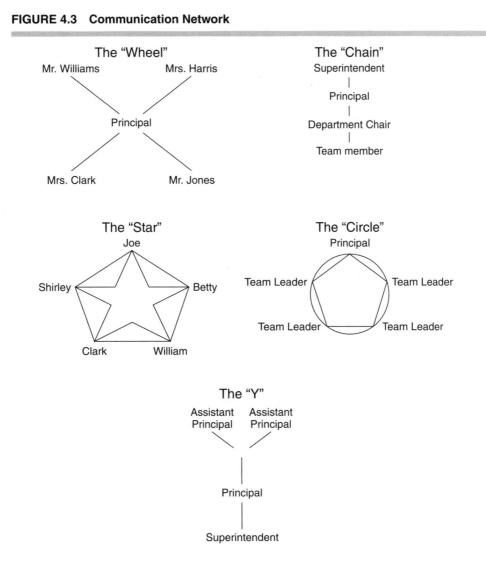

Two-way communication and open accessibility to all network members best characterize the star network. This type of network is likely to be practiced in a learning community because status is not an issue, and the benefit to be derived is high faculty morale. For example, if all fourth-grade curriculum team members communicate with each of the others regarding the development of the new curriculum, the star network would be operable.

With the circle pattern, there is also flexibility in the flow of communication. As an individual communicates in two directions (right and left), there is equal communication, and each individual is considered a decision maker. This pattern might also be found in a learning community.

The last network in the pattern is the Y network, which allows communication similar to that of the chain. A principal may get directions from the superintendent to complete a task and give directions to each of two assistant principals who may be part of his staff. In such an instance, each assistant principal could discuss the task with the principal but not with each other or the superintendent.

Regardless of the pattern selected for use by school leaders, it is important for them to have a communication plan that can be used to clearly articulate objectives and strategies that will achieve the vision and goals of the school. This plan must be one that allows the leader to demonstrate a sense of understanding, trust, and respect for the potential worth of the individuals affiliated with the school (Standards 3 and 4).

Reducing Barriers to Effective Communication

To utilize the process of communication in reaching the ISLLC Standards, school leaders must acquire accurate pictures of how they are perceived as communicators and constantly assess those pictures to refine their communication skills (Stech, 1983). It is also necessary for leaders to acquire an understanding of the individuals with whom they work and be willing to continuously examine their own assumptions, beliefs, and practices (Standard 1). As was illustrated in Chapter 3, individuals who make up a school faculty can represent many different eras. To enhance communication effectiveness, it is important for the leader to recognize the variety of ideas, values, and cultures of people from these different eras. This is critical if leaders want followers to act on what is being transmitted, as every message sent by the leader will be given meaning by the receiver, based upon the receiver's characteristics and the conditions under which the message is being received (Barge, 1994).

Because of the above-mentioned factor, barriers can form, and depending on the nature of the situation, these barriers can interfere with the effectiveness of the transmittal process and cause a breakdown in communication. By being sensitive to the barriers that exist and knowledgeable of strategies that can be employed to eliminate them, school leaders can enhance their communication effectiveness. A list of barriers that frequently interfere with effective communication in schools appears in Table 4.2. The reader will be able to view many of these barriers in Scenario 7 wherein the lack of effective communication skills became a roadblock to the implementation of a new professional development plan. In reading that scenario, the reader will want to particularly note the activities ongoing in the administrative meeting and the consequences of a leader using a communication style that does not afford her the benefit of appropriate feedback.

TABLE 4.2   Common Barriers That Frequently Interfere with Effective Communication in Schools

Information overload: A situation wherein an individual receives more information than he/she can cognitively process in the given period

Status difference: A situation wherein the free flow of information between personnel at different levels in the organization is inhibited because of their position (Note: The greater the disparity in status, the less likelihood that communication will occur openly and effectively)

Semantics: A situation wherein the spoken word has a different meaning for the receiver than the sender (Note: This is likely because of the varied backgrounds, knowledge, and experience of individuals in the organization)

Filtering: A situation wherein the message from the sender is altered (intentionally or unintentionally) or partially transmitted to the receiver

Paralanguage: Situations wherein stress, the speed of speech, grunts, sighs, and other such clues that are vocal but not really verbal are displayed

Interpersonal relationships: The quality of the relationships of the individuals interacting and the interpersonal style of the parties in a relationship

Strategies for Reducing Barriers to Communication

Leaders can often remove barriers, prevent breakdowns in communication, and improve communication effectiveness by:

1. establishing effective interpersonal relationships;
2. managing position power;
3. acquiring feedback;
4. being active listeners;
5. displaying empathy; and
6. understanding the ethics of conversation.

Using these strategies, the leader can safeguard against communication barriers, develop communication confidence, and avoid unexpected problems, while benefiting from a variety of ideas, values, and cultures. In so doing, the leader works to influence the type of school climate that enhances decision quality and acceptance. To provide additional insight into barriers to effective communication, each of the aforementioned areas will be briefly discussed.

Interpersonal Relationships

In learning organizations of the type suggested by the ISLLC Standards, in order to acquire the information necessary to effectively administer schools, leaders have to interact with individuals inside and outside of the schoolhouse. In communicating with these individuals, it is helpful when positive interpersonal relationships are established.

The interpersonal style of parties in a relationship can be a significant determinant of the quality of that relationship. The manner in which individuals interact creates an emotional climate that characterizes their interaction and determines whether or not communication problems emerge (Rogers & Farson, 1995). In communicating with individuals and/or groups, what may seem to be a challenging task becomes considerably less challenging when the school leader has developed interpersonal relations skills sufficient to acquire information that is necessary to make quality decisions.

The quality of decisions, to a large extent, depends on the information (data) used to make those decisions. Poor information results in poor decision quality. It is better to have no data than to have bad data. Therefore, the leader can ill afford to have poor interpersonal relations with the faculty.

Given that much of the information needed to make quality decisions will come from teachers, the relationship between teachers and the principal becomes paramount. For example, if principals have a poor relationship with teachers, and teachers do not respect the principal's judgment, or if the principal is making decisions in the zone of concern of teachers without their involvement, the quality of the information teachers provide the principal may not be sufficient for the principal to adequately address the issue in question. Barth (1990) suggests that no relationship in a school has a greater effect on the quality of life in that school than the relationship between teacher and principal.

Building a Climate of Trust   In order to foster effective interpersonal relationships and open the lines of communication, school leaders must build a school culture of trust. Ciancutti and Steding (2001) advise that in a culture of trust, the leader is consistent in words, actions, and deeds, and there are no gaps between what the leader says and does. The same leader appears in every faculty meeting, enabling the faculty to develop an appreciation for what spoken statements mean and an understanding of the various actions taken. As a result of the trust developed between the faculty and the leader, faculty members begin to trust one another, and a framework for interacting is developed. They begin to communicate directly and openly and do not withhold information or participate in sharing information that has not been verified. When the leader builds a school culture of trust and everyone is treated with dignity and respect, the full potential of the faculty is developed, and the school benefits from informed decision making.

This type of communication begins with leaders acquiring an understanding of their own communication style and the style used by others. It is the match in styles that leads to effective communication (Greenberg & Baron, 2003). Therefore, the more effective leaders become in developing an understanding of the communication style of others, the more effective they are likely to be in matching their styles with the styles of others. With a deeper understanding of communication styles, the door is open for effective two-way communication. A summary of six communication styles reported by Greenberg and Baron (2003) appears in Table 4.3 In reviewing these styles, it will be beneficial for readers to assess each to determine the style that is likely to enhance their communication effectiveness.

Position Power

Like interpersonal relations, position power can be a barrier to effective communication. The position held by the leader and the power that is associated with that position (position power) could invoke fear in followers. Because leaders are in a position to reward or punish, individuals will sometimes refrain from providing them information, or to say the least, they will filter the information if it is negative. Ryan and Oestreich (1991) reported accounts of followers in schools who were reluctant to speak out about certain issues because of the possible negative reaction to their comments by the principal. If the behavior of the leader places fear in individuals who work in the schoolhouse, a barrier to effective communication is likely to occur. Faculty members may put off having a conversation with the principal because they believe it will be confrontational. It is extremely difficult to have a high level of quality in the organization when people are afraid (Deming, 1986).

TABLE 4.3 Communication Styles

▶ The Noble: Leaders with this style use few words, go directly to the point, speak directly, stating just what is on their mind.

▶ The Socratic: These leaders think through issues before reaching a conclusion. They like details, are not afraid to engage in long debates, and will argue their point.

▶ The Reflective: Reflective communicators strive to avoid conflict. They are concerned with interpersonal relations and communicate in a manner that will not offend others. They are excellent listeners and are likely to say nothing before saying something that causes conflict.

▶ The Magistrate: These leaders combine aspects of the Noble style with aspects of the Socratic style. They communicate in a dominating manner, displaying an air of superiority. These individuals tell you exactly what they think and will go into great detail to get their point across.

▶ The Candidate: Candidates combine aspects of the Socratic style with aspects of the Reflective style. They display a warm and supportive disposition, communicating in a very likable manner. However, they are analytical and chatty and base their interaction on a great deal of information.

▶ The Senator: These leaders have skillfully developed both the Noble and Reflective styles of communication. The two styles are not mixed. Rather, the leader skillfully moves between the two as the situation warrants.

SOURCE: Greenburg & Baron.

Staying Connected   The school leader has to stay connected with the faculty, interact, and exchange information. When the leader and the faculty are connected, the faculty feels empowered and is more likely to commit to goal attainment. When the leader does not stay connected with the faculty, conflict will emerge and become a disruptive force in the communication process, and some very innovative ideas can be lost because individuals are afraid of repercussions. In order to keep the lines of communication open, the leader has to stay connected with each faculty member. "Staying connected means that leaders do more than listen to the facts and circumstances being discussed. It goes beneath surface matters and engages deeper emotional levels. It says to the other person that he or she is valued as a human being" (Ciancutti & Steding, 2001, p. 90).

When leaders enter a room, they should not enter demonstrating power; rather they must realize that everyone in the room has some type of power (expertise, charismatic, or position) and can use that power to negatively or positively influence the attainment of school goals. Dr. Raines, President of The University of Memphis, does this exceptionally well. When entering a meeting, she individually greets as many people as possible, shakes hands, and makes warm comments. This type of behavior conveys respect for the individual and acknowledges that all individuals can make a contribution to the attainment of university goals.

An example of a less effective approach appears in the Scenario in Chapter 3 (p. 66) wherein the principal gave Mrs. Harmon an assignment that she did not complete to his expectation. In opening the meeting with the assistant principals, he exhibited position power. He was very directive and used "The Noble" style in communicating his message. This style of communication proved to be ineffective. To be effective communicators, leaders must sustain a collaborative position displaying "acts of caring about what the other person says, without seeking to either fix the situation or to discord or discount it" (Ciancutti & Steding, 2001, p. 91).

When leaders place themselves in a collaborating position, they can influence, facilitate, and acquire support from the entire school community. If individuals in the internal or external environment refrain from communicating with the leader, school goal attainment will be extremely difficult.

Acquiring Feedback

The leader can reduce the likelihood of position power interfering with effective communication by creating the type of supportive environment that was discussed in Chapter 3 (learning environment). Such an environment promotes effective communication because there is a feeling that individuals listen to one another, welcome comments, and respect and appreciate each other. In this type of environment, leaders can anticipate meaningful feedback regarding their behavior.

Feedback is literally defined as the information provided to the sender by the receiver conveying how the message was received and acted upon (Cusella, 1987). It is a process that can be used to give individuals and groups important information about their level of performance, and its skillful use is critical to leaders' successful management of relational obstacles (Barge, 1994).

Feedback is also used to solicit ideas from teachers. Teachers have excellent ideas about how to improve school programs, and effective leaders establish a process for that information to reach them. Once the process is in place, they use it in defining roles, motivating and empowering individuals, managing conflict, seeking the opinions and concerns of followers, and providing a comfort level for stakeholders to express their true feelings regarding messages being communicated. However, it cannot be overemphasized that for feedback to be provided in a manner that fosters effective communication, the climate must advance a sense of equity, allowing participants to feel trust, acceptance, and warmth.

Ciancutti and Steding (2001) suggest that in such a climate, individuals feel safe enough to be open and share their true feelings and concerns. If the climate is hostile or threatening, emotions can become a factor, resentment might exist, and defensiveness builds, making it difficult for the parties to communicate effectively. To openly address an issue, individuals must feel that there is no need to fear exposure of themselves to members of the group. If this fear is removed, the individual is likely to speak freely and openly.

Practicing Active Listening

Active listening enhances communication effectiveness. When leaders are active listeners, they acquire the total meaning of the message and observe the underlying feelings while noting and being sensitive to all verbal and nonverbal clues displayed by the sender. If they do not understand the message being sent, they raise questions and provide the sender an opportunity to clarify his or her position. During the communication process, they provide feedback to indicate the extent to which the message is being received. Such feedback may be in the form of a nod or responding to the sender by rephrasing the sender's words into their own words. When school leaders model active listening, they assist faculty members in gaining a clear understanding of their roles and responsibilities and demonstrate a cooperative attitude toward others (Rogers & Farson, 2001). Also, they encourage other individuals to become active listeners, thereby enhancing communication effectiveness throughout the school.

Another way for the leader to become an active listener is to view communication as a people process, rather than a language process (Gibbs, 1995), and develop a clear understanding of the networks used in a social system to transmit messages. They cannot be passive, simply observing words that are spoken; rather, they must actively try to grasp the facts and the feelings in what is being said and help the speaker work out any problems that may exist (Rogers & Farson, 2001).

Understanding how to convey a message is as important as the content of the message. Often the way things are said is more important than what is said. Although individuals do a lot of listening, only a small percentage of what is heard is comprehended (Rowe & Baker, 1984). Consequently, the benefit to be derived from developing the skills of active listening cannot be overemphasized. Standard 2 stipulates that the disposition of school leaders should emphasize student learning as being the fundamental purpose of schooling. When school leaders practice active listening, they are likely to display this type of disposition.

Displaying Empathy

Also, individuals are less likely to communicate openly when others (especially leaders) convey a feeling of superiority in position, power, wealth, and intellect, or arouse some type of defensive position. Such defensive actions interfere with the communication flow, making it difficult for the leader to move the agenda effectively, solve problems, and make decisions using the best data available. Simply put, it causes a breakdown in communication.

Followers tend to be receptive to leaders who display empathy in the communication process. Empathy is best described as the ability of the senders of messages to put themselves in the positions of the receivers (Stech, 1983). An important aspect of empathy involves conveying to receivers that their feelings are acknowledged and understood and that both the meaning and feeling behind what is being said are appreciated. It is a way in which the leader can demonstrate a spirit of genuine respect for the potential worth of the individual, conveying that the individual has rights and can be trusted to be self-directed. Most definitely, a leader in a learning community would be an individual who showed empathy in appropriate situations.

The Ethics of Conversation

Leaders can also remove barriers and enhance the communication process by bringing ethics to school conversations. In schools, communication is very pervasive, as people accept or reject each other based on words used and the context in which individuals use them. To reduce as much controversy as possible, school leaders need to advocate the addition of an ethical dimension to school conversations.

When individuals participate in an ethical conversation, certain qualities of character are exhibited, and the process of conversing reinforces these qualities. The conversation is governed by reason, and participants are willing to provide evidence for their position, take responsibility for the statements they make, be open to persuasion, and yield to the better argument (Grant, 1996).

In schools, the type of conversation that best lends itself to ethics is dialogue (Grant 1996). A dialogue presumes that all participants are equally open to persuasion and will yield to the better argument. With dialogue, participation in the conversation becomes important within itself as the conversation process recognizes the value of each participating faculty member and reinforces the quality of and respect for that individual.

In schools, for communication to be as effective as possible, the act of receiving information must be separated from the act of judging information. Whereas both functions are important, if they are not kept separate during the transmittal process, the flow of information may be discontinued or altered, and important information could be lost. (Ciancutti & Steding, 2001).

When leaders advocate a conversation process that includes ethics, they advance a sense of value, equity, trust, and acceptance. When these ethical qualities do not exist, some people do not communicate effectively because they feel unappreciated, misunderstood, defensive, hostile, frustrated, or distressed (Sobel & Ornstein, 1996).

Leadership in Today's Schools

In summary, communication is very pervasive in today's schools; it is the lifeblood of relationships, which are a lifeline to accomplishing the goals of the school. When members of the school team communicate effectively, they feel connected, understood, valued, trusted, and respected. Messages are transmitted, and the organization moves toward goal attainment. When people do not communicate effectively and are not in the communication channel, they often feel unappreciated, misunderstood, defensive, hostile, frustrated, or distressed (Sobel & Ornstein, 1996). Therefore, it is important for the school leader to be skilled in the process of communication.

The Scenarios

The scenarios that follow hold implications for how ineffective communication prohibits the establishment of the type of educational community supported by ISLLC Standards 1 and 2.

In Scenario 6, many issues are at hand. Among them are school climate, culture, and barriers to student learning. These characteristics and how they influence ineffective communication in Merry High School are the focus of this scenario. The reader is challenged to identify others.

In Scenario 7, the lack of effective communication skills becomes a roadblock to the implementation of a new professional development plan. The focus of the scenario is Standard 1. In the scenario, this standard was not met. What happened? What went wrong, and what could have been done differently? These are the underlying questions to which the reader might seek an answer. Also, the reader will be able to see what can happen in a school district when communication is ineffective and the vision is not shared. The activities ongoing in the administrative meeting and the consequences of a communication system that does not afford the leader the benefit of appropriate feedback should be of particular interest to the reader.

SCENARIO 6
"THE TARDY POLICY KILLED KATO"

STANDARD 2

A school administrator is an educational leader who promotes the success of all students by advocating, nurturing, and sustaining a school culture and instructional program conducive to student learning and staff professional growth.

Kato, a senior at Merry High School, is a recent immigrant and star athlete. He makes friends easily and is very well liked by his teachers and peers. His class work is average, and discipline is not a problem for him. Unfortunately, Kato has been tardy for his first-period class (English, Mrs. Clark) three times this quarter (tardy 1—overslept, late 5 minutes; tardy 2—Mom drove him to school, late 10 minutes; tardy 3—left a book at home and had to return to get it, late 8 minutes).

On November 11, when Kato came to his first period class 8 minutes late, his third tardy, Mrs. Clark advised him that he would have to report to the On Campus Suspension Class (OCS). Kato begged and pleaded with Mrs. Clark, saying, "I really want to be in class because the midterm examination in this class is scheduled for next week, and I want to be prepared." Mrs. Clark, thinking about the last faculty meeting and the strong emphasis that Principal Johnson placed on strict adherence to the new tardy policy, politely stated the consequences and directed Kato to OCS. Kato refused to go to OCS and was sent to the principal's office.

When Kato reached the office, he spoke with Mr. Martin, Vice Principal at Merry High. Kato explained, "Mr. Martin, I really do not want to go to OCS; I must get ready for midterm. Please allow me to return to class. I don't want to miss a day out of class!"

"You know the rules, Kato. This is your third tardy. I am going to insist that you serve your time in OCS during your first period."

"Mr. Martin, I want to go to class. If you will not permit me to go to class, then I refuse to go to OCS."

"Then, Kato, if you refuse, I will have to send you home."

"Fine, Mr. Martin."

"Fine, then that's what we will do, Kato."

Mr. Martin filled out the necessary paperwork and sent Kato home. Kato did not have a car and had to walk home. As Kato walked out the door, Mr. Martin headed toward the phone to contact Kato's parents. On the way to the phone, his office assistant advised him that a fight was in progress in the quad, and he was needed out there at once. Mr. Martin headed to the quad without intending to break the district's rule that parents must be contacted when a student is suspended.

One hour later, Mr. Martin found out that Kato had been killed.

Apparently, Kato was on his way home when an older "gang member" friend, Serge, drove by and offered Kato a ride home. Kato accepted because he did not want to walk the two miles home. As the boys drove to Kato's home, Serge saw a rival gang member walking on the sidewalk, pulled up next to him, and starting talking "trash." The rival gang member pulled out a gun, fired it at Serge, missed, and hit Kato, killing him instantly.

The media got the story right away. They asked, "Why was Kato going home? Who authorized his dismissal from school, and why were his parents not contacted? Is it true that he was killed because he was tardy three times?" Final message to the public: The Tardy Policy Killed Kato.

REFLECTIVE THINKING

The ISLLC Standards

The following are indicators of the ISLLC Standards addressed in the scenario:

2: The culture of the school was not based on trust; cultural diversity was not valued; communication was not very effective; operational procedures were not effectively carried out; people were not trusted to make good decisions; there was a lack of collaboration with families; the community of the school was not very caring, and the dialogue between decision makers was ineffective.

Reflective Questions and Scenario Analysis

1. Looking at the big picture, was Mr. Martin's behavior representative of an educator who influences an environment that focuses on the needs of students and their families? What evidence can you provide to support your conclusion?
2. If you were making management decisions to enhance teaching and learning, what action would you have suggested to Mrs. Clark? In your response, give consideration to the concept of trusting people and their judgment.
3. In your judgment, which is more important, meeting the needs of individual students or following the letter of policy? Provide a rationale for your response.
4. If it is true that administrators, faculty, and staff should develop a caring community in schools, were the consequences created by the tardy policy too severe for the offense? If so, why? If not, why not?
5. Given that school leaders should view families as partners in the education of their children, in what ways could school personnel collaborate and communicate with families to prevent a situation of this nature from occurring?
6. How could the tardy policy be changed to serve the same purpose but allow some flexibility for teachers and assistant principals to reflect their judgment in its implementation?
7. What kind of message would be sent to the larger community (parents, students, teachers, and citizens) if the administration of the school completely dropped the tardy policy?

ADDRESSING THE CRITICAL ISSUES

The Influence of Leader Behavior in Communication

The communication medium used by a principal to convey a message to the faculty concerning the implementation of a new policy may pose advantages and/or disadvantages for the effective implementation of that policy (Cunningham & Cresco, 1993). In a situation such as the one occurring at Merry High School, the type of communication used to convey the policy to the faculty likely influenced the manner in which the policy was implemented. It determined, to a large degree, the flexibility each faculty member elected to use in the implementation process.

The directive from the principal to strictly adhere to the tardy policy presents itself as a downward or top-down, authoritarian communication approach. This approach can create barriers because members of the faculty decoding the principal's message do not provide feedback on their understanding of the message (McPhee & Thimpkins, 1985). Faculty members are likely to view the directive based on their perceptions of the principal's character, personality, motivation, and style and give these factors priority as they implement the policy. Once again, we note that leaders must be aware of the influence their behavior has on the faculty.

In school settings, different situations warrant different actions, and whereas policies must be followed, the faculty often needs room to make judgments. Therefore, the mode of communication used to emphasize the new policy should have been one that allowed interaction and feedback from the faculty, providing the principal an opportunity to check for understanding, expectations, and level of comfort in the implementation process. The leadership style of the principal was less than effective.

The Effects of Climate on Communication

School climate is a relatively enduring quality of the school environment that refers to people's perception of the general work environment. The formal organization, informal organization, personalities of participants, and organizational leadership influence this perception. Considering that the quality of the environment can have a major effect on the behavior of people who work in the school (Lunenburg & Ornstein, 1996), a primary focus of the school leader should be the development of a school climate that is nurturing and caring. The design and implementation of policies, procedures, and programs must take this factor into consideration.

The development of a new tardy policy tends to suggest that tardiness is a problem at Merry High School. In the last faculty meeting, the principal's action of emphasizing strict adherence to a new tardy policy tends to suggest that attention is being given to resolving the problem. However, the manner in which a principal communicates new policy and emphasizes its importance denotes a style of organizational leadership (Hoy & Miskel, 1991), and the leadership style of the principal contributes to the climate of the school. Therefore, it is necessary for the principal to continuously examine the effect his behavior has on personalities in the school.

Organizational leadership must influence the climate in a positive manner in order to assure decision effectiveness (McPhee & Thimpkins, 1985). For this to occur, the principal must possess three general skills: (a) diagnosing—understanding the problem situation, (b) adapting—altering behavior and other resources to meet the contingencies of the situation, and (c) communicating—interacting with others in a way that they can easily understand and accept the decision (Gorton & Schneider, 1994). The leadership style of the principal, the manner in which the decision on the tardy policy was communicated to the faculty, and the climate of the school are all possible contributors to the problems and concerns at Merry High School.

Capturing the Feeling in Kato's Message

At Merry High School, it is questionable whether Mrs. Clark ever considered Kato's feelings, as her primary concern was implementation of the policy as directed by the principal. Following the rule appeared to be more important than identifying a cause of Kato's problem. Mrs. Clark's perception of what was best for her, Kato, and the school was, to some extent, influenced by her perceptions of the principal's character, personality, motivation, and style. She gave these factors priority as she implemented the policy. Under different circumstances, she might have taken different actions. Kato expressed concern that he was missing out on the review in class. His expressed intentions were not to avoid On Campus Suspension Class, but to attend English class. Mrs. Clark exercised no flexibility in policy implementation. The school climate at Merry High appeared to have influenced the behavior of Mrs. Clark to the extent that no consideration was given to the feelings of the message transmitted by Kato.

Mr. Martin took the same position as Mrs. Clark—follow the rules. He never considered any alternatives to On Campus Suspension Class or indicated that he really understood what Kato was saying. Very seldom, if ever, should a rule be so hard and fast that an alternative cannot be considered (Hersey & Blanchard, 1993). When this occurs, the lines of communication often close, and the situation turns into one of confrontation. Effective school leaders never allow this to occur, as they are always attempting to ensure that students have the knowledge, skills, and values needed to become successful adults (Standard 1).

Avoiding Communication Barriers

The situation with Kato should never have progressed to the confrontation stage; an either/or situation is rarely, if ever, in the best interest of effective problem solving and decision making (Bormann & Bormann, 1972). In this situation, the emotions of both individuals became a barrier to effective communication. Both parties became defensive, and neither was willing to set aside his concerns and be understanding of the other's concerns.

Time pressure was also a problem for Mr. Martin. He did not take the time to advocate, nurture, or make Kato feel valued and important. Also, he failed to call Kato's parents. The policy and the climate of the school were the guiding factors as opposed to the problematic concerns of Kato. Failure to call Kato's parents was a policy violation on Mr. Martin's part, even though it was unintentional. Pupil personnel policies should be designed to meet the needs of students and their families, and the implementation procedures should foster the same.

As we view the key issues in this scenario, quite clearly the major barrier that most likely prevented Mr. Martin from reaching a different solution to Kato's problem was his failure to use effective communication skills that removed the barriers to achieving the vision of the tardy policy. Barriers to achieving the vision were not identified, clarified, and addressed. The dialogue that occurred between Mr. Martin and Kato became confrontational and defensive, creating still another communication barrier.

A Schoolwide Perspective

The climate at Merry High School forced strict compliance to the policy in an authoritarian manner. The end objective (enforcement of the tardy policy) was achieved while the needs of the student went unattended, creating a more challenging situation. Although it is understandable that policies are needed and must be enforced, one must also recognize that "a school administrator is an educational leader who promotes the success of all students by advocating, nurturing, and sustaining a school culture and instructional program conducive to student learning and staff professional growth" (Standard 2). This standard is not being met at Merry High School. In schools where students are nurtured, rules, regulations, and procedures are matched with the needs, personality, and desires of the student (Greenberg & Baron, 1997). Student learning is the fundamental purpose of schooling; thus, the school has to be organized and aligned for success (Standard 2).

Once Kato reached the office, he reinforced his desire to remain in school and attend class. However, the policy and strict adherence to the policy again became the dominant issues. Mr. Martin failed to address Kato's real concern—missing class. His position of strict adherence to the policy and the rules of the school provoked a confrontational win/lose situation.

An assistant principal has legitimate power. Mr. Martin could have utilized legitimate power in a manner consistent with good human relations. Consistency in leadership does not mean taking the same position all the time; it may mean taking the position appropriate for the follower's level of readiness in a manner that allows the follower to understand why a particular behavior is occurring (Gorton & Schneider, 1994). In school situations, it is often helpful to try to see the other person's point of view, to be open to influence, and to be prepared to alter one's position (Bormann & Bormann, 1972).

When school personnel are nurturing, they show concern for the unique problems of their students and a willingness to assist them in finding solutions to their problems (Greenberg & Baron, 1997). Mutual trust exists, and finding the cause of the problem is more important than enforcing the policy (Arnold & Feldman, 1989). After all, "a school administrator is an educational leader who promotes the success of all students by advocating, nurturing, and sustaining a school culture and instructional program conducive to student learning and staff professional growth" (Standard 2).

SCENARIO 7
THE NEW PROFESSIONAL DEVELOPMENT PLAN

STANDARD 1

A school administrator is an educational leader who promotes the success of all students by facilitating the development, articulation, implementation, and stewardship of a vision of learning that is shared and supported by the school community.

Dr. Georgia Edwards is superintendent of Oakville, a large metropolitan school district. Her central staff recently developed a new set of instructional goals and outlined an ambitious professional development program. This new professional development program was the topic of discussion at the April administrative meeting, which included principals who were not members of the superintendent's central office staff. After considerable discussion of the program, Dr. Edwards asked the principals to share the program concepts with their faculties and to promote their implementation.

The assistant superintendents and departmental directors expressed a great deal of excitement about the new program and agreed to share the program with their staffs. The principals, on the other hand, did not seem as excited about the program, but, nevertheless, agreed to promote its implementation.

Three weeks later at a parent meeting, Dr. Edwards was talking with teachers from several of the buildings and found that they knew little or nothing about the new professional development program. In fact, a number of them complained that they rarely heard anything from her office, other than rumors. "Unless there is a problem or a new mandate from the Board of Education, we do not hear from your office," one teacher advised. The teachers also expressed frustration over the lack of opportunities to share their opinions about issues that affected them and their classrooms.

Dr. Edwards was unsure how to proceed. Until now, she was confident that the channels of communication were open—both those leading to and from her office. "Why didn't principals share the new program as they promised they would? Why am I not receiving teachers' opinions? How can I open the channels of communication?"

REFLECTIVE THINKING AND SCENARIO ANALYSIS

The ISLLC Standards

The following are indicators of the ISLLC Standards addressed in the scenario:

1. Effective consensus-building skills were not used; effective communication skills were not used; the vision was not developed with and among stakeholders; and barriers to achieving the vision were not identified, clarified, and addressed.
2. Applied motivational theories were not employed; all individuals were not treated with dignity and respect, and a variety of supervisory and evaluation models were not employed.

Reflective Questions

1. Based on your knowledge of effective operational procedures at the district level that influence effective operational procedures at the school level, which approach would you suggest Superintendent Edwards use in facilitating the development, articulation, and implementation of her vision for a professional development plan?
2. What are some consensus-building and negotiation skills that might prove to be helpful to Dr. Edwards in this situation? Support your response with indicators from ISLLC Standard 1.
3. Based on the indicators of ISLLC Standard 1, how did Superintendent Edwards compromise the implementation of the professional development plan?
4. Giving consideration to components of implementation plans that enhance goal attainment, what strategies and objectives could Dr. Edwards have used to improve the flow of information, data collection, and analysis?

5. Giving consideration to the formal communication network, if teachers felt comfortable in voicing their concerns to the superintendent, what other problems might Dr. Edwards find to exist in Oakville? If Dr. Edwards is interested in demonstrating that she is professionally ethical, how should she have responded to the teachers?

6. As superintendent, how important is it to maintain a continuous dialogue with other decision makers regarding the implementation of a new program plan? Justify your response based on principles of effective communication.

ADDRESSING THE CRITICAL ISSUES

Communicating the Implementation Process

In her approach to implementing the new professional development plan, Dr. Edwards minimized its success potential. She failed to communicate an implementation plan in which objectives and strategies to achieve the vision and goals were clearly articulated. Communication cannot be considered effective just because the leader delivers a message. Individuals who receive the message must understand it and be willing to act on it in an efficient and effective manner. To ensure that this occurs, the leader might take several courses of action, among which is having a detailed communication plan that effectively eliminates barriers and secures feedback sufficient to evaluate communication effectiveness.

The Communication Plan

The initial administrators' meeting was a good start toward introducing the new program information; the problem developed when the information did not continue down the chain. As a mode of communication, the verbal mode, or speech, tends to be spontaneous, flexible, and permit an immediate response (Stech, 1983). However, when a new plan is presented, often after a period of reflection, new insight into a message may be acquired and need discussion and reinforcement through a form of repetitiveness. Such reinforcement will improve communication effectiveness (Barge, 1994). At Oakville, a districtwide newsletter, in addition to the original meeting, may have assisted greatly in dissemination of the message. Also, a written mode of communication is more permanent and involves more thought and preparation; a newsletter could have served as a point of reference throughout the implementation process.

Also, Dr. Edwards could have improved the implementation process by establishing building-level employee meetings that included representatives of all role groups in the community. In so doing, she would be able to enhance program implementation by assessing the extent to which information was being disseminated, the accuracy of communication, and other relationship concerns. Also, her presence at these meetings would have emphasized the importance of the program. McCaskey (1979) advises that face-to-face contact is very important in the communication process, as senders of messages are able to look the receiver in the eye and enhance the impact of their presentation. As a follow-up to her on-site visits, information obtained could be used to systematically evaluate districtwide communication effectiveness. Principal Johnson in Chapter 2 was very effective in using repetitiveness in her communication process.

Utilizing an Effective Mode of Communication

Dr. Edwards used a form of communication that involved the transmission of information from people at one level in the school district to people at different levels (downward communication). This type of communication is frequently plagued with difficulties because information provided is incomplete, and no effort is made to evaluate the accuracy of the message (Sobel & Ornstein, 1996).

If accurate information is the key to effective communication, a form of communication that would generate evaluative data sufficient to analyze the success of the implementation process should have been utilized. Once the information was received (feedback data), any necessary changes could have been made, and all administrative personnel could have been informed of the changes. An effective communication system contains each of these components, and the absence of any one of them is likely to contribute to communication ineffectiveness.

Even though there was considerable discussion in the initial meeting, the superintendent did not clearly articulate an implementation process. In fact, the principals were not very receptive to the plan, and little effort was made by the superintendent to acquire feedback about their lack of interest, the implementation approach the principals would use, or the evaluation of the success of the implementation process. Ending her presentation, she simply instructed principals to communicate to their faculties information regarding the implementation of her program. Her vision was not clear; nor did the principals share it.

School leaders must have a way of judging the effectiveness of the communicated message. It is imperative that the leader acquires feedback from the faculty sufficient to judge the effectiveness of the message and make any necessary modifications. When the leader demonstrates openness to receiving feedback, the communication process is enhanced throughout the school.

Status Differences at the Parent Meeting

At the parent meeting, status differences could have been a restrictive barrier to communication between the superintendent and teachers. The superintendent, at a very high level in the organization, received information from individuals (teachers) at a different level, which was much lower. Dr. Edwards, as well as the teachers, would be especially prone to status differences because of their positions in the organization. However, in this instance, the superintendent was a sensitive listener. She did not display a sense of power nor indicate in any manner that she was superior in position or intellect. Therefore, the teachers focused on the message they wanted to deliver, rather than the person to whom the message was being delivered. They described their attitudes regarding the district's communication system and their lack of knowledge about the plan. The superintendent created the climate for this to occur; if there had not been an acceptable comfort level between the teachers and the superintendent, status would have become a barrier, and free exchange would not likely have occurred. Nevertheless, this process of communication does not replace the operational procedures that must govern the formal communication process at the school and district levels. Frequently, this mode of communication can become a barrier to effective organizational communication.

Quite clearly, in Oakville, the flow of information needs to be improved. The following are three strategies that Dr. Edwards could use to improve the communication process.

1. Adopting a districtwide communication program would improve the flow of communication. Processes that would assist individuals in understanding messages communicated between all administrators could be put in place. The program might also focus on the development of active listening skills that require participation, openness, and receptivity. It is more than just keeping quiet, smiling, and hearing someone else's words; rather, it means actively participating and providing meaningful feedback to the sender of the message (McPhee & Thimpkins, 1985).

2. Dr. Edwards might also improve communication by implementing quarterly visits to each school. Information could be transmitted on a firsthand basis, and misunderstandings could be discussed immediately. Sometimes employees need face-to-face contact with superiors to feel respected and informed. Dr. Edwards might find the practice of "management by walking around" to be an effective way of keeping in touch with all employees and promoting an effective communication system. Certainly, visibility on the part of the superintendent, principal, or any key administrator can lead to the development of a positive and trusting relationship throughout the entire district.

3. Conducting regular staff meetings, with agendas disseminated well in advance of the meeting, is another way of providing information and receiving meaningful feedback. These meetings could assist an administrator in identifying, analyzing, and solving problems in collaboration with staff members. Members of the faculty and staff are more inclined to voice opinions when they have had an opportunity to research agenda items.

In summary, regardless of the method used, information must be communicated to the individuals that need that information to effectively fulfill their responsibilities. When school leaders hold back information, directions can become unclear, vague, and open to different interpretations and rumors. Individuals often feel unappreciated, misunderstood, defensive, hostile, frustrated, or distressed (Sobel & Ornstein, 1996). If information does not flow freely, followers are likely to sense a lack of trust and confidence in the leader and lose faith in the integrity of the communication channels.

Communication of the Vision

Dr. Edwards made the professional development program a priority in Oakview. The program plan was introduced in a manner that conveyed to the principals that it was the superintendent's plan, designed to implement a new set of goals, which they may or may not have supported. Quite clearly, even though the principals agreed to implement the plan, they had not bought into it.

The total school community did not share the vision. The principals' lack of excitement, tone of voice, mumbling, and hesitation in the exchange of information transmitted this message. In the communication process, these are clues that the effective school leader must be able to identify and consider. The transmission of nonverbal messages is very prevalent in school systems; often half of the messages communicated are nonverbal (Covey, 1989).

The real challenges for Superintendent Edwards are listening with feeling, showing empathy for staff, and creating a climate that fosters the kind of feedback from her staff that will inform the decision-making process. Superintendent Edwards' decision lacked quality that could have been acquired from the involvement (in the planning stage) of individuals knowledgeable of teacher needs. It lacked acceptance that could have been obtained by initially involving the people who would ultimately have to implement the plan. Both decision quality and acceptance can be improved through effective communication. With these improvements, Dr. Edwards would take a major step toward becoming a school administrator who is "an educational leader who promotes the success of all students by facilitating the development, articulation, implementation, and stewardship of a vision of learning that is shared by the school community" (Standard 1).

CHAPTER SUMMARY

Communication is the lifeblood of the school. It is the glue that holds the other administrative functions together. Through effective communication, the school family can work collaboratively to achieve the vision of the school by openly identifying problems and seeking solutions, while trusting, respecting, and valuing the diversity that comprises the school family.

Communication can occur verbally or nonverbally. When leaders use words in a written or oral manner, a form of verbal communication is being used. School leaders communicate verbally in faculty meetings, staff conferences, parent meetings, and in discussions with students about various matters. This type of communication is very effective when it is done in a two-way mode. It allows interaction to occur between both the sender and the receiver of messages.

Verbal communication also occurs when the leader sends out newsletters, parent notices, and other written materials. However, this form of communication is one way and often does not generate instant feedback. Its effectiveness lies in conveying information that needs to be retained and used as a point of reference or for directions. When the faculty, staff, students, parents, and others need information regarding the implementation of policies, procedures, and directives, the written mode of communication tends to work well.

When a message is transmitted without the use of words, the form of communication is considered nonverbal. Nonverbal behavior is very important, as more than half of what is communicated is conveyed by body language. More often than not, the feelings of the sender are conveyed nonverbally. Therefore, for the dynamics of communication to have the greatest impact, both the content of the message and the feelings of the sender must be considered. Communication has to occur with the sender giving the highest level of attention to the feelings that underlie the content.

The school has both a formal communication network and an informal one. The formal network is directed by the structure of the organization, and individuals who function in the organization direct the informal network.

The major function of the formal network is to convey information sanctioned by the system. Members of the organization use the informal network to convey messages of interest often called rumors. The leader should be aware of rumors, as they can be detrimental to goal attainment. Both networks serve a meaningful purpose, and the school leader should be knowledgeable of both and the manner in which they function.

Information in schools flows in several directions—upward, downward, horizontally, and diagonally. The flow of information is very important, as it provides task coordination and furnishes emotional and social support. However, regardless of the flow, barriers interfere with communication effectiveness and must be removed. Managing the use of power, eliminating fear, encouraging feedback, and establishing a climate of openness and trust can remove barriers.

When people communicate effectively, fear is removed from the workplace, and creativity comes alive. Positive emotions stimulate creativity, and the communication process can be used as a catalyst for effectiveness.

MOVING INTO PRACTICE

Review the scenarios in Chapter 4. Using the pros and cons of the various situations, identify several approaches that you would use to address the following school-related issues in an actual situation. Project yourself in the role of the principal and take care to formulate a rationale for your selected behavior.

- ◆ Select a local school district policy that addresses school attendance and tardiness and relate the requirements of that policy to the ones in the policy at Merry High School.
- ◆ Hold a mock press conference and explain the Kato incident to the media and the general public.
- ◆ How can the school climate problem that is likely to exist as a result of Kato's death best be addressed? What community resources would prove valuable?
- ◆ It has recently come to your attention that one of your teachers has some good ideas for closing the achievement gap but is reluctant to communicate those ideas to you. What would you say to her to persuade her to share her ideas with you?

ACQUIRING AN UNDERSTANDING OF SELF

- ◆ What does your body language communicate to individuals?
- ◆ How do you assess the manner in which people perceive you?
- ◆ Are you communicating the message that you want to convey to people? What evidence do you have to support your conclusions?

DEEPENING YOUR UNDERSTANDING

Now that you have read this chapter, visit the Companion Website for this book at **www.prenhall.com/green** *and take the Self-Assessment Inventory for this chapter.*

Completing this inventory will give you an indication of how familiar you are with the ISLLC Standards knowledge indicators that relate to this chapter.

SUGGESTED READINGS

Ramsey, R.V. (2002). *How to say the right thing every time: communicating well with students, staff, parents, and the public.* Thousand Oaks, CA: Corwin Press.

Shaver, H. (2004). Organize, communicate, empower. Thousand Oaks, CA: Corwin Press.

Weller, D. L. & Weller, S. J. (2001). The assistant principle: Essentials for effective School leadership. Thousand Oaks, CA: Corwin Press.

AVAILABLE POWERPOINT PRESENTATIONS

After completing this chapter, log on to the Companion Website for this book at **www.prenhall.com/green** *and click on the PowerPoint module.*

- • The Communication Process
- • Can Talk Make Us Better?

WEBSITES

Communication Process and Leadership
http://edis.ifas.ufl.edu/pdffiles/CD/CD01300.pdf

Communication Structure and its Effects on Task Performance
http://www.analytictec.com/mb021/commstruc.htm

PRACTICE ISLLC EXAMS

After reading this chapter, log on the Companion Website for this book at **www.prenhall.com/green** *to take the practice ISLLC exams.*

REFERENCES

Arnold, H. J., & Feldman, D. C. (1989). *Organizational behavior.* New York: McGraw-Hill.

Barge, J. K. (1994). *Leadership: Communication skills for organizations and groups.* New York: St. Martin's Press.

Barth, R. S. (1990). *Improving school from within: Teachers, parents, and principals can make the difference.* San Francisco: Jossey-Bass.

Bormann, E. G., & Bormann, N. C. (1972). *Effective small group communication.* New York: Burgess.

Ciancutti, A., & Steding, T. (2001). *Built on trust: Gaining competitive advantage in any organization.* Chicago: Contemporary Books.

Covey, S. R. (1989). *The 7 habits of highly effective people.* New York: Simon & Schuster.

Cunningham, W. C., & Cresco, D. W. (1993). *Cultural leadership: The culture of excellence in education.* Boston: Allyn & Bacon.

Cusella, L. P. (1987). Feedback, motivation, and performance. In F. M. Jablin, L. L. Putnam, K. Roberts, & L. W. Porter (Eds.), *Handbook of original communication: An interdisciplinary perspective* (pp. 130–164). Newbury Park, CA: Sage.

Deming, W. E. (1986). *Out of the crisis.* Cambridge, MA: MIT Center for Advanced Study.

Gibbs, J. R. (1995). Defensive communication. In D. A. Kolb, J. S. Osland, & I. M. Rubin (Eds.), *The organizational behavior reader* (pp. 225–229). Upper Saddle River, NJ: Prentice Hall.

Gibson, J. L., Ivancevich, J. M., & Donnelly, J. H., Jr. (1976). *Organizations: Behavior, structure, and progress* (Rev. ed.). Dallas, TX: Business Publication.

Gorton, R. A., & Schneider, G. T. (1994). *School-based leadership: Challenges and opportunities.* Upper Saddle River, NJ: Prentice Hall.

Grant, R. W. (1996). The ethics of talk: Classroom conversation and democratic politics, fearless cause. Record volume 97, number 3.

Greenberg, J., & Baron, R. A. (1997). *Behavior in organizations.* Upper Saddle River, NJ: Prentice Hall.

Greenberg, J., & Baron, R. A. (2003). *Behavior in organizations.* Upper Saddle River, NJ: Prentice Hall.

Guarino, S. (1974). *Communication for supervisors.* Columbus: The Ohio State University.

Hersey, P., & Blanchard, K. H. (1993). *Management of organizational behavior: Utilizing human resources* (6th ed.). Upper Saddle River, NJ: Prentice Hall.

Hoy, W. K., & Miskel, C. G. (1991). *Educational administration: Theory, research and practice* (4th ed.). New York: McGraw-Hill.

Interstate School Leaders Licensure Consortium of the Council of Chief State School Officers. (1997). *Candidate information bulletin for school leaders assessment.* Princeton, NJ: Educational Testing Service.

Kmetz, J. T., & Willower, D. J. (1982). Elementary school principal work behavior. *Educational Administrative Quarterly, 18,* 62–78.

Lewis, P. V. (1980). Organizational communication: The exercise of effective management. Columbus, OH: Grid.

Lewis, P. V. (1987). *Organizational communication: The essence of effective management.* New York: Wiley.

Lunenburg, F. C., & Ornstein, A. C. (1996). *Educational administration: Concepts and practices* (2nd ed.). Belmont, CA: Wadsworth.

McCaskey, M. B. (1979). The hidden messages managers send. *Harvard Review 57,* 135–148.

McPhee, R. D., & Thimpkins, P. (1985). *Organizational communication: Traditional themes and new directions.* Thousand Oaks, CA: Sage.

Myers, M. T., & Myers, G. E. (1982). *Managing by communication: An organizational approach.* New York: McGraw-Hill.

National Association of Elementary School Principals (2001). Leading learning communities: Standards for what principals should know and be able to do. Alexandra, VA: Author. www.naesp.org

Rogers, C. R., and Farson, R. E. (1995). Active listening. In D. A. Kolb, J. S. Osland, & I. M. Rubin (Eds.), *The organizational behavior reader* (pp. 203–214). Upper Saddle River, NJ: Prentice Hall.

Rogers, C. R., & Farson, R. E. (1995). J. S. Osland, D. A. Kolb, & Rubin (Eds.), *Active listening in the organizational behavior reader* (7th ed.). Upper Saddle River, NJ. Prentice Hall.

Rowe, M. P., & Baker, M. (1984). Are you hearing enough employee concerns? *Harvard Business Review 127–135.*

Ryan, K. D., & Oestreich, D. K. (1991). *Driving fear out of the workplace: How to overcome the invisible barriers to quality, productivity, and innovation.* San Francisco: Jossey-Bass.

Sobel, D. S., & Ornstein, R. (1996). *The healthy mind healthy body.* New York: Time Life Medical.

Stech, E. L. (1983). *Leadership communication.* Chicago: Nelson-Hill.

5

DECISION MAKING: QUALITY AND ACCEPTANCE

In today's schools, decision making is one of the primary leadership functions. Leaders are continuously making decisions about individuals, groups, school structure, the instructional program, and many other factors that ultimately determine if schools function effectively. If the process of decision making is not conducted in an effective manner, the entire school stands to be negatively impacted. Therefore, understanding the decision-making process and how to effectively utilize it is of paramount importance to school leaders.

The purpose of this chapter is to examine the process of decision making in schools and to discuss practices and procedures used by school leaders to make quality decisions that are acceptable to all stakeholders. First, the reader is provided with a definition of decision making that includes a general overview of several approaches school leaders use to make decisions. Then, a discussion is held on the involvement of faculty members and other stakeholders in the decision-making process. The chapter concludes with a description of barriers and traps that can inhibit decision effectiveness.

The scenarios in the chapter approach decision making from three different perspectives: (a) establishing and implementing policies that ensure educational success for all students; (b) acting with integrity, valuing diversity, and bringing ethical principles to the decision-making process; and (c) effectively communicating with all stakeholders to ensure decision quality and acceptance.

Through these scenarios, the reader will have an opportunity to practice selecting appropriate decision-making alternatives and involving faculty and other stakeholders in the decision-making process. Also, the reader will be able to examine the activities in these scenarios and relate them to ISLLC Standards 5 and 6. In processing information regarding these activities, the reader will want to note instances of fairness, ethical practices, and situations when the characters, especially the leader, act with or without integrity. Special attention should be given to the connection between communication and decision making and how each process has the potential of negatively impacting the other.

Defining Decision Making

Decision making is defined as a systematic process of choosing from several alternatives to achieve a desired result (Kamlesh & Solow, 1994). Within this definition, three elements are presented: (a) choice (choosing from options), (b) process (electing to make the decision independently or involving others), and (c) purpose (the results or desired outcome). In view of the importance of these elements to the process of decision making, a brief discussion of each follows.

Selecting Among Options

Selecting among options often involves providing resources to some individuals and groups while denying them to others. A choice has to be made, and making choices in schools has far-reaching implications. For example, if a principal in a school with multiple grade levels only has funds sufficient to purchase computers for one grade level, a choice must be made as to which grade level receives the computers. When the principal makes that choice, some faculty members will receive material resources and others will not; thus, conflict that negatively affects the instructional program could result. Therefore, in making such a choice, the objective of the school leader should be to minimize negative consequences and maximize positive outcomes. The probability of achieving this objective can be enhanced if the leader makes informed choices and acts with integrity and in an ethical manner (Standard 5).

Informed choices are likely to be made when the leader has a thorough understanding of decision processes and uses that knowledge to select and implement alternatives that will result in quality decisions that are accepted by stakeholders. The process selected may entail the leader making the decision independently or involving others. For example, there are times when leaders have knowledge sufficient to make a decision independently, and there are times when they can enhance the quality of the decision by acquiring information from other individuals or groups. Also, there are instances when the involvement of others will enhance the acceptance of a decision. The pivotal point is that individuals and/or groups should be involved in the decision-making process when their involvement will enhance the quality and/or acceptance of the decision.

Decision Outcome

The purpose of any decision is achieving a desired outcome. Leaders would be very effective in achieving this goal if they knew in advance the outcome of every decision alternative implemented. Although there are times when school leaders are more certain of the outcome than others, there are also times when leaders have absolutely no knowledge of the outcome. Thus, the difference between effectiveness and ineffectiveness is the degree of uncertainty that lies between the alternative selected and the desired outcome. In order to reduce the uncertainty and enhance the probability of achieving the desired outcome, the school leader has to acquire the best information possible. With good data, the leader can select effective decision alternatives and avoid having to address unanticipated consequences. Figure 5.1 summarizes a model that many researchers and writers offer for use in making decisions (Barge, 1994; Gorton, 1987; Hoy & Tarter, 1995; Yukl, 1994). By reviewing this model, the reader will be able

FIGURE 5.1   Steps in an Analytical Decision-Making Model

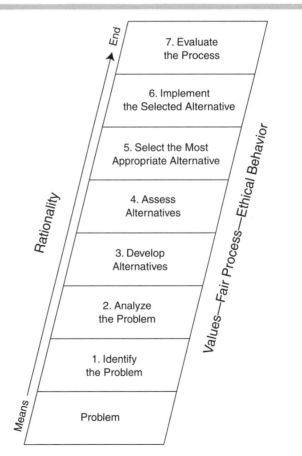

to develop an understanding of the complex nature of problem analysis, selecting a solution and effectively implementing the solution.

An Analytical Model of Decision Making

Scientists have traditionally conceptualized decision making as a process that individuals and groups use to solve a problem by moving through a series of analytical steps as seen in Figure 5.1 (Harrison, 1987). In the first step, the leader identifies the problem. The next step is to analyze the problem to determine the critical issues. Then a thorough analysis is needed to identify a satisficing alternative. The analysis should take into account individuals who are affected, situations that are impacted, and the type and sources of data that are needed to select an appropriate solution.

In the third step, the leader develops problem solution alternatives. A note of caution, at this juncture, is that the alternatives seldom, if ever, appear in an either/or manner. If the problem is carefully analyzed as described in step two, the leader will likely come to the realization that several alternatives exist. Also, in some instances, leaders have a tendency to resort to past experiences, selecting an alternative that has worked previously. This temptation should be resisted, as problems may seem alike but in actuality are different, thus warranting a different alternative. Therefore, it is advisable for the leader to explore all possible alternatives.

Once the alternatives have been identified, the decision maker is ready for step four, assessing the alternatives in terms of their match with the problem. At this stage, the leader is seeking to identify the most satisficing alternative. Simply put, the leader is attempting to determine which one of the generated alternatives will most effectively address the problem (decision quality) and which one will produce the least amount of conflict (decision acceptance). After assessing all alternatives, step five—selecting the most appropriate alternative—is taken.

The sixth step involves the implementation of the alternative and should be carefully planned, as decisions of high quality serve no meaningful purpose if they are not implemented effectively and in a manner that is acceptable to stakeholders.

Finally, step seven is an evaluation of the process used to make the decision. The entire process should be assessed, and the decision alternative implemented should be monitored to determine if the problem is being adequately addressed. The leader needs to know that the decision alternative selected solved the problem and that the process used to identify it was not flawed. If the leader fails to evaluate the process and the success of the alternative chosen, flaws in the process, if any, will not be identified, and the errors that influence them are likely to be repeated.

The Leader's Disposition

Simply following the sequential steps of a decision-making model is not sufficient. Effective decision making also depends on the judgment and disposition of the leader. As school leaders make selections from various alternatives, they reveal their preferences for particular values, interests, and beliefs (Barge, 1994). For example, when school leaders administer to students disciplinary action that they believe will attain the desired outcome, they are making value judgments (Willower, 1991). Given this factor, leaders have to be concerned with the biases, values, interests, and beliefs that they bring to the decision-making process. To avoid the influence of these biases, they have to be knowledgeable of various ethical frameworks, establish standards, and hold themselves to those standards (Standard 5). Consider the following examples of how biases of leaders can affect individuals and school programs.

School leaders make decisions regarding the rooms to which teachers are assigned, the students they teach, the time of day specific subjects are taught, any extra assignments teachers are required to fulfill, and a number of other activities too numerous to mention. In making those assignments, judgments are made about the individuals affected. School leaders make a number of judgments during the course of a year and the effect those judgments have an effect on the instructional program, as well as the life of individuals inside and outside of the schoolhouse. Therefore, one can appreciate how important it is for school leaders to refrain from allowing their personal interests and beliefs to influence decision outcomes.

It should also be noted that other individuals and/or groups inside and outside of the schoolhouse bring biases, values, interests, and beliefs to the table when they ask the leader to make decisions. Thus, the leader must use a decision-making approach that considers the impact that these ideas, values, and cultures will have on the decision outcome. The approach should also protect students' rights and improve their opportunities for success (Standard 6).

In practicing the art of leadership through decision making, more than good intentions are required. School leaders have to bring good judgment and ethical principles to the decision-making process and be willing to use the influence of their offices constructively and productively in the service of all students and their families (Standard 5). In some instances, they may even have to subordinate their own interests in order to make decisions of quality that the faculty and the larger school community will accept (Standard 5).

In summary, it is of value for the school leader to understand that there is no one best way for leaders to make effective decisions. The process of decision making in schools is influenced by the complexity of issues, time frame, and a number of other demands that influence leader behavior in one way or another (House & Dessler, 1974; Maier, 1963; Yukl, 1994). Consequently, in applying judgments or the leader must give consideration to factors influencing the decision-making process, the decision outcome, and the probable consequences (Hoy & Tarter, 1995).

The section of Chapter 3 entitled "Organizational Structure and Leader Behavior" focused on the leader's understanding of self and the need for leaders to assess the influence of their values on the actions they take, as well as how their behavior influences others. As we continue our exploration of decision making, a review of that section, as well as the constructs in Figure 2.3 of Chapter 2, may be beneficial.

Approaches to Decision Making

It is conceivable to believe that most school leaders want to develop nurturing school communities that enhance teaching and learning. The challenge is identifying ways to make decision choices that move the school in that direction. Acknowledging that this is a complex task, school leaders need to be proficient in making effective decisions. Several writers and researchers (House & Dessler, 1974; Maier, 1963; Yukl, 1994) have noted that there is no one best way to make effective decisions. The complexity of school situations and time frames that demand decisive actions often influence leader behavior in a manner quite different from that suggested by theory and research. More often than not, making good decisions in schools is contingent on the nature of the situation and the process used by the leader.

Although there is no one best way to make decisions, there are a number of theoretical models that, if appropriately applied, can improve one's decision-making capability. In applying theoretical models, the leader may elect to use either a normative (rational) or a descriptive (nonrational) one. "These two theories of the nature of decision making have dominated social science thinking about the topic" (Gorton, 1987, p. 3). Each presupposes that the decision maker will reach a decision by proceeding through a series of steps like or similar to those outlined in Figure 5.1. Given the popular use of these two models, a summary of each is presented in the following section.

The Normative Theory

According to the normative theory, leaders follow a series of prescribed actions to make a decision or reach a solution to a problem. They begin with a problem that is logically addressed by engaging in a series of sequential steps that lead to an effective problem solution (Gorton, 1987). Using a normative model in a school situation, the principal would identify the problem and its causes, analyze it, develop alternatives or possible solutions, evaluate the alternatives, select and implement the alternative that seems most satisfactory, and then evaluate the outcome.

The theory offers the decision maker varying degrees of rationality. "Decisions are rational if there is a reasonable connection between the means and ends, that is, if decision makers choose wisely the appropriate means for achieving the goals" (Hoy & Tarter, 1995, p. 3). The decision models derived from this theory are often referred to as rational models because the steps taken in reaching a solution are sequential, and it is assumed that the leader will be rational in following them (Gorton, 1987). The

Classical, Administrative, and Mixed Scanning theoretical decision-making models are popular normative models that vary in their degree of rationality. A summary of each of these models will appear later in the chapter. First, we discuss the descriptive models.

The Descriptive Models

Commonly referenced models derived from "descriptive theory" are the Garbage Can, Political, and Incremental models. Descriptive models are somewhat nonrational, and if the leader chooses one, the focus is on the manner in which the decision is *actually* reached, rather than how the decision *should* be made (Gorton, 1987). Individuals who support this theory question whether the complex nature of school problems and the lack of leader control over elements in the environment of the schoolhouse permit decision making in a rational sequential manner (Gorton, 1987). For example, if an irate parent enters the principal's office requesting an explanation of a previous action taken that involved her child, a set of sequential steps may not be plausible.

In summary, both the normative and descriptive models presuppose that certain actions and situations will apply. However, because the behavior of school leaders influences the lives of so many individuals, *Practicing the Art of Leadership* recommends that the process used in making all school-related decisions be as rational as possible and governed by ethical principles. In the following section, we identify the characteristics of the six models previously mentioned and note situations in which they can be appropriately used.

The Classical Model

One of the primary objectives of the school leader is to make management decisions to enhance learning and teaching (Standard 3), and in that process, finding satisfactory solutions to multifaceted issues in a rational manner is desirable. The Classical Model is completely rational and has as its prime objective maximizing achievement of the goals of the organization by finding the best solution from among all possible alternatives. This process, which presupposes that all alternatives are identifiable, consists of a series of sequential steps that begin with problem identification and end with the achievement of the desired outcome. However, most accounts of the Classical Model in the literature on decision making suggest that it is unrealistic for use by school leaders, as complete rationality in school decision making is not possible (Bolman & Deal, 1997; Hoy & Tarter, 1995; Yukl, 1989). School leaders never have access to all the information about an issue; nor are they able to identify all the possible alternatives. However, the model does offer school leaders a rational plan of action that is preferable to arbitrary and biased responses. This is an asset to school leaders, given that one of their primary objectives is to make management decisions to enhance learning and teaching (Standard 3). Thus, finding satisfactory solutions to multifaceted issues in an efficient and effective manner is desirable. However, if complete rationality is not possible (Classical Model), where can the school leader turn? What is an acceptable alternative that is suited for issues that occur in the day-to-day operation of schools? To some extent, Herbert Simon (1982) answered these questions when he presented the strategy of satisficing, which is reflected in the Administrative Model.

The Administrative Model

The Administrative Model offers a systematic process that can be used to enhance the identification of the appropriate alternative when competing alternatives exist. Simon (1982) theorized that there are instances when the decision maker selects a decision alternative that does not reflect everything desired. In such instances, if the alternative is not totally unsatisfactory, a form of satisficing comes into play. When a strategy of satisficing is employed, it is an acceptable alternative to the classical process.

Because leaders do not always have the data necessary to find the one best alternative to complex issues, they may settle for what is known as "bounded rationality." In such cases, the leader uses a rational sequential process to find the most satisfactory solution possible. The process consists of distinct phases: (a) recognition and definition of a problem, (b) analysis of difficulties, (c) establishment of the criteria for success, (d) development of an action plan, and (e) the appraisal of the plan.

Using such a process, school leaders can, more often than not, obtain wise solutions to problems. Decisions can be reached using a means-ends analysis; the leader selects a means to reach a desired end. Although the solution reached may not be optimal, it is satisfactory. For example, a principal of a high school is interested in purchasing new football uniforms for the school's team and has identified five companies to contact regarding the purchase. After completing the call to the third company, he stopped calling and made a purchase. Consequently, he made a decision with limited information, as he did not make the fourth and fifth calls.

On some occasions, the school leader finds problems that are very complex in nature—so much so that decision outcomes are difficult to predict. In such instances, the leader may turn to the nonrational incremental decision-making model.

The Incremental Model

Hoy and Tarter (1995) describe the Incremental Model as one that allows the school leader to make changes in small increments to avoid unanticipated negative consequences. The means-end analysis found in rational decision making is inappropriate. Decision objectives and alternatives are intertwined, and alternatives are selected when they are only slightly different from current reality and lie between current reality and the desired goal. Outcomes of decisions made are assessed and compared to the desired direction or what is accepted before other decisions are attempted. Lindblom (1959), who refers to this type of decision making as the "science of muddling through," argues that administrators are only able to muddle through many issues because of their complexity, uncertainty, and the amount of conflict that is likely to be provoked. Therefore, they make small decisions and evaluate the consequences of each, proceeding until they reach the ultimate desired alternative. Because of the pressure of time, the risk of selecting a particular decision alternative, and the void that exists within the information base, school leaders often turn to this descriptive model of decision making. To illustrate the point, consider that a superintendent is interested in implementing a new computer program for all schools in the district at a cost of two million dollars. However, he is not quite sure how teachers, parents, and other stakeholders will receive this new program concept or if it will enhance student achievement. Therefore, he installs the computers in two schools and evaluates their use; then, after a period of time, installations are made in five additional schools, and their use in those schools is evaluated. The decision regarding installation in the remaining schools is based on the evaluative information from the first two installations.

The Mixed Scanning Model

The Mixed Scanning Model offered by Etzioni (1967) allows the school leader to combine the flexibility of the incremental model with the rationality of the satisficing model. By responding to the questions: What is the basic mission of the organization? and What incremental decisions will move the organization in that direction?, leaders can make decisions and stay within the realm of the organization's mission and policies. Problems can be surveyed, difficulties analyzed, and a tentative action plan initiated. If the plan fails, something new can be attempted.

The Mixed Scanning Model seems appropriate for use by school leaders, as the approach guides the decision process, allowing the school leader to remain focused while reflecting on consequences of the selected alternative and the common good. The school leader who meets the ISLLC Standards will have to be willing to take risks in the pursuit of the school's vision, and that seems acceptable as long as personnel are perceived as placing student success first and acting with integrity, fairness, and in an ethical manner.

The Garbage Can Model

The Garbage Can Model and the Political Model are often used in school situations. March (1982) reasons that the Garbage Can model allows individuals to act without thinking through an issue. This is an action that should be infrequent in its occurrence but is sometimes necessary. In instances when it is used, rather than beginning with a problem and ending with a solution, decision outcomes are products of independent streams of events. As problems occur and alternatives are formed, they are deposited into what is referred to as a garbage can. When the solution, the problem, and the participant just happen to connect, making a fit, the problem is solved. If the solution does not fit, then the problem remains unsolved (Cohen, March, & Olsen, 1972). For example, Principal Green, observing student decorum in the cafeteria, was very displeased with his observation. To improve student decorum, he implemented a solution alternative that had worked effectively in a similar situation in the past. However, student decorum in the cafeteria did not improve, and the solution alternative was not retained.

Three days later he tried a second alternative that had worked in a similar situation in the past. When the faculty expressed concern with this decision alternative, it was not retained. Then, Principal Green implemented a third alternative. His third decision alternative, one previously used, improved student decorum in the cafeteria and also met with the approval of the faculty. Because of its effectiveness and acceptance, the third decision alternative was retained for the remainder of the year.

The Garbage Can Model relies on chance and provides an explanation for the actions of school leaders who appear to make decisions in an irrational manner.

The Political Model

The Political Model becomes the decision-making tool when organizational goals are replaced by personal influence, and power is the overriding force (Kanter, 1982). Most organizations have defined goals, which they strive to achieve. However, in some instances, the power and influence of individuals and/or groups suppress organizational goals. In such instances, personal perspectives and preferences influence decisions in the organization. The prevailing order of the day is manipulation. Individuals and/or groups maneuver to influence organizational outcomes so that the objectives they favor might be achieved, rather than the objectives of others in the organization. Conflict, bargaining, and game playing are intensive and pervasive, and satisficing organizational decision making gives way to influence, power, and persistence (Kotter, 1985).

As one might realize, selecting a model to utilize in reaching a decision of quality that will be accepted by stakeholders takes considerable thought on the part of the leader. In addition to selecting an approach, the leader must also determine whether to make the decision independently or to invite assistance. We now turn to a discussion of the styles leaders might use. Two noteworthy styles are autocratic and participatory.

Autocratic or Participatory Decision Making

Consider for a moment that you are the principal of an elementary school and a decision has to be made regarding the use of one of three basal texts in teaching first grade reading. A group of teachers reviewed each of the three series and expressed different levels of satisfaction with them. Would you select the series to be used (autocratic) or would you involve other individuals (participatory) in the selection process? If you elected to involve other individuals in the selection process, who would you involve and why? Making this determination can be a challenging decision within itself. Also, if the incorrect approach is selected, it could prove to be quite problematic.

When a leader uses an autocratic style and makes the decision with little or no involvement of faculty or other stakeholders, contingent on the situation, decision quality and/or acceptance could become problematic. Stakeholders may perceive that the leader simply wants to achieve success without regard to how others feel or will be affected. If the situation is reversed and the leader chooses to use a participatory style involving faculty members and/or other stakeholders and such involvement is not warranted, the decision reached could also be of poor quality and not well received. In such instances, the stakeholders may not have an interest in the issue or the expertise necessary to provide meaningful input. Consequently, the school leader should not conclude that an autocratic style or a participatory style will always be either inferior or superior. Rather, the goal should be to involve faculty members or stakeholders in the decision-making process when their involvement will improve the quality and/or acceptance of the decision. In other instances, the leader should make the decision independently. Choices range from totally autocratic behavior to joint participatory behavior. These choices, as described by Yukl (1994), appear in Table 5.1.

Selecting a Decision-Making Style

In recent years, with the widespread acceptance of the reform movement, participatory decision making has increased in importance. Involving faculty members and

TABLE 5.1   Approaches to Decision Making

1. Autocratic: The leader reaches a decision without any assistance from followers. Followers have no influence over decisions.

2. Consultation: The leader seeks the opinion of followers and asks them for their ideas. After giving consideration to the ideas, opinions, and suggestions of subordinates, the leader makes the decision.

3. Joint Decision Making: The leader meets with followers, discusses the problem, and together they develop a workable solution to the problem. The leader serves as a group participant and has no more influence than any other member of the group.

4. Delegation: The leader gives the authority and responsibility for making the decision to the group. Limits are specified, and prior approval may or may not be required for decision implementation.

SOURCE: Material compiled from the work of Yukl, 2002.

other stakeholders in the decision-making process is an approach that has been informed by many researchers and writers (Gorton, 1987; Hoy & Miskel, 1991; Maier, 1963; Vroom & Jago, 1988; Vroom & Yetton, 1973; Yukl, 1989). From the work of these individuals, evidence suggests that, under certain conditions, groups outperform individuals. The challenge for school leaders is determining when and under what conditions faculty members and other stakeholders should be involved. As was explained in the earlier section "Autocratic or Participatory Decision Making," there are some instances when school leaders should make decisions autocratically, and in some instances, they should invite the participation of stakeholders. Some writers have reported that the question of whether a group will do a better job of making a decision than the leader acting independently depends, to a large extent, on the complexity of the issue, the expertise of the participants selected, and whether or not the issue is in the participant's zone of concern (Hersey, Blanchard, and Johnson, 1996; Johnson & Johnson, 1982; Yukl, 1994). The following models offer suggestions that may be used by the leader in selecting a decision style.

The Vroom and Yetton Model   Vroom and Yetton (1973) offered a normative model that distinguishes between individual and group decision making. The model addresses how the behavior of the leader affects decision quality and acceptance. The originators of the model also suggest when leaders should involve followers in the decision-making process and to what extent. The school leader is offered five decision procedures. Two procedures are autocratic in nature, two speak to consultation in decision making, and one speaks to leaders and followers making decisions jointly.

The Vroom and Yetton Model addresses two basic assumptions: (a) The more influence followers have, the more they will be motivated to implement a decision, and (b) when decision acceptance is not already high, follower participation will increase decision acceptance (Yukl, 1989). This model is considered the best-known model for management of participation in organizational decision making (Hoy & Tarter, 1995).

The Vroom and Jago Model   Vroom and Jago (1988) offered a revision to the Vroom and Yetton Model, adding the dimensions of time and follower development. Participatory decision making is very time consuming, and the leader must give consideration to the importance of making the decision in a timely manner. The revised model adds these criteria as critical factors to be considered in determining the optimal decision procedures to utilize.

1. If a decision needs to be made with expediency, then selecting a participatory style may be counterproductive.
2. If followers have the skills and attributes necessary to participate in the decision-making process, then, under certain conditions, they should be invited.

Such conditions would suggest that an immediate decision is not necessary and followers' participation would enhance decision acceptance and quality.

Even with these two models, the challenge around participation and the inclusion of faculty members in the decision-making process remain a complex issue. Whereas it is touted in research as one of the few approaches leaders can use to increase morale and productivity, its use creates issues in other areas of the organization. The two major concerns regarding the use of a participatory approach are designing a system in which followers can effectively function and the fear from leaders that if followers are allowed to participate too frequently, they will abuse the privilege (Bolman & Deal, 1997). In spite of these issues, leaders must be concerned with decision quality and decision acceptance, and follower participation is a factor in each of these areas. In the following section, these factors and their influence on the decision-making process are discussed.

Decisions of Quality and Acceptance   Group performance is jointly affected by the intervening variables of quality and acceptance (Maier, 1963). Decision quality takes into account the objective aspects of decisions that affect the performance of the group. These objective aspects are considered aside from any effects mediated by decision acceptance. Using the group process depends on the contribution of group members and their ability to communicate effectively, use good judgment, be accurate in their assessment of the concerns and issues, and remain focused.

Decision quality (Maier, 1963) also refers to the expertise of members of the group—the extent to which group members are able to contribute to the selection of a decision alternative of quality. On some occasions, individuals are assigned to groups and do not have the expertise to make a contribution. In other instances, individuals who have the required expertise are not invited to participate as a member of the group. Both situations have the potential of negatively impacting decision making in schools.

Decision acceptance refers to the degree to which followers are committed to implementing a decision in an effective manner (Maier, 1963). In some instances, decisions made by the leader are accepted by followers simply because the decisions are beneficial to them or because of the approach used by the leader in reaching the decision. In other instances, followers refuse to accept a decision because it was made in an autocratic manner. As is the case with decision quality, in such instances, decisions in schools can be negatively impacted by these factors.

To address these concerns, a two-dimensional approach is widely accepted for use by leaders in determining if followers are to be involved in the decision-making process. First, the leader determines if followers have the expertise to contribute to finding an appropriate solution to the problem being addressed, and second, the leader determines if the problem lies within the zone of concern of followers (Yukl, 1989).

Expertise of Participants   In schools, a variety of tasks have to be completed. Some of the tasks are complex and require that individuals and/or groups have considerable training or experience. To be effective, leaders must be knowledgeable of the skills and attributes of faculty members and carefully select individuals to perform tasks independently or to assume a role as a group member.

If select members of the faculty are assigned a task or asked to become a member of a group and do not have the expertise necessary to complete the task or to make a contribution to group discussion, lack interest in the topic, or function in conflict with other members of the group, decision quality is likely to be less than desired (Maier, 1963). Conversely, if an individual is interested in performing a task and has the expertise needed and the leader fails to identify that individual to work independently or as a member of a group, then a valuable resource is lost. Also, the individual in question may lose respect for the leader.

Participants' Zone of Concern   The second part of the equation is zone of concern and refers to the extent to which followers will be affected by the decision and/or expected to implement the decision. A decision is within the zone of concern or interest of followers when they are affected by the decision and/or expected to be involved in the implementation process. If a decision is within their zone of concern and followers are excluded from participating in the process, they are likely to feel deprived and develop a level of dissatisfaction for the school leader.

Conversely, when decisions are outside of the zone of concern or interest of followers, they are not likely to be highly motivated to participate in the decision-making process. Thus, including them is not likely to enhance decision quality or acceptance. The critical point for school leaders to remember is that followers included in the decision-making process should not only have a stake in the outcome of the decision, but they should also be able to contribute to the decision outcomes and implementation (Bridges, 1967). With this point in mind, if the school leader elects to involve members of the faculty in the decision-making process, several different group decision techniques can be employed.

Group Decision Techniques

The Dialectical Inquiry Technique, the Nominal Group Technique, the Delphi Technique, and the Brainstorming Technique are among the most popular group decision-making techniques. Gorton (1987), Yukl (1989), and Barge (1994) report that these techniques have been found to be very effective in generating ideas from group members to enhance participatory decision making.

The Dialectical Inquiry Technique

The Dialectical Inquiry Technique is most appropriate for addressing complex problems when two completely different and contrary approaches are identifiable. The leader can operationalize the technique with direct involvement of the opposing groups or elect to use the technique independently of the opposing groups. Whereas this technique has proven to be effective, its negative aspect may be a lack of group cohesiveness (Yukl, 1994). Nevertheless, it is a technique worthy of consideration. Barge (1994) characterizes the technique in the following manner:

1. All available information regarding a specific problem or event is collected by the leader and presented to two subgroups. The makeup of each group is as homogenous as possible, but the groups are as different as possible.
2. The groups meet separately, analyze the information, and develop a list of assumptions in the order of their importance. The assumptions are written and presented to the opposing group. The groups then meet together to debate the merit of their theses and/or proposals. After the debate, each group presents a refined proposal to the leader. The proposal should be in writing and include all relevant information, assumptions, and key facts.
3. The leader reviews the information provided by the groups in search of arguments and positions that are counter to or negate the theses. The leader also looks for recommendations counter to those developed in Step 2 and conditions under which the original analysis would be in error or open to question. The antithesis of the original analysis is thus identified.
4. The leader compares the two lists constructed in Steps 2 and 3 and engages in a systematic critique of the competing assumptions. The validity of both sets of assumptions is examined. Ultimately, a list of assumptions consistent with both analyses is identified. A synthesis of the two competing positions is developed.
5. On the basis of the remaining assumptions, the leader can develop a set of recommendations.

To observe a practical situation wherein this technique can be applied, the reader's attention is called to the scenario "The Requested Change" (p. 136). This scenario contains a challenge for the school leader that could be addressed using this technique.

The Nominal Group Technique

When using the Nominal Group Technique, six steps are followed. The leader generates ideas in a silent manner by asking group members to write their ideas on slips of paper without engaging in discussion. Several minutes are allotted for the ideas of group members to be written. After the allotted time (5–10 minutes), each member contributes an idea in a round-robin manner. As ideas are suggested, they are written on a blackboard or flip chart. No evaluation or discussion of ideas is permitted during the posting period. The posting process continues until all ideas are presented. Members may pass if they have no additional ideas. After all ideas are posted, the leader reviews the list, inviting discussion on each by asking for questions, statements of clarification, or statements of agreement or disagreement regarding the relevance of the ideas to the problem. After the group has finished, ideas can be combined through a preliminary vote. Additional discussion is held on the combined ideas, and this leads to a final vote (Delbecq, Van de Ven, & Gustafsen, 1986).

The Delphi Technique

The Delphi Technique, developed by researchers at the Rand Corporation in 1969, is a technique that has proven to be very effective when expert advice concerning an issue is needed from a large number of people (Dalkey, 1969). It is a process that generates ideas and allows individuals to react to program proposals or raise questions concerning a project. Individuals are able to think through complex issues and submit high-quality ideas without the influence of individuals in positions of status. The technique involves the following five steps:

1. The leader defines the problem, decision, or question to which individuals and/or groups are to react.
2. The leader identifies those individuals and/or groups whose opinions, judgments, or expert knowledge would be valuable to obtain in the process of making a decision.
3. The leader asks for responses of identified individuals and/or groups using a written format, often a questionnaire.
4. The results received are summarized and redistributed to the individuals and/or groups, and they are asked to review and indicate any changes in their initial responses.
5. Step 4 is repeated until there is a reasonable consensus on the problem or decision (Gorton, 1987).

This is an excellent technique to use in acquiring curriculum ideas for new programs. It allows for the input of a large number of teachers (generating quality ideas and ownership for the new program) while utilizing the expertise of outside professionals and acquiring the endorsement of central administration and or State Department officials.

Brainstorming

Brainstorming is a technique used to encourage group members to contribute to finding solutions to problems by spontaneously suggesting any and all ideas that come to mind (Osborn, 1957). When ideas are suggested, they are written on a blackboard or flip chart. The rules of effective brainstorming do not permit any positive or negative evaluative comments, scowls, groans, sighs, or gestures. All ideas are accepted, and value judgments are deferred. Members of the group are also encouraged to combine or improve on ideas suggested.

In summary, there is little doubt that using groups in the decision-making process holds many advantages. Groups tend to generate more ideas and make higher-quality decisions. Working with others often causes members to perform better; they receive support and encouragement and tend to look at alternatives more thoroughly. They acquire a greater understanding of the issues and take ownership of the decisions, realizing they will have to live with the outcomes.

Barriers and Traps That Inhibit Decision Effectiveness

Although there are a number of advantages to both autocratic and participatory decision making, there are also a number of barriers and traps that interfere with decision effectiveness or cause decisions to be flawed when either is used. Some worthy of note are groupthink, the overuse of groups, and fair process.

Groupthink

Groupthink can become a barrier because sometimes groups become so cohesive that members resist challenging ideas to maintain the integrity of the group. Because members do not want to risk disrupting the stability of the group, information from outside of the group that would possibly enhance decision quality is rejected, and creative thinking is stifled.

Overuse of Groups

The leader must also safeguard against involving too many people in the decision-making process. Some leaders have so many committees operating that they spend the major portion of their time in committee meetings. Involving individuals in decisions that should be made by the leader can be as problematic as not involving individuals when the situation warrants their involvement. This constitutes poor leadership.

Fair Process

Fair process is another issue to which leaders should give special attention as decisions are reached. In many instances, individuals on the faculty of a school will like the outcome of a decision that has been reached by the principal or others but will not like the process that was used to produce the decision. The process that produces a decision is a major concern of many individuals. People care about decision outcomes, but they also care about the process that is used to reach those outcomes. They want to have their say, and they want to feel that they had an opportunity to participate in the process, even if their point of view is rejected. When this does not occur, the process can profoundly influence the attitudes of faculty members in a manner that negatively impacts the success of the school (Kim & Mauborgne, 1997).

Without fair process, school goals can be difficult to achieve because when the faculty does not trust the process, they are likely to see only the negative side of the issue. Kim and Mauborgne (1997) report three principles of fair process that are worthy of consideration by the school leader. They are:

1. *Engagement*: Individuals are involved in decisions that affect them. The leader asks for their input and allows them to refute the merits of one another's ideas and assumptions.
2. *Explanation*: Everyone involved and affected should understand why final decisions are made as they are.
3. *Expectation Clarity*: Once a decision is made, managers state clearly the new rules of the game (p. 69).

Regardless of individuals' roles in the school district or position on the faculty, they want to be treated with respect and appreciated for the expertise brought to the organization. Individuals want their ideas and opinions to be seriously considered, and they want to understand the reasoning behind decisions that are made.

Avoiding Hidden Traps

Leaders should also be aware of hidden traps in decision making. Decisions are often flawed because of hidden traps that get in the way of effectiveness. From the work of Hammond, Keeney, and Raiffa (1998), eight traps that leaders might consider in attempting to safeguard against flawed decision making are:

1. *Status Quo*: We all carry biases, and those biases influence the choices we make. The source of the status-quo trap lies deep within our psyches, in our desire to protect our ego from damage.
2. *Sunk Cost*: We make choices in a way that justifies past choices, even when the past choices no longer seem valid.
3. *Confirming Evidence*: We seek out information that supports our existing instinct or point of view while avoiding information that contradicts it.
4. *Framing*: We can use different frames to assess a problem. The same problem can elicit very different responses when frames use different reference points. A poorly framed problem can undermine even the best-considered decision.
5. *Estimating and Forecasting*: We often fail to get clear feedback regarding the accuracy of our estimates and forecasting.

6. *Prudence*: When we are faced with high-stakes decisions, we tend to adjust our estimates to be on the safe side.
7. *Recallability*: We frequently base our predictions about future events on our memory of past events, and we can be overly influenced by dramatic events—those that leave a strong impression on our memory.
8. *Overconfidence*: We tend to be overconfident about our accuracy relative to our estimates. This can lead to errors in judgment and, in turn, bad decisions (pp. 47–58).

Leadership in Today's Society

The demands on education today are placing pressure on leaders in the field to be effective decision makers and to communicate those decisions in a manner that will improve teaching and learning and promote the success of all students (ISLLC, 1996). Guarding against groupthink, using groups only when appropriate, insuring a system of fair practice, and safeguarding against hidden traps can assist greatly in improving decision quality and acceptance in schools. In making and communicating decisions in the manner the ISLLC Standards require, leaders will have to take a number of factors under consideration. They will need to understand the values and the culture of the school and community they serve, identify appropriate decision-making models, and act using a professional code of ethics. Their primary objective will necessarily have to be the involvement of all stakeholders in a manner that will generate decisions that reflect the common good. To develop a deeper understanding of the contents of this chapter, we analyze the behavior of individuals and groups in two scenarios.

The Scenarios

The scenarios in this chapter approach decision making from three different perspectives: (a) establishing and following policy to provide educational success for all students in a safe environment, (b) acting with integrity, valuing diversity, and bringing ethical principles to the decision-making process to ensure success for all students, and (c) effectively communicating with all stakeholders to ensure that decisions are of quality and will be accepted. The reader will be able to observe two leaders with different styles make different decisions, all of which have some effect on the environment of the school and student learning. Also, the reader can analyze the activities of these scenarios as they relate to ISLLC Standards 5 and 6. Particular attention should be given to the connection between communication and decision making and how each process has the potential of negatively impacting the other.

In Scenario 8, a principal is faced with making a decision concerning the instructional program. He is new to the school and is not very clear on the political, social, economic, and cultural context of the community. Nevertheless, the decision he is asked to make will impact students, teachers, and the organizational structure of the school. In responding to the issue and reaching a decision of quality that will be accepted, he will need to be guided by indicators of ISLLC Standards 5 and 6.

In Scenario 9, respect for the work that has been completed in the past challenges a principal who must make a decision regarding work that must be completed in the future, lest the state of student discipline compromises the learning environment of the school. The challenge faced by the principal is one of accepting the responsibility for school operations while demonstrating appreciation for the work of others. He is also challenged to accept the thesis that his faculty can be inspired to perform at a higher level.

SCENARIO 8
THE REQUESTED CHANGE

STANDARD 5

A school administrator is an educational leader who promotes the success of all students by acting with integrity, fairness, and in an ethical manner.

STANDARD 6

A school administrator is an educational leader who promotes the success of all students by understanding, responding to, and influencing the larger political, social, economic, legal, and cultural context.

Mr. Robert Miller was recently appointed principal of Springview Elementary School (July 1 of the current year). Springview is a school with a student population of 800. The students are from across the city, as Springview has an open enrollment policy.

Everyone appears to be pleased with the racial make-up of the faculty, which is 90% Caucasian and 10% African-American. They are also pleased with the racial composition of the student body, which is 90% Caucasian, 8% African-American, and 2% Asian-American. Mr. Miller is only the second principal. Mr. Williams, the former principal, opened the school 10 years ago. Under his authoritarian leadership and firm control, the school became the pride of the Springview School District.

The second week of school, Mr. Miller looked at his calendar to find that he had an appointment with a group of parents from the east section of the city, the area everyone refers to as the "old money part of the city." He was also scheduled to meet with a group of parents from a new area of the city called Lakehills. Lakehills was recently developed, and a large number of minority first-time homeowners have moved into the area.

Mr. Miller was wondering why these two groups wanted a meeting. "Perhaps to welcome me to the school," he said as he asked his secretary to show the first group of parents into his office.

Very little was said in the first meeting. Indeed, the parents welcomed Mr. Miller to the school and advised him that he could depend on their support. However, they had one request, which was to establish ability grouping at the school. They gave a number of reasons for wanting this change; however, the major reason expressed was instructional time. It was their contention that the slow children took up a large portion of instructional time, and there was not enough left to challenge the gifted students. The meeting ended with Mr. Miller saying he would consider the request and give them a response in the next several days.

In the second meeting, Mr. Miller was met with quite a different situation, no direct request at all. The parents welcomed him to the school and advised him how pleased they were with the education their children were receiving. They also said that they would provide any assistance he needed and hoped there would be no major changes in the instructional program. The meeting ended with all smiling.

REFLECTIVE THINKING AND SCENARIO ANALYSIS

The ISLLC Standards

The following are indicators of the ISLLC Standards addressed in the scenario:

1: Effective consensus-building and negotiation skills are needed; information sources, data collection, and data analysis strategies must be utilized; and consideration must be given to all members of the community.

2: Consideration must be given to principles of effective instruction; diversity, its meaning for educational programs, and the benefit it brings to the school community must be given consideration; the change process for systems, organizations, and individuals must be understood and utilized; and student learning must be accepted as the fundamental purpose of schooling.

5: Ethical principles must be included in the decision-making process; the focus must be the development of a caring community; and laws and procedures must be applied fairly, wisely, and considerately.

6: The political, social, cultural, and economic systems and processes that impact schools must be given consideration; legal systems must be used to protect students' rights; and there must be ongoing dialogue with representatives of diverse community groups.

Reflective Questions

1. What are the primary issues in this scenario, and what information is Principal Miller likely to need in order to demonstrate appreciation for and sensitivity to the diversity in the school community?

2. What decision-making approaches could Principal Miller use to ensure decision quality while involving families and other community stakeholders in selecting a decision alternative?

3. What action, if any, should Principal Miller take to demonstrate that he is an educational leader who treats people fairly, equitably, and with dignity and respect? Justify your position.

4. What information sources, data collection, and data analysis strategies would you advise Principal Miller to utilize to ensure decision quality and acceptance?

5. What action should Principal Miller take to ensure that the final alternative selected will give consideration to principles of effective instruction and influence the implementation

of a curriculum based on research, expertise of teachers, and the characteristics of a learned society?

ADDRESSING THE CRITICAL ISSUES

Framing the Situation

Principal Miller is faced with making a decision concerning the instructional program. He is new to the school and is not very clear on the political, social, economic, and cultural context of the community. Information concerning these areas would contribute greatly to the selection of a decision alternative. Nevertheless, even without information in these areas, a decision has to be made, and that decision will impact students, teachers, and the organizational structure of the school. With this in mind, Principal Miller must select a decision-making model to use in responding to the issue and reach a decision of quality that will be acceptable to stakeholders. Of the six models presented earlier in the chapter, three are worthy of consideration, two are not practical for this situation, and the use of one is a definite no.

Selecting a Decision Approach

Mr. Miller is faced with the challenge of selecting an approach to use in identifying a decision alternative to address the complex issue of ability grouping. Obviously, selecting a decision model is an important part of that process because it will determine the information sources, data collection technique, and the data analysis strategies that will inform the selection of the decision alternative.

Given that the outcome of the decision will have implications for many individuals and groups, as well as the school's instructional program, it is advisable that Mr. Miller be as rational as possible in seeking a solution and keep in mind that the fundamental purpose of schooling is student learning (Standard 2).

The Administrative Model is an appropriate model for Mr. Miller to consider. Using this model, he can proceed through a series of steps and select between the competing requests. However, being certain that the alternative selected will produce the desired outcome is another issue. Because of the nature of human dynamics in schools, school leaders cannot always be certain that implementing a selected decision alternative will produce the desired outcome. The degrees of uncertainty are expressed in terms of risk. As the degree of difficulty increases, so does the risk of selecting the best decision alternative.

The degree of risk can be controlled by acquiring information on the probability of the selected alternative producing the desired outcome (Amit & Wermerfelt, 1990). Therefore, considering the importance of the issues around ability grouping and the void in Mr. Miller's information base, to "manage" the risk factor, he might give consideration to using the nonrational incremental decision-making model. He could work with the faculty and other individuals to establish instructional goals for the school. Before selecting a decision alternative, he could return to the issues of ability grouping to determine if it will enhance goal attainment, before selecting a decision alternative.

The Mixed Scanning Model also seems appropriate for use by Mr. Miller. Using this model, he could review the mission of the school, determine if ability grouping is aligned with the mission, and select a decision alternative in accordance with the mission. The rationale for selection of the decision alternative could be the mission of the school, as it is important for the leader to use the influence of his or her office constructively and productively in the service of the school (Standard 5).

The model that is a definite no in terms of use by Mr. Miller is the Political Model. Because of Mr. Miller's lack of certainty of the first groups' motivation and power base and the impact the decision being requested will have on teaching and learning, he could make a political decision that would shape policy in a manner detrimental to the quality of education for all students. One responsibility of the school leader is to be knowledgeable of the political, social, cultural, and economic systems and processes and how they impact schools (Standard 6). In the absence of this knowledge, a political decision seems unwise.

It is clear that selecting a model to utilize in reaching a decision of quality and acceptance involves many factors and will take considerable thought by Mr. Miller. His challenge can be summarizied in the following manner: (a) his status as a new principal, (b) the complexity of the issue, (c) insufficient information to make an autocratic decision, (d) uncertainty concerning the motivation and power of the groups, and (e) the decision being in the zone of concern of the faculty. Because of these factors, he is not likely to be able to make a decision based on complete rationality, and the issue is too volatile to risk chance decision making. Therefore, he will have to resort to a form of satisficing. His concern necessarily becomes one of acquiring and processing all relevant information to ensure decision quality, and the Administrative Model appears to be the most appropriate for that purpose.

Selecting a Decision Style

In addition to selecting an approach for use in identifying a decision alternative, Mr. Miller must determine whether to make the decision independently or to invite assistance from faculty members and/or other stakeholders. The following facts should influence that determination.

To select a decision alternative regarding the requests of the two parent groups, Mr. Miller will need to obtain information from a variety of sources inside and outside of the schoolhouse. In addition, he will need to have some idea of how the alternative selected will affect various other individuals and groups, as well as the school's instructional program over the long term. Considering these factors and given the nature of his position, he will need to "manage" the risk he takes, and he can manage that risk, to some extent, by inviting other individuals and/or groups into the process. In doing so, he can acquire relevant information concerning the issues while involving individuals who will be affected by the decision. Recognizing these facts, a consultation or joint decision-making style as advocated by Yukl (1998) appears to be most appropriate for use by Mr. Miller. The use of either of these styles is likely to improve both the quality and acceptance of his decision (Bolman & Deal, 1997). To provide the reader with a deeper understanding of why this is the case, we review the complexity of the issue in question.

The Complexity of the Issue

Researchers have struggled for decades to find answers to questions about ability grouping. For every research reviewer who has concluded that grouping is helpful, another has concluded that it is harmful. Schools that group according to ability tend to use two basic approaches: (a) Students are grouped according to like characteristics between classes, often called tracking, or (b) students are grouped within classes based on assessed ability (Parkay & Stanford, 2001).

Within-class ability grouping is often used in elementary classrooms for instruction in reading and mathematics. Students who experience this type of grouping are assigned to classes on the basis of achievement that is usually determined by standardized test scores. High school leaders who practice ability grouping assign students to classes based on their goals after graduation. Such classes are divided into areas that may include a college preparatory track, a vocational track, and a business education track (Parkay & Stanford, 2001).

For the most part, between-class ability grouping does not contribute to greater achievement (Good & Brophy, 2000). However, teachers are better able to meet the needs of diverse groups of students. Conversely, negative expectations can be derived from such group labels, as some students may tend to feel inadequate, inferior, and limited in their ability to learn (Parkay & Stanford, 2001).

From the discussion above, it is easy to see that ability grouping is a complex and controversial subject that extends beyond the schoolhouse, into the community. Because of the complex nature of the subject, the concerns of the two parent groups should be explored in an objective manner. If large discrepancies exist between students' abilities and achievement, as perceived by one group of parents, programs should be designed to address those discrepancies. Still, ability grouping may not be the most effective instructional approach to use. For those reasons and others, it is clear that the decision to be made is not one that the leader should make using an autocratic style. Other individuals with expertise in the area could contribute greatly to the quality of the decision.

The Vroom and Yetton Model provides a theoretical rationale for this position. In reviewing the model, there are several factors that suggest that Rule 3 is applicable in Mr. Miller's situation. Some of these factors are the need for teacher expertise, the high probability of teacher interest, the extent to which they will be affected by the decision, and the certainty that teachers will be involved in the process of implementing the decision. These factors place the issue in the zone of concern of teachers and offer evidence that they should be involved in the decision-making process.

In summary, the decision concerning ability grouping is larger than the classroom, spreading into the community of the school. The ultimate responsibility for its implementation lies with the classroom teacher. Mr. Miller's primary responsibility is schoolwide, while teachers (in addition to new teacher-leader roles) devote their time and attention specifically to the teaching and learning process. Quite clearly, teachers have expertise in the area of ability grouping, and the end results of the decision will greatly affect them and the children they teach. Therefore, ability grouping is an issue that is in their zone of concern, and Mr. Miller would be well advised to involve them in the decision-making process.

Mr. Miller must also be concerned with the involvement of parents on both sides of the issue, as each group should have an opportunity to present their point of view. It is important for families and other stakeholders to be involved in the decision-making process (Standard 3). Therefore, he should select and utilize a group decision-making technique that will allow the opinions of parent groups, as well as other individuals and groups, to be heard. In this way, both sides of the issue will be presented. The Dialectical Inquiry Technique would facilitate this outcome. We continue our review of participatory decision making through the following scenario.

SCENARIO 9
RETAINING THE STUDENT RECOGNITION PROGRAM

STANDARD 5

A school administrator is an educational leader who promotes the success of all students by acting with integrity, fairness, and in an ethical manner.

Overfield High School is a large 9–12 urban high school with a student population of 3000. Over the past 6 years, the school has experienced an increase in discipline problems and a decline in student achievement and attendance. At least two students have been expelled for having weapons on campus.

In an attempt to change this trend, the principal and staff made a commitment to implement a student recognition program. The program has been in operation for 4 years. During the first 2 years of the program, there was a decline in discipline problems, attendance increased, and the faculty was pleased with the classroom work of their students. However, the past 2 years of the program have been quite different. Discipline problems are increasing; attendance has fallen by two percentage points, and Principal Jones has noticed signs of waning faculty enthusiasm for the program. In fact, the original, energetic and enthusiastic core of 15 teachers who conceptualized the program and influenced the faculty and student body to adopt it has now dwindled to a group of 5 overworked individuals. Principal Jones realized that something had to be done or the program would fall apart, and all the original gains would be lost. Therefore, early in the spring, he scheduled a series of meetings to review the program.

During the spring review, teachers voiced concerns that the students were losing their excitement about the rewards associated with the program. The faculty also reported instances where they had heard students complain about boredom—too much time sitting still, the "same old prizes," and too-stiff attendance guidelines. Relative to their involvement, the faculty expressed concerns regarding the behavior of some of the students during assembly programs and the need for a change in the program guidelines. On the positive side, the faculty reported that students expressed enjoyment of the use of field trips, tickets for special events, dances, and food as "prizes." At the conclusion of the review, it was decided that the student recognition program was a good program that simply needed to be revitalized.

Once the faculty recognized which areas of the program they needed to revise, they spent hours in five different meetings, generating and evaluating ideas and identifying possible changes to the program. After the fifth meeting, Principal Jones looked at his exhausted faculty and said to them, "You have done an excellent job. I will take all your suggestions, compile them, and send you a copy of the compilation during June for your review. We will meet in late August to discuss and finalize the program for next school year."

The faculty appeared very energized, and everyone left school feeling a sense of accomplishment and voiced satisfaction with the outlook for the new school year.

Reflective Thinking and Scenario Analysis

The ISLLC Standards

The following are indicators of the ISLLC Standards addressed in the scenario:

1: Knowledge of learner goals in a pluralistic society will be needed, as well as information sources, data collection, and data analysis strategies. Effective communication, consensus-building, and negotiation skills are critical components, and the core beliefs of the school vision will need to be modeled for all stakeholders.

2: Principles of effective instruction will have to be applied, as well as change processes for systems and organizations, and all individuals must be treated with fairness, dignity, and respect.

3: Management decisions that enhance learning and teaching will have to be made, and stakeholders will need to be involved in those decisions.

5: The value of the diverse community must be respected and ethical principles brought to the decision-making process. The principal will need to demonstrate a professional code of ethics.

6: There must be ongoing dialogue with representatives of the diverse community, and a variety of ideas, values, and cultures will have to be recognized.

Reflective Questions

1. What were some early indicators that the student recognition program needed attention?
2. What were some early decisions that could have been made to reduce the likelihood of the problem escalating to the level that signaled a need for the spring review?
3. If it is true that low faculty morale existed before the spring review, what leadership behavior possibly led to the level of satisfaction expressed by the faculty at the end of the spring review?
4. In the scenario, can you cite passages that would serve as evidence that ethical principles were included in the decision-making process?
5. What effect did the disposition of Principal Jones have on his attempt to address this situation? From the scenario, cite passages to support your response.
6. Cite instances from the scenario that suggest that faculty participation increases decision quality and acceptance.

Addressing the Critical Issues

Factors Influencing a Decision at Overfield High

When one considers the dynamics and the inner workings of the social system at Overfield High School, it is quite clear that any decision reached by Principal Jones would be in the zone of concern of the faculty. It is also clear that the faculty had the expertise to assist him in reaching an acceptable decision. Therefore, the Joint Decision Making approach presented in Table 5.1 is the appropriate choice. If he had made an autocratic decision, he would likely have met strong resistance. Discipline is in the zone of concern of the faculty, and in this instance, because of their past involvement, continued involvement is warranted. Obtaining ideas from the faculty on the merits of the existing program would not have been sufficient. In instances of this nature, faculty members will develop respect for the principal who consults and participates with them in generating ideas concerning the solution to a problem. This is important since the relationship between principals and teachers can enhance the potential for school improvement (Barth, 1990).

Using a Group Decision Technique

In reaching a solution to the discipline, achievement, and attendance problems at Overfield High School, Principal Jones used the Nominal Group Techniques. He asked the faculty for suggestions concerning the solution and gave them an opportunity to develop them. All members of the faculty had an opportunity to contribute their ideas. The faculty spent several hours generating ideas and putting them in writing. After all ideas were submitted, the principal took them with the intent of compiling them and reaching a decision alternative.

In a more formal approach to using the technique, during the spring review, he could have given the faculty an opportunity to think through the issues and write suggestions on slips of paper and post them on the board. Post-it notes work well for this type of activity. After all ideas were posted, he could have held a discussion on each idea, eliminating the ones the faculty did not deem worthy of retaining. From the remaining suggestions, a decision alternative could have been selected.

Avoiding Barriers and Traps at Overfield High School

At Overfield High School, the principal avoided a decision trap. A large number of faculty members were involved in the origination of the student recognition program. These faculty members demonstrated creativity and interest in resolving a challenge faced by the school. The principal did not allow failure of the program to reflect negatively on the creators. If this had occurred, it is likely that faculty creativity would have been stifled, and future attempts by the faculty to solve schoolwide problems would have been negatively impacted. In addition, the program was evaluated; without some type of program evaluation, it would have been difficult for the principal to determine the causes of the lack of success.

The principal avoided another trap when he kept the original group involved. Inviting other faculty members to provide the leadership for the program would have possibly embarrassed the initial group of teachers, leading them and their colleagues to believe that they were responsible for the failure of the program. Such an approach is not likely to be well received by the initial group or motivational to other faculty members.

When Principal Jones engaged the faculty in a participatory decision-making approach, he showed respect for their expertise and acknowledged the importance of their involvement. In making a decision, when quality is important and followers have the expertise to make the decision, a participatory decision-making style leads to more effective decisions than does an autocratic style (Yukl, 1989).

Motivating Faculty Creativity Through Fair Process

When assessing the issue from the viewpoint of motivating faculty creativity, the most critical factor to be considered by Principal Jones was to ensure decision fairness, quality, and acceptance. He accomplished these outcomes by selecting a decision-making approach that
included all stakeholders. The faculty was initially committed to the student recognition program (especially the original 15), and at one time it worked well. Before altering the program or changing to a completely different one, it was wise of him to acquire the faculty's
assistance in conducting an analysis of the current program, determining the critical issues,
and developing and evaluating possible alternatives. This action was likely considered as fair
by the faculty, especially the 15 faculty members who originally conceptualized the program.

In selecting his decision alternative, Principal Jones likely gave consideration to the impact
of his behavior on the faculty members assuming responsibility for the initial program. In so
doing, he ensured that individuals who had worked to achieve success with the initial program were treated with fairness, dignity, and respect. Students and staff need to feel valued
and important, and the leader must assume the responsibility of ensuring that the contributions they make are acknowledged (Standard 5).

In summary, the leadership style of Principal Jones followed closely one that is informed by
the ISLLC Standards. He was not directive, issuing mandates and stressing rules and regulations; rather, he was collaborative and sought input from stakeholders. His emphasis was not
on the performance of the teachers or placing blame. More specifically, his disposition indicated that he was committed to finding a solution to a problem using a fair and equitable
process. When the leader displays this type of disposition, using procedures that provide the
faculty with an opportunity to have input into decisions that are in their zone of concern,
teaching and learning are likely to be enhanced.

CHAPTER SUMMARY

All decisions in schools have some influence on the performance of both faculty
and staff. Therefore, it is important for the school leader to realize the magnitude
of the problem and to be as rational as possible in selecting a decision alternative.
The basic decision-making model includes the following steps: (a) identification of
the problem, (b) analysis of the problem, (c) identifying alternative solutions,
(d) assessing the alternatives, (e) selecting an alternative, (f) implementing the selected alternative, and (g) evaluating the process.

In the process of making decisions, the leader can elect a normative or descriptive approach. Also, the leader may elect to make decisions independently or

involve others. The determination should be based on several factors, among which are time, the situation, the issue, and the expertise needed. As challenging as decision making is, the leader can minimize its negative impact by eliminating barriers and traps that inhibit effectiveness.

Working independently, leaders can improve the decision-making process by recognizing their own biases and those of others and being fair and displaying ethical principles in the process. Using group decision-making techniques and safeguarding against groupthink and the overuse of groups, the leader can enhance participatory decision making. In either instance, the leader must know that the quality of the decision reached and the manner in which it is implemented will not only have an impact on the faculty, staff, and students, but will also have an impact on the perceived effectiveness of the leader.

MOVING INTO PRACTICE

Review the scenarios in Chapter 5. Using the pros and cons of the various situations, identify several approaches that you would use to address the following school-related issues in an actual school situation. Project yourself into the role of the principal and/or superintendent and take care to formulate a rationale for your selected behavior.

◆ It is early September at Frost, and you have all the students assigned to classes. A parent group enters the school, insisting that many special students have been inappropriately placed. In fact, they make claims that the inclusion laws have not been followed. They demand to see the master schedule and to work cooperatively with you in rescheduling the children. They threaten to carry the issue to the superintendent if you do not comply with their request. What action do you take, and upon what do you base your decision?

◆ Develop a list of decision alternatives that could be used by Mr. Miller at Springview Elementary.

◆ Make a list of five situations in which a leader should involve others.

◆ Draft a statement that would inform the school and community of the enactment of a zero tolerance policy banning weapons on campus.

◆ Design a shared decision-making model that involves students, faculty, staff, parents, and community members in meaningful decision making. Take care to establish the relationship that must exist between role groups as they function as members of the team.

ACQUIRING AN UNDERSTANDING OF SELF

◆ What decision-making style works best for you?

◆ What safeguards do you have in place to ensure that you are making the best possible decisions?

◆ What is your position regarding fair process, and what steps do you take to ensure that your position on issues is fair, equitable, and gives consideration to the rights of others?

DEEPENING YOUR UNDERSTANDING

Now that you have read this chapter, visit the Companion Website for this book at **www.prenhall.com/green** *and take the Self-Assessment Inventory for this chapter.*

Completing this inventory will give you an indication of how familiar you are with the ISLLC Standards knowledge indicators that relate to this chapter.

SUGGESTED READINGS

Hammond, J. S., Keeney, R. L., & Raiffa, H. (1998). *Smart choices: A practical guide to decision-making.* Boston: Harvard Business School Publication.

Rebore, R. W. (2001). *The ethics of educational leadership.* Upper Saddle River, NJ: Prentice Hall.

Shapiro, J. S. & Stefkovich, J. (2000). *Ethical leadership and decision making in education: Applying theoretical perspectives to complex dilemmas.* Mahwah, NJ: Lawrence Erlbaum Associates.

AVAILABLE POWERPOINT PRESENTATIONS

After completing this chapter, log on to the Companion Website for this book at **www.prenhall.com/green** *and click on the PowerPoint module.*

• The Decision-Making Tool Kit
• Nominal Group Technique
• Cause and Effect Diagram
• Decision-Making Strategies
• How to Identify a Problem
• How to State a Problem

WEBSITES

Decision Making Techniques
http://www.cs.tcd.ie/courses/ism/sism/resource/papers/knoll/techniq.htm

School Based Shared Decision Making
http://www.uni.edu/coe/iel/sdsum.html

The Delphi Technique: What Is It?
http://www.learn-usa.com/acf001.htm

PRACTICE ISLLC EXAMS

After reading this chapter, log on the Companion Website for this book at **www.prenhall.com/green** *to take the practice ISLLC exams.*

REFERENCES

Amit, R., & Wermerfelt, B. (1990). Why do firms reduce business risk? *Academy of Management Journal, 25,* 443–451.

Barge, J. K. (1994). *Leadership: Communication skills for organizations and groups.* New York: St. Martin's Press.

Barth, R. S. (1990). *Improving school from within: Teachers, parents, and principals can make the difference.* San Francisco: Jossey-Bass.

Bolman, L. G., & Deal, T. E. (1997). *Reframing organizations: Artistry, choice, and leadership* (2nd ed.). San Francisco: Jossey-Bass.

Bridges, E. A. (1967). A model for shared decision-making in the school principalship. *Educational Administrative Quarterly, 3,* 49–61.

Cohen, D. K., March, J. G., & Olsen, J. P. (1972). A garbage can model of organizational choice. *Administrative Science Quarterly, 17,* 1–25.

Dalkey, N. (1969). *The Delphi method: An experimental study of group decisions.* Santa Monica, CA: Rand Corporation.

Delbecq, A. L., Van de Ven, A., & Gustafsen, D. H. (1986). *Group techniques for program planning: A guide to normal group and Delphi processes.* Middleton, WI: Green Briar Press.

Etzioni, A. (1967). Mixed scanning: A third approach to decision making. *Public Administration Review, 27,* 385–392.

Good, T. L., & Brophy, J. E. (2000). *Looking in classrooms* (8th ed.). New York: Longman.

Gorton, R. A. (1987). *School leadership and administration: Important concepts, case studies, and simulations* (3rd ed.). Dubuque, IA: McGraw-Hill.

Hammond, J. S., Keeney, R. L., & Raiffa, H. (1998, September/October). The hidden traps in decision-making. *Harvard Business Review,* 47–58.

Harrison, E. F. (1987). *The managerial decision-making process* (3rd ed.). Boston: Houghton Mifflin.

Hersey, P., Blanchard, K. H., & Johnson, D. E. (1996). *Management of organizational behavior: Utilizing human resources* (7th ed.). Upper Saddle River, NJ: Prentice Hall.

House, R. J., & Dessler, G. (1974). The path-goal theory of leadership: Some post hoc and a priori tests. In J. G. Hunt & L. L. Larson (Eds.), *Contingency approaches to leadership* (pp. 29–55). Carbondale: Southern Illinois University Press.

Hoy, W. K., & Miskel, C. G. (1991). *Educational administration: Theory, research and practice* (4th ed.). New York: McGraw-Hill.

Hoy, W. K., & Tarter, J. C. (1995). *Administrators solving the problem of practice: Decision-making concepts, cases, and consequences.* Boston: Allyn & Bacon.

Interstate School Leaders Licensure Consortium of the Council of Chief State School Officers. (1997). *Candidate information bulletin for school leaders assessment.* Princeton, NJ: Educational Testing Service.

Johnson, D. W., & Johnson, F. P. (1982). *Joining together: Group theory and group skills.* Upper Saddle River, NJ: Prentice Hall.

Kamlesh, M., & Solow, D. (1994). *Management science: The art of decision-making.* Upper Saddle River, NJ: Prentice Hall.

Kanter, R. M. (1982, July/August). The middle manager as innovator. *Harvard Business Review, 60*(4), 95–105.

Kim, C., & Mauborgne, R. (1997, July/August). Fair process: Managing in the knowledge economy. *Harvard Review, 75*(4), 65–75.

Kotter, J. P. (1985). *Power and influence: Beyond formal authority.* New York: Free Press.

Lindblom, C. E. (1959). The science of muddling through. *Public Administrative Review, 19,* 79–99.

Maier, N. R. (1963). *Problem solving discussions and conferences: Leadership methods and skills.* New York: McGraw-Hill.

March, J. G. (1982). Emerging developments in the study of higher education. *Review of Higher Education, 6,* 1–18.

Osborn, A. F. (1957). *Applied imagination.* New York: Scribner's.

Parkay, F. W., & Stanford, B. (2001). *Becoming a Teacher.* Boston: Allyn & Bacon.

Simon, H. A. (1982). *Models of bounded rationality.* Cambridge, MA: MIT Press.

Vroom, V. H., & Jago, A. G. (1988). *The new leadership: Managing participation in organizations.* Upper Saddle River, NJ: Prentice Hall.

Vroom, V. H., & Yetton, P. W. (1973). *Leadership and decision making.* Pittsburgh, PA: University of Pittsburgh Press.

Yukl, G. A. (1989). *Leadership in organizations* (2nd ed.). Upper Saddle River, NJ: Prentice Hall.

Yukl, G. A. (1994). *Leadership in organizations* (3rd ed.). Upper Saddle River, NJ: Prentice Hall.

Yukl, G. (2002). *Leadership in organizations* (5th ed.). Upper Saddle River, NJ: Prentice Hall.

Will Ower, D. (1991). Micropolitics and the sociology of school organizations. *Education and Urban Society, 23,* 442–454.

6

MANAGING CONFLICT IN TODAY'S SCHOOLS

Conflict is a major occurrence in today's schools, and the most astute school leaders are discovering that managing it can be a challenging process. As schools increase in diversity and people exercise their rights to present and challenge issues, divergent views surface, giving rise to conflict.

In contrast, supporters of the current educational reform movement are advocating massive changes in the way schools are structured; the curriculum format; and the role of faculty, staff, and leader (Riley, 2002; SREB, 2001). These suggested changes, in one way or another, emphasize empowerment, participation, and collaboration, all of which suggest that individuals and groups in the schoolhouse can work in harmony. Also, in order to perform their required functions on a daily basis, school leaders, as well as other individuals, interact with a variety of personalities performing many different functions. If conflict is allowed to become a harmful force in the schoolhouse, individuals can be consumed by negative feelings and hostile actions that adversely affect their performance, as well as the school program.

However, the solution does not lie in the avoidance of all conflict in schools, but rather in reducing the incidence of conflict and minimizing its disruptive effect. Therefore, in practicing the art of leadership, a major goal of school leaders should be to organize the school in a manner that facilitates the performance of all functions with minimum conflict.

In this chapter, we (a) present, in summary format, a definition of conflict; (b) discuss the nature and types of conflict that frequently occur in schools; (c) analyze the sources of those conflicts; and (d) identify strategies commonly used to manage them. Because the literature refers to most conflict occurring in today's schools as organizational conflict (Barge, 1994; Fullan, 1999; Goodlad, 1984; Greenberg, 1996a; Katz & Lawler, 1993; Sashkin & Morris, 1984), the scenarios of the chapter are focused on the disposition, decision-making behavior, and communication skills of the leader and the leader's interactions with individuals and groups. The primary intent of the scenarios is to affirm that the negative effects of conflict in schools can be minimized. As a result of working through the scenarios, the reader will develop a greater appreciation for the influence of leader behavior on conflict in schools and gain insight into how effective management, collaboration, and the use of ethical principles can reduce the negative dysfunctional aspects of conflict. Reflected in these scenarios are indicators of ISLLC Standards 3, 5, and 6.

A Definition of Conflict

Putnam and Poole (1987) define conflict as "the interaction of interdependent people who perceive opposition of goals, aims, and views, and who see the other party as potentially interfering with the realization of these goals" (p. 352). It is a social phenomenon that is heavily ingrained in human relations, expressed and sustained through communication, and occurs when individuals and/or groups become dependent on one another to meet identified needs (Barge, 1994). Because of the interdependent nature of individuals and groups, conflict in organizations is inevitable, endemic, and often legitimate. It is a normal part of social relations and can be either functional (positive) or dysfunctional (negative). Since schools are open social systems composed of individuals and groups with opposing interests but dependent on each other to achieve individual and school goals, conflict is understandably inevitable and all-pervasive.

The Nature of Conflict in Schools

There is general agreement that conflict occurring in schools is latent (ever present) and exists because of divergent (or apparently divergent) views and incompatibility of those views (Owens, 1995; Sashkin & Morris, 1984). The issue that must be given consideration is whether the conflict is functional or dysfunctional.

Functional Conflict

When conflict is functional, there is a win–win attitude, and harmony exists. Functional conflict facilitates the accomplishment of goals by members of the organization and/or generates new insights into old problems (Putnam & Poole, 1987). For example, a school leader has the responsibility of shaping the school's educational programs. In order for this to occur, the leader may find it necessary to make changes in teacher assignments, the curriculum, and/or existing instructional materials. When these changes are presented to the faculty, some members who do not support them might become motivated to seek other program ideas as an alternative in the decision-making process. As a result of divergent points of view, the organization benefits; new ideas surface, individuals are motivated, and decision making is enhanced.

Dysfunctional Conflict

Dysfunctional conflict occurs when discussions are focused on individuals and when individuals adopt inflexible positions on key issues (Witteman, 1990). There is a win-lose attitude, producing hostility (Owens, 1995) that can negatively affect a faculty to the extent that their productivity is disrupted. For example, Ms. Devine, a teacher at Walton High School, requested a 3-day leave of absence to attend a religious conference. The principal denied the request, advising her that he was denying the request because the annual achievement tests were scheduled for the following week, and students needed her to lead them in a review. After being denied the leave, Ms. Devine contacted the teacher's union and filed a grievance, stating that her religious rights had been violated. The complaint spread through the school and divided the faculty. The school climate became disruptive just before the annual achievement tests were to be administered.

Regardless of whether the conflict is functional or dysfunctional, individuals affected may feel a sense of deprivation and respond in a manner that negatively impacts student success. Therefore, if schools are to effectively achieve established goals, a major concern of school leaders must be developing an understanding of the sources of conflict that occur in schools and acquiring skills in minimizing the disruptive effect.

Sources of Conflict in Schools

Conflict in schools often occurs over situations in which individuals and/or groups experience some degree of difficulty in obtaining an action alternative (March & Simon, 1958). It can occur within a faculty member, between faculty members, or among faculty members of a particular grade level. Conflict can also be experienced between groups, within the larger faculty, between school and central office leadership, between school personnel and parents, or between the faculty of one school and the faculty of another school. Because of their impact on school effectiveness, each of the above-mentioned instances in which conflict can occur will be examined.

The Context and Content of Conflict

The type of conflict that occurs in schools can be differentiated in two ways: context (the type of conflict that might occur) and content (the issues over which the conflict occurs). Then, there are the feelings and responses of the individuals involved in the conflict. According to Gross (1958), individuals involved in conflict may feel deprivation and respond in a reactive or proactive manner. To ensure that the organization's resources are managed in a way that promotes a learning environment that is safe, efficient, and effective, leaders should seek to understand each of these areas and their implications for behavior in schools.

The Context of Conflict   Conflict occurs in three contexts:

1. *Interpersonal*: conflict that exists between individuals within a group or organization;
2. *Intergroup*: conflict between two groups within a larger social system, and
3. *Interorganizational*: conflict that exists between two organizations (Barge, 1994, p. 163).

Interpersonal and intergroup conflict can be observed to some extent in all organizations, as these types of conflict are seen as a natural part of social relationships. Interorganizational conflict is a somewhat infrequently occurring phenomenon (Wexley & Yukl, 1984). In each of the areas mentioned, conflict might emerge because of the following reasons:

1. *Competition for scarce resources*: Often in school situations, decisions have to be made regarding who will receive space in a given building, who will receive the new computers, or who will be assigned the last bell as his/her planning hour. Such issues are competitive in nature, and conflict is produced.
2. *A desire for autonomy*: There are instances in schools in which teachers, administrators, and parents are so committed to a program or activity (allocating booster club funds, directing the senior play, facilitating curriculum planning) that they lay claim to it and want total autonomy over its operation. If there is interference with the activity, conflict occurs. In such an instance, the conflict is over a desire for autonomy.
3. *Divergence in views and/or goals*: If individuals in the primary unit of a school have different views over which approach to use in the teaching of reading—whole language or phonetics—and cannot agree on which of the approaches to use, divergent goal conflict occurs (Pondy, 1967).
4. *Social factors*: Schools consist of a group of individuals with different personalities, and as they interact to complete tasks, in some instances, these differences engender conflict (Lindelow & Scott, 1989; Pondy, 1967).

Two other contexts in which conflict might occur are intrapersonal conflict and intragroup conflict (Barge, 1994). Intrapersonal conflict refers to conflict that is occurring within an individual. In such instances, the individual is at odds with himself/herself because of uncertainty about the action to take regarding a particular issue or competing goals. For example, imagine that the principal of Clark High School has spent 2 years working with the faculty and community establishing a set of long-range goals for the school. The goals have been developed, and sufficient progress has been made toward their attainment. However, because of his success at Clark, at the end of his second year, the superintendent offers the principal a position in the central office. If he accepts the position, he would have developmental responsibilities for the district's curriculum with a sizable increase in pay.

Making the decision to stay and finish the job at Clark, keeping a commitment to that school and its constituency, or taking the new assignment and fulfilling a career dream is one that is likely to require much thought. The challenge of making such a decision could produce considerable intrapersonal conflict.

During the tenure of a school leader, there will be many instances when the leader will be faced with situations of a similar nature. These situations may concern school programs, personnel, or issues in the community. Because these issues require decisions involving morals, values, and/or personal goals, and the outcome is of an impending nature, the leader may experience frustrating intrapersonal conflict.

In such instances, intrapersonal conflict can be addressed by conducting an in-depth analysis of self, which might prove to be beneficial. The analysis entails ranking the advantages and disadvantages of the situation using a point system. Two columns are formed, one positive and one negative. All factors are placed in one of the two columns and given a point value on a scale from one to ten. The difference in the sum of the two columns is likely to provide insight into the decision.

Intragroup Conflict   Intragroup conflict occurs when there are divergent opinions within a group on a particular issue (Barge, 1994). For example, if some members of the senior faculty support the seniors' desire to hold the after-prom party at a local nightclub, as opposed to other faculty who prefer the school gym, intragroup conflict has occurred. If the conflict is not resolved in an effective manner, communication between the two groups may be adversely affected, compromising any coordination of efforts.

The Content of Conflict

According to Barge (1994), conflict content refers to the issues over which the conflict occurs, of which there are two fundamental types—substantive and affective. He describes substantive conflict as being related to the issues, ideas, and positions of a conflict. Later in the chapter, in reading the scenario "The Discipline Plan," you will come to understand that at Barnsbury, the issue was the discipline plan, whether it should be changed, and who should be involved in the change process. Ideas were presented by various members of the faculty, and each faculty member took a different position on the ideas presented. This issue over the discipline plan resulted in substantive conflict.

A second example, illustrating substantive conflict, relates to a team of teachers discussing curriculum. Let us say there are several teachers engaging in a discussion concerning the merits of a curriculum program. The teachers may have different ideas concerning the content of the curriculum and take different positions regarding the appropriate grade level the curriculum should serve and the amount of instructional time that should be allotted for its use. These differences of opinions can also provoke what is classified as substantive conflict.

Affective or social conflict, the second type, concerns the emotional aspects of the problem and may affect the interpersonal relationships among members of the faculty (Barge, 1994; Lindelow & Scott, 1989; Pondy, 1967). When disagreements occur among members of a school faculty over power, status, role development, or personality issues, affective conflict can occur. Emotions are involved as individuals strive to achieve their own preferred outcome, which, if achieved, will deny another's desired outcome, thus producing hostility. Such is the case when individuals engage in a struggle for control of a group or express concern about the attitude that an individual brings to the group.

How Individuals Respond to Conflict

The content of an issue, whether it is substantive or affective, can influence the behavior of individuals in schools, swaying them to respond in a reactive or proactive manner (Greenberg, 1996a). Therefore, the leader should seek to become knowledgeable about the diversity that exists in the school so that operational procedures can be designed and managed to ensure that opportunities for successful learning are maximized.

The Reactive Response

If individuals respond to a particular conflict, displaying behavior in an attempt to escape or avoid a perceived unfair state or occurrence, the behavior is considered reactive. An example of reactive behavior would be the negative responses by some members of the faculty to the principal's distribution of new computers to other members of the faculty. For example, if a principal acquires new computers and distributes them to select members of the faculty with the expectation that other faculty members would continue to use old and somewhat out-of-date computers, the individuals expected to use the old computers may tend to feel that they have been treated unfairly. In a general sense, they may feel that unfair and inequitable treatment exists among all school personnel. As a result of these feelings, they may display certain negative emotions, which will motivate them to initiate action to eliminate the experienced inequity.

The conflict just described is not between the two groups of individuals, but rather with the state of affairs in the school. Berger, Zelditch, Anderson, and Cohen (1972) advise that individuals in organizations make comparisons with a generalized order, rather than with other individuals. Such comparisons relate to status and value, and, as a result, individuals can develop a feeling of inequity to which they respond. When this occurs, faculty effectiveness can be compromised, negatively affecting the academic achievement of students. If there are not enough computers for all faculty members, the program goals might inform the allocation. In the absence of program goals, the faculty might meet and establish priorities for the use of technology in the school. In that way, the school leader becomes the facilitator of the plan, rather than the maker of the plan. In response to this type of situation, Standard 5 stipulates that school leaders should bring ethical principles to the decision-making process and treat all individuals fairly, equitably, and with dignity and respect; the leader should have a program plan in place to meet this standard.

Further informing leader behavior regarding the feelings of followers, Martin, (1981), in addressing the "theory of relative deprivation," asserts that certain reward distribution patterns in schools could encourage individuals to make certain social comparisons. When social comparisons are made, they can lead to followers feeling a sense of deprivation and resentment, causing a variety of reactions, ranging from depression to the outbreak of violent riots. To eliminate the possibility of such feelings occurring, the effective school leader strives to identify and implement procedures that ensure fair and equitable treatment of all individuals, another indicator of ISLLC Standard 5.

The Proactive Response

There are also instances in schools when individuals and/or groups display behavior in an effort to promote justice and create fair treatment and equitable distribution of resources when they do not exist in quantities sufficient for everyone. In such instances, this type of behavior is considered proactive (Greenberg, 1996b). Individuals observing inequity in the treatment of school personnel relative to the reward system and/or the distribution of resources sometimes proactively strive to create an equitable distribution system. Such action is taken because these individuals feel a positive change in the distribution system is ultimately in the best interest of all parties (Leventhal, 1976).

Freedman and Montanari (1980), addressing the equity norm, offer a possible solution to such occurrences in schools. They theorized that when it is perceived that resources are being distributed in a manner that is not equitable, as was the case in the previously mentioned computer distribution plan, leader behavior can improve the situation. For example, a leader who values maintaining social harmony among the faculty would advocate the equity norm. In so doing, an attempt would be made to apply strategies that would facilitate the equal division of computers among the faculty, regardless of their possible differential contributions.

In summary, individuals and groups in schools, as well as those served by the school, tend to seek and appreciate just and fair treatment. If they have a negative experience with another individual or group, they may hold a grudge and plan an action of retaliation. This type of behavior consumes energy that could be employed in more productive school endeavors. Therefore, the school leader should seek to become knowledgeable about the diversity that exists in the school so that operational procedures can be designed and managed to ensure that individuals and groups do not respond to issues in a manner that adversely affects student learning (Standard 2). Rather, all individuals are treated fairly, equitably, and with dignity and respect (Standard 5).

Role Conflict

Another type of conflict that frequently occurs in schools is role conflict. School leaders and their followers face conflicts and pressures, not only because of change, but also because of the roles and expectations that people hold for them and the expectations they hold for themselves. Individuals and groups, inside and outside of the schoolhouse, also have expectations for the school in terms of goals the school is expected to achieve and the roles various individuals and groups are expected to play in achieving those goals. Often, it is by these expectations and the extent to which goals are met that the effectiveness of the school is measured (Hoy & Miskel, 1991). When the goals of the school are not achieved to the extent expected and the roles of individuals and groups do not meet expectations, conflict can occur. A factor in these instances is the behavior definition of the leader.

Role Expectations for the School Leader

The behavior definition of school leaders is composed of two sets of role expectations, one formal and the other informal. The formal role is defined by the school district in the form of a job description and is governed by school policies, whereas individuals and groups who hold expectations for the leader define the leaders informal role. These individuals and groups reside inside the schoolhouse and within the greater school community. Together, the formal and informal expectations comprise a behavior definition that characterizes how different individuals and groups affiliated with the school believe the leader should perform in a given situation (Getzels, 1958).

School leaders must be knowledgeable of these expectations, as they represent a powerful source of influence on their behavior and serve as informal evaluation standards that are applied to their performance. Failure of leaders to assess current conditions and develop an understanding of the expectations that followers have for them can inhibit their ability to establish directions with any degree of certainty of how those directions will be received by the faculty (Gorton, 1987). In fact, without this understanding, the leader could actually create dysfunctional conflict or exacerbate existing conflict. The expectations influencing such a conflict can vary in direction, clarity, and intensity.

Direction   Direction refers to the extent to which school leaders and faculty are in agreement on the decision of a particular issue, program, activity, or problem (Gorton, 1987). Because of the direction of a decision, the leader and followers may either totally agree on the manner in which a problem decision is addressed, or they may be in total disagreement. The point to be given consideration is the situation and the perception of individuals as to the right of the leader to behave in the selected manner (Gorton, 1987). In making judgments regarding a particular situation, the leader might give consideration to the nature of the situation and make a determination relative to the perceived direction in which it falls.

Clarity

Clarity refers to the adequacy of communicating expectations (Gross, 1958). When expectations are not clearly communicated, role ambiguity becomes a factor, making it difficult for leaders to determine the behavior expectations held for them. For example, in a faculty meeting, an agreement was reached that seniors would complete their work and end school 2 weeks prior to the last day of school. However, no details were presented. The faculty left the meeting with the expectation that written directions would follow from the principal. However, the principal delegated the task to the assistant principal for the twelfth grade, who sent written instructions to the faculty. In the final 2 weeks of the school year, even with written instructions from the assistant principal, the faculty was not quite certain as to how to handle the situation because they expected instructions from the principal. It would have been beneficial to the principal to have had an understanding of the expectations that the faculty held for his role. When the leader misperceives the expectations held by the faculty, disagreement and/or misunderstanding can occur, producing role conflict.

Intensity

The intensity of a conflict refers to the depth of interest and/or concerns that an individual or group holds for the issue in question (Gross, 1958). The magnitude of feelings determines the intensity of the conflict. When an individual or group feels strongly about an issue and is adamant about the actions they expect from the leader, their behavior might be quite different from a situation in which an individual or group only has casual feelings regarding a situation, with little or no expectations for the leader.

School leaders will also find that it is in their best interest to recognize the importance of being knowledgeable of the expectations of others regarding their role and to diagnose possible conflicts involving direction, clarity, and intensity. Developing an understanding of expectations and diagnosing conflict for direction, clarity, and intensity can enhance the leader's ability to anticipate and assess the reactions of others relative to their behavior regarding specific decisions (Campbell, 1968). It is not likely that school leaders will be able to develop an understanding of all individuals in the school community. However, it is imperative that they have an understanding of individuals who can impair or enhance their effectiveness (Standard 6).

The Leader's Expectations for Self

In addition to the formal and informal expectations of others, leaders must understand and address the expectations that they hold for themselves. Consistent with the need for leaders to have an understanding of self as presented in Chapter 3, they need an understanding of the expectations that they hold for their roles. Self-expectations are influenced by the manner in which leaders perceive they should behave and may be more important than the expectations of others in the determination of the decisions they make in a given situation (Greenberg, 1996b). This behavior is derived from the leader's personal needs as illustrated in Scenarios 10 and 11, appearing later in this chapter.

In summary, the personal needs of the leader and the expectations of members of the organization and the larger culture are major factors that influence role behavior (Getzels, 1958). The interactions between the leader's needs disposition, the role expectations of other individuals in the organization, and the larger culture influence the leader's behavior (Getzels, 1958). Given Getzels's theory, it seems reasonable to believe that the greater the compatibility between the leader's needs disposition and the expectations of individuals affiliated with the organization, the greater the overall compatibility. Therefore, leaders' knowledge of the expectations of others for their behavior should prove to be helpful in managing the school.

The Ability to Manage Conflict

Quite clearly, as was previously stated in the section of this chapter entitled "A Definition of Conflict," because of the interactive behavior in schools, the question is not whether conflict will surface—it will, for it is a natural part of social relationships. Rather, the question becomes one of whether school leaders have the skills to manage it. In essence, a primary skill needed by today's school leaders is the ability to manage conflict.

Conflict Management

Conflict management is the process of resolving and minimizing disagreements resulting from perceived or real differences. A conflict has been managed when its cognitive barriers have been changed to agreement (Greenhalgh, 1986). The parties involved reach a level of commitment that enables the barriers of the conflict to be removed and allows for a dissipation of the forces that caused the initial stress (Hanson, 1996). Approaches to conflict management can range from a win–win orientation (both parties achieving some or all of their desired goals) to a win–lose orientation (only one party clearly achieving the desired goal). The determining factor is the extent to which the parties desire to satisfy their own concerns versus the concerns of the other party (Daft, 1999).

The approaches used by the leader to resolve conflict vary, as no one style will fit all situations. However, much of the theoretical literature strongly suggests the contingency approach—diagnosing a conflict to identify the optimal ways of managing it under the given conditions (Owens, 1995). Using this approach, the primary objective of the school leader is to first determine if a conflict really exists; if it does, the conflict should be diagnosed, various management strategies reviewed, and the strategy that will lead to an effective solution selected. As a result of using this approach, the leader is able to identify a conflict management strategy that will acquire optimal results under the prevailing conditions. The following section contains a description of how a leader might manage a conflict using the contingency approach.

The Contingency Approach to Conflict Management

First, the leader determines if a conflict really exists—if the goals of the involved individuals or groups are truly incompatible. In many instances, the goals of the parties only seem incompatible, and having them engage in a general discussion can result in a satisfactory solution. However, in instances where the goals are truly incompatible, the leader should seek to determine how the parties have conceptualized the situation and how they really feel about the issues involved. When individuals are involved in a confrontational situation, the way they view the situation will determine, to a large extent, the way they will respond regarding finding a solution (Owens, 1995). These uncertainties can be removed by diagnosing the conflict. Through such diagnosis, the specific pattern of behavior of the individuals involved can be identified.

Making a determination as to the extent and magnitude of the feelings of the individuals and/or groups involved in the conflict will allow the leader to fully conceptualize the conflict and apply a strategy that is likely to resolve the disagreement. According to Thomas (1976), when engaged in a conflict, individuals may display cooperative behavior, indicating the degree to which they are interested in reaching a satisfactory solution to the concerns of others. In other instances, individuals may display assertive, uncooperative behavior, which displays the extent to which they are desirous of satisfying individual interests.

There are also instances in which one of the parties engaged in conflict will display complete apathy toward a situation, ignore it, and eventually completely withdraw. Then, on other occasions, that individual might feel a high sense of cooperation and will be accommodating, displaying a willingness to attend to the concerns of the other party while sacrificing his or her own concerns.

Individuals might also be very competitive and fight to satisfy their own concerns at the expense of the other party. If the parties are willing to collaborate and engage in mutual problem solving to satisfy their concerns, still another option is available for use by the leader. If the parties are moderately assertive and moderately cooperative, they may be willing to engage in a sharing orientation that often leads to compromise. As a result of diagnosing the conflict, specific patterns of behavior of the parties involved can be identified and an appropriate management strategy applied.

Applying the Appropriate Management Strategy

After the conflict has been diagnosed, it must be managed, and the style of the leader is a key factor in that process. Consequently, various sources were consulted (Barge, 1994; Gorton, 1987; Hanson, 1996; Owens, 1995; Rahim, 1986; Thomas, 1976) to identify styles that could be used to successfully manage conflict after it had been diagnosed. Although different terminology was often used, these sources offered the following five approaches as those best suited for leaders to use in managing conflict, contingent on the desired outcome:

1. *Avoidance*: The leader has a desire to maintain a rational climate and copes with the conflict by avoiding it completely. The issues are so minimally important that investing the time and resources necessary to resolve the conflict appears unwise. The desire for a peaceful coexistence and the avoidance of a hostile aftermath are given priority. There are both advantages and disadvantages to using this approach. Although the conflict and the possible hostility that could result are avoided at the present time, the potential for conflict remains and could resurface at any given time.
2. *Smoothing*: The leader has a desire to maintain positive interpersonal relationships. In order to maintain these positive relationships, disagreements and differences of opinions on substantive issues are minimized.

3. *Bargaining*: Moderate levels of concern for both task and relationship are displayed. The parties must voluntarily agree to enter a problem-solving approach. A solution to the conflict is reached as a result of both parties making concessions. Neither party is a winner, but neither party is a loser. Sometimes, a third party may be called in to serve as a mediator and be given the responsibility of providing assurance that everyone is treated fairly and an equitable compromise is reached.

4. *Power struggle*: There is little concern for interpersonal relationships between the parties involved. The major focus is on task accomplishment. Power and force are used to break down the opposition and win, regardless of the consequences to the other party.

5. *Problem solving*: Problem solving is a collaborative approach to managing conflict. Both parties collaborate in an attempt to achieve the best solution to the conflict. The primary concern is accomplishing the task in a manner that is rational and allows a positive climate to be maintained.

Leadership in Today's Schools

In summary, there is no one best approach to conflict management. However, it is commonly agreed among many conflict management theorists that the problem-solving approach is the most effective (Lunenburg & Ornstein, 1996). Nevertheless, selecting the appropriate approach cannot be overemphasized, for if the approach selected is not appropriate for the situation, not only will the conflict remain unresolved, but it is likely to be exacerbated.

The Scenarios

Scenario 10 addresses conflict that emerges as a result of Principal Smith's decision regarding a discipline plan for the school. The intent of this scenario is to demonstrate how leader behavior can positively or negatively affect the learning environment of the school. In analyzing the scenario, the reader might seek to determine the best approach to use in implementing a new discipline program while minimizing conflict among faculty, parents, and students.

In Scenario 11, an individual transitioning into a different school as principal uses an approach that is counterproductive to acquiring the type of school environment that promotes the success of all students. Given that every school leader is likely to transfer from one school assignment to another, identifying an approach that can be used to make the transfer in a manner that creates an effective learning environment should be beneficial.

Scenario 12 presents a clear picture of the relationship between decision making and conflict. A leader made a poor decision that resulted in conflict. Then, the strategy selected for use in managing the conflict was inappropriate, causing the problem and the conflict to escalate. In addition, several of the indicators of the ISLLC Standards are violated.

SCENARIO 10
THE DISCIPLINE PLAN

STANDARD 3

A school administrator is an educational leader who promotes the success of all students by ensuring management of the organization, operations, and resources for a safe, efficient, and effective learning environment.

The parents of Barnsbury Elementary School left the office of the superintendent smiling because the superintendent had informed them that a new principal had been assigned to their school with specific instructions to give discipline top priority. For several years, discipline had been a problem at Barnsbury Elementary; however, over the past 2 years, this situation had really escalated. Parents and students became concerned about student safety. The Parent-Teacher Organization had scheduled this meeting with the superintendent to demand action.

The previous principal had operated with very few discipline rules and regulations. In fact, the student handbook on discipline had not been updated during his 5-year tenure. Discipline consequences were out of line with the offenses, and students were aware of this fact. Parents believed the principal was not fulfilling his role.

The PTO members had voiced this concern on several occasions, but their complaints fell on deaf ears because many senior faculty members had control of their classes and were content with the status quo. The major discipline incidents occurred before school, during lunch, and after school, and it was the unofficial position of the faculty that discipline during these periods was the responsibility of the administration. Even though teachers new to the school wanted a change in policy, it had been resisted by many senior faculty members because a change in discipline policies might mean teacher duty at these times. The superintendent informed the PTO that he had given the new principal a free hand to improve discipline at the school. Thus, they were pleased with the news of Principal Smith's appointment.

Principal Smith, having been appointed in late June, worked all summer organizing a new list of expected school behavior regulations and a discipline plan for the school. He read books, talked with other principals in the district, and studied several discipline programs offered by various companies before putting together what he felt was the best overall method to maintain a well-disciplined school. Having discussed discipline with the superintendent and other principals, he felt, as principal, it was his responsibility to develop a workable plan for the faculty.

When Mr. Smith presented his completed discipline plan to the faculty at their first meeting, he was instantly bombarded with resistance from several faculty members. According to Mrs. Jones, "This discipline plan is too rigid. It doesn't allow me the flexibility to address the differences in the ages of students or extenuating circumstances that often occur. I want to have flexibility; I don't want my hands tied when it comes to disciplining my students. I want to be in control."

Mrs. Moore complained, "I've been teaching for almost 20 years now, and I certainly feel I can control my students. I've never had any complaints before, and I don't expect any this year."

"Although a schoolwide discipline plan might be helpful to all of us, I feel teachers should have input. I resent having a plan forced on me. I think I've earned the right to have a voice in the way I manage discipline in my classroom. However, I do agree that we need a workable plan in place before school begins," stated Mrs. Hall.

"Well, that may be true! However, you must agree things are out of control with all the fights and children out in the halls all times of the day; it really is difficult to teach," voiced Mrs. Green.

Other faculty members also had negative comments. "The plan is too lenient for many of our students. Things were bad enough last year, and we need to lay down the law."

Mrs. Williams stated, "If it's going to work, it should definitely allow some flexibility for the teachers. You probably won't get much cooperation without giving teachers some flexibility."

Mr. Frank offered, "I just don't think it's right for someone to tell us how to manage our classrooms. It might have been okay if we had been asked our opinion first, but I don't think you asked anyone."

"We really need a change. I believe we should form committees and study the situation, then implement a plan that is acceptable to all faculty members. I don't think we should conduct an extensive study for the purpose of improving discipline," offered Mrs. Williams.

Mr. Smith was perplexed after hearing the various comments from the faculty.

REFLECTIVE THINKING AND SCENARIO ANALYSIS

The ISLLC Standards

The following are indicators of the ISLLC Standards addressed in the scenario:

1: Effective communication, consensus-building and negotiation skills are needed, and leaders have to be willing to continuously examine their assumptions, beliefs, and practices.
2: Consideration must be given to the change process for systems, organizations, and individuals; the culture of the school must be taken into consideration; all individuals must be treated with fairness, dignity, and respect; and barriers to student learning must be identified and removed.
3: Risks must be taken and management decisions that enhance learning and teaching must be made; operational procedures must be designed and managed to maximize opportunities for successful learning; problems must be confronted in a timely manner; and effective conflict resolution skills must be used.
5: Ethical principles must be brought to the decision-making process, and a caring school community must be developed.
6: Models and strategies of change and conflict resolution, as applied to the larger political, social, cultural, and economic context of schooling must be utilized.

Reflective Questions

1. After reviewing Mr. Smith's behavior, which of the ISLLC disposition indicators did he fail to meet? Give a rationale for your response with consideration to factors that are relevant to a principal implementing a new program plan at a school with characteristics similar to those at Barnsbury.
2. What are the different types of conflict occurring in the scenario?
3. Judging from the comments of various faculty members, how would you assess the intensity of the conflict between the principal and the faculty?
4. What conflict management strategies would you use at Barnsbury to reduce the negative effect of the conflict? Justify your response.
5. What is likely to be the result if Mr. Smith uses position power to ensure the implementation of his plan? Cite evidence for your response.

ADDRESSING THE CRITICAL ISSUES

The Cause of Conflict at Barnsbury

In an attempt to improve discipline at Barnsbury Elementary, Mr. Smith, the new principal, designed a discipline plan for implementation during the first year of his principalship. However, when he presented the plan to the faculty, it met with resistance that incited conflict. The type of conflict (context) was interpersonal, and it occurred because of divergent views and role expectations.

Divergent Views

The discipline plan (conflict content) was being revised because of a needed change (level of student behavior) in the environment of the school. The change proposed was in the discipline rules and regulations. Rules and regulations are often used to prevent or manage conflict by clarifying such issues as how to proceed, when to proceed, and who should assume responsibility for specific tasks (Owens, 1991). In contrast, when individuals disagree with the substance of the rules and regulations, and/or the process in which the rules and regulations were developed, the individuals or the rules can become dysfunctional and cause or exacerbate conflict. This was the case at Barnsbury Elementary. Some members of the faculty disagreed with components of the plan, and others disagreed with the manner in which the plan was developed.

Role Conflict

Several members of the faculty viewed discipline as being in their zone of concern. Therefore, when the principal took unilateral action in developing the plan, role conflict emerged. Faculty involvement in a change process when the change is in their zone of concern is of utmost important, as the faculty is interested in the benefits the change holds for them (Fullan, 1993).

In schools, the manner in which any plan is developed or modified can either generate conflict or facilitate problem solving. Conflict is likely to be minimized and problems resolved when the faculty is appropriately involved and there is compatibility between the leader's decision behavior and the expectations stakeholders hold for the leader's role.

Diagnosing the Conflict

At Barnsbury Elementary, the faculty is exhibiting proactive behavior. They view the principal as being unjust in his action in that he developed and/or modified a discipline plan that lies in the zone of concern of teachers. The vision for a safe and supportive learning environment should be developed with stakeholder involvement (Barth, 1990). Given that this did not occur and considering that he is a new administrator, the faculty is likely to believe that this type of behavior will be repeated.

The Intensity of the Conflict

Quite clearly, based on the comments made by various faculty members, they held certain expectations for the principal, and those expectations were not met. In fact, there was considerable disagreement on the plan the principal had developed (causing a variance in role direction). In addition, the intensity of the concerns of teachers has reached the point that if he does not alter the plan, they are likely to attempt to avoid implementing it, using whatever sanctions are available to them. At this point, the principal must be concerned with direction and intensity. Mr. Smith would better serve the school program by seeking to determine the level at which the conflict is rooted, what outcome will foster a smooth opening of school, and how he can achieve that outcome.

Managing the Conflict

In managing the conflict, Mr. Smith should use a problem- solving collaborative approach. The faculty has already expressed disagreement with his plan. If he competes with them (insisting that the faculty implement the plan in its current format), a power struggle will develop, and someone will win and someone will lose. Eventually, the students will lose, as the teachers, under forced conditions, would not be fully committed to implementation of the plan. One major responsibility of educational leaders is to promote the success of all students by using the influence of their office constructively and productively (Standard 5). Therefore, they do not champion issues that provoke conflict.

Mr. Smith would be well advised to subordinate his interest in the existing plan and initiate the design of a new plan, using a collaborative approach that acknowledges the faculty's expertise and communicates to them the importance of their role in school discipline.

In summary, Mr. Smith provoked conflict between himself and members of his faculty and among the faculty members, primarily by his leadership style. Whereas any change in the existing discipline plan is likely to initiate some conflict, a more inclusive style of leadership would have minimized the disruption. Given that the action has been taken and the conflict exists, it must be managed. A contingency management approach appears to be appropriate.

SCENARIO 11

I AM YOUR NEW PRINCIPAL

STANDARD 5

A school administrator is an educational leader who promotes the success of all students by acting with integrity, fairness, and in an ethical manner.

Lakeside Elementary School is a large inner-city school with the highest suspension rate in the district. Over 90% of the faculty has been in the building for 15 years or more. The current principal, Mr. Downey, is retiring after serving the district for 40 years, the past 6 at Lakeside Elementary as principal.

In a reorganization of the district's administrators, Principal Early was assigned to Lakeside Elementary School. The assignment was made in June to become effective in July. Principal Early, a veteran administrator with over 20 years experience, knew Mr. Downey and had discussed various issues with him at district meetings over the years. Therefore, in the interest of a smooth transition, Mr. Downey invited her to the final staff meeting of the school year at Lakeside Elementary.

Principal Early attended the meeting wearing a suit and very high-heeled shoes. She walked toward the front of the group and began passing out papers to the faculty. On the paper was printed the Board of Education's policy regarding faculty appearance and dress, which she proceeded to read to the group. She explained her philosophy on dressing "professionally" and informed the faculty that some of them dressed inappropriately, and this would have to change.

She then passed out lists of expectations; one list contained what she expected from the faculty, and one contained what the faculty could expect from her. She informed the faculty that she had read the personnel files of all faculty members and knew all the "troublemakers" in the building. She also stated that she would be watching test scores, and if faculty members were not effective in their current placements, they would be transferred to another school. She further emphasized that teachers who had been in the same classroom for many years would be moved because they did not own their rooms.

After admonishing the faculty several times about current practices within the building and informing the faculty that it was not too late to apply for a transfer, she asked the faculty for questions, waited 15 seconds, and when there were none, she walked out of the room, leaving a stunned and speechless group of teachers.

When the new school year began, Principal Early filled seven of nine open faculty positions with individuals from her former school. These included positions that were not posted for the entire faculty, a practice inconsistent with district policy. The new faculty members were given special treatment and were permitted privileges that continuing faculty members were not allowed.

In one of her first faculty meetings as the new building administrator, Principal Early informed the "continuing faculty" that the "incoming faculty" members did not feel welcome in the building, and that it was their fault. At the end of the first quarter, Principal Early wondered why there was conflict between the two groups and why the year had not gotten off to a smooth start.

Reflective Thinking and Scenario Analysis

The ISLLC Standards

The following are indicators of the ISLLC Standards addressed in the scenario:

3: Potential problems and opportunities have to be identified; human resources have to be developed and managed; management decisions that enhance learning and teaching have to be made; effective conflict resolution and communication skills have to be used; and human resource functions have to be aligned in a manner that supports school goals.

5: A caring school community has to be developed; the principal has to serve as a role model and give consideration to the impact his or her behavior has on the behavior of others; and laws and procedures have to be applied fairly, wisely, and considerately.

Reflective Questions

1. In your judgment, what was the substance of the initial conflict at Lakeside?
2. In the scenario, can you cite instances where members of the faculty would be justified in feeling a sense of deprivation?
3. In the scenario, what information, implied or stated, could you use to justify the disposition of Principal Early?
4. Reflecting on the indicators of the ISLLC Standards, what justification might be offered to support Principal Early's decision to fill the vacant positions with teachers from her former school?
5. Cite three of Principal Early's actions that directly contributed to the conflict that existed at Lakeside after the beginning of the school year. Justify your selection with indicators from the ISLLC Standards.
6. What influence, if any, might the past stability of the faculty and the climate of the school have on the nature of the current conflict?

Discussion of the Critical Issues

Factors Influencing Conflict at Lakeside

The initial conflict at Lakeside occurred for a number of reasons. First, the equilibrium of a well-established faculty (with very little turnover) was disrupted by a change in principals. It is not uncommon for the uncertainty of the personality of a new principal and the idea of having to meet a new set of expectations to be stressful for a school faculty (Gorton, 1987). Therefore, the initial presentation of the arriving principal is a key factor in the principal's acceptance by the faculty. Consequently, entering school leaders should give considerable thought to the content and style of delivery of their initial presentations.

The Second Factor

Principal Early's initial presentation was not only stress- producing, but it created a hostile climate and set the stage for conflict. The nature of the situation in terms of the expectations the faculty had for their new principal was extremely different from what they heard in Principal Early's initial presentation. Thus, it became clear to the faculty that her norms, beliefs, and expectations were different from those that previously existed. Role expectations differed in terms of direction, setting the stage for conflict. The way individuals perceive that others will treat them may lead either to increased or decreased conflict (Luthans, 1992). Also, if individuals in a school have different views of the role that the principal should play, conflict is likely to exist (Barge, 1994).

Leader Disposition

Dr. Early's presentation was directive and boss-centered, setting a tone for a power struggle to emerge. Her statement concerning the personnel files gave the impression that she was looking for "troublemakers" so she could "deal with them." Announcing that she would be looking at test scores implied that teachers were solely responsible for test scores, and threatening to move teachers to different rooms worsened an unsettled situation resulting from the retirement of Mr. Downey.

She introduced fear into the workplace, as opposed to removing fear. Principal Early's disposition in the initial meeting, coupled with the content of her presentation, created a "we-they" climate, thus initiating conflict between her and the faculty. Emotions got involved, and hostility was produced, resulting in affective conflict.

A Third Factor

A third conflict-producing factor emerged when Principal Early established expectations for the faculty before making a determination of the faculty's expectations for her role. Failure of leaders to assess current conditions and develop an understanding of the expectations that followers have for them will inhibit their ability to establish directions with any degree of clarity of how those directions will be received by the faculty (Gorton, 1987).

She created an atmosphere of distrust, and the faculty developed the attitude that the new principal was out to get them. Having developed this attitude, it became difficult for Principal Early to create a positive relationship with them. Trust started to erode, and the climate of the school became riddled with conflict. The negative reactions, besides being quite stressful, became problematic in that they diverted the attention of the faculty from teaching and learning to social and survival issues.

In general, when a new leader enters a school, the leader strives to build a level of trust, realizing that schools that are considered great places in which to work are characterized by high levels of trust between the faculty and the principal and among members of the faculty (Ciancutti & Steding, 2001).

Social Conflict

Once the school year started, decisions made by Principal Early, the organizational structure of the school, and the communication process aggravated the initial conflict. The faculty became divided, and social conflict emerged between individuals and groups.

Intraorganizational Conflict

Before the new school year began, Principal Early recruited members from the faculty of her former school to fill vacant positions that existed at Lakeside. Focused recruitment is an acceptable practice, and it is understandable that a principal faced with the challenges posed at Lakeside would want several individuals on staff with whom rapport had already been established. However, the acquisition of these individuals must occur within the realm of policy. This was not the case at Lakeside, and the end result was intraorganizational conflict.

A Reactive Response

When Principal Early elected to bring members of her former faculty to Lakeside, they became members of the Lakeside faculty organization and should have been identified as such. Principal Early should have taken definitive steps to unite the two groups. Leaders should use the influence of their office to develop faculty cohesiveness.

A major problem was created when the faculty became identified as consisting of two groups. The distinct identification of the two groups led to intraorganizational conflict (conflict between two groups within the faculty). The matter was further complicated when the "continuing faculty" members perceived the incoming faculty members to be getting special treatment. The perceived treatment of the incoming faculty members fueled the conflict.

The Equity Norm

Allowing special privileges to the incoming group further built resentment and angered members of the faculty who were not receiving them. The "continuing faculty" members perceived the action to be unfair and sought to promote justice. They believed that the equity norm had been violated. When an individual or group perceives an action to be unfair, they will often react in a proactive manner in an attempt to achieve fair treatment (Greenberg, 1996b).

Martin (1981) asserts that certain reward distribution patterns will encourage individuals to make certain social comparisons. The "continuing faculty" made such comparisons, and as a result, they developed feelings of deprivation and resentment. A faculty does its best work when the level of interpersonal tension is low to moderate and participants are able to share their opinions with one another in a climate of acceptance (David, 1994).

Principal Early's Leadership Style

Principal Early entered Lakeside using a leadership style based in classical theory. She was directive and structured and used her position power to set the tone for her first year as principal of the school. She took a very strong position prior to obtaining an understanding of the individuals on the faculty or allowing them to participate in any restructuring efforts that were to occur. She did not factor into her actions the power of informal groups. As we observed in Chapters 2 and 3, failure to understand the behavior of informal groups can be counterproductive.

Now, if Principal Early wants to change the faculty's perception, she might be well advised to consider a leadership style that is less directive, more people centered, considerate, and one that reflects an understanding of and a respect for the behavior of faculty members functioning as individuals and members of informal groups. Productivity in organizations tends to improve when human factors, such as morale, a feeling of belonging, participative decision making, and effective communication are factored into leader behavior (Standard 1). A leadership style incorporating these characteristics would be based in human relations theory. The behavior displayed by Principal Johnson in Scenario 2 could serve as an example.

SCENARIO 12

THE ASSIGNMENT OF AN ASSISTANT SUPERINTENDENT OF INSTRUCTION

STANDARD 6

A school administrator is an educational leader who promotes the success of all students by understanding, responding to, and influencing the larger political, social, economic, legal, and cultural context.

Superintendent Morgan of the Bellwood School District (a district that had undergone considerable controversy as a result of a city-county school district merger) sat in his office, realizing that the new school year was only a month away. Considering the parent and student complaints from the previous year, there was simply no way to enter the new school year without changes in the assignment of principals. Given that the director of human resources had just advised him of a letter of retirement from Walter Robins, Assistant Superintendent of Instruction, and resignation of the assistant principal at Clark Middle School, he believed this to be an excellent opportunity for some districtwide changes to improve the district's effectiveness. After all, he thought "Wilma Henderson, principal at Williamsburg High, is an excellent person to assume the role of assistant superintendent of instruction. The achievement scores of students in her school are the best in the district and above the state average. She is very knowledgeable about curriculum issues, attends state and national meetings, and appears to command the respect of administrators and teachers. Filling this position with Wilma would mean the best of all worlds. It would add an excellent person to the central office team and, at the same time, create an opportunity to reassign principals and enhance the climate in the school district."

After calling the director of human resources and acquiring the personnel files of all current principals and assistant principals, Superintendent Morgan began his deliberations. He looked at various strengths and weaknesses and compared successes to projects attempted. He reviewed parent, student, and teacher complaints of the previous year, looked at student achievement scores, discipline problems occurring in the various schools, and even the attendance records of administrators, teachers, and students. After completing the review, he compiled a list of personnel changes to be made by the director of human resources. He did not seek board approval, as the law in the state where he was employed empowered the superintendent to make personnel changes, under certain conditions, without board approval. The following changes were made:

- Wilma Henderson from principal of Williamsburg High to assistant superintendent of instruction in the central office
- Allen Harris from principal of Walker High to principal of Williamsburg High
- Anthony Reed from principal of Northside High to principal of Walker High
- Linda Hart from principal of Central City High to assistant principal of Clark Middle
- Evelyn Morris from assistant principal of Clark Middle to principal of Northside High
- Charles Adams from assistant principal of Clark to principal of Clark Middle
- A posting for an assistant principal at Clark Middle

Three days after Superintendent Morgan announced the changes to school district personnel and the general public, he began to receive a number of complaints. On the fourth day, in a meeting with the director of human resources, he discussed the following complaints, some of which had been presented to him and others that were appearing in the local newspaper.

One of the board of education members was complaining that the position of assistant superintendent was not posted. Bill Johnson, Assistant Principal of Williamsburg High (who happens to be African-American), complained that once again he had been passed over for promotion. Charles Walker, a teacher in the district and a longtime seeker of an administrative position, expressed concerns that all of the positions should have been posted. Linda Hart (also African-American) was believed to have had at least two meetings with Bill Johnson, as he was attempting to get her to join him in filing a class action suit.

Over the next several days, the local newspaper, which is not very supportive of the school district, printed articles concerning fairness, the superintendent's annual evaluation, in-fighting, and unethical personnel practices. One headline read, "Superintendent's Evaluation Drops in Twenty-two of Twenty-three Areas." Another read, "Superintendent Loses Favor with Some Board Members over Fairness Issue." In one article a board member stated, "The superintendent makes his own rules." In responding to the superintendent's evaluation, the article quoted one board member as saying, "The only area in which the superintendent's evaluation increased was sense of humor and the ability to laugh at personnel mistakes." Another article quoted still another board member as having said, "The superintendent should resign as he is unethical in his behavior."

In his soft jolly mannerism, Superintendent Morgan comments, "I will not speak to these charges. The law gives me the right to make personnel changes, and I followed the law. As far as posting, the assistant principal's position was posted, and that is sufficient."

The debate over the issue continued at the board level and in the community for weeks. As time passed, the conflict became more intense, pressure mounted, and the superintendent resigned.

REFLECTIVE THINKING AND SCENARIO ANALYSIS

The ISLLC Standards

The following are indicators of the ISLLC Standards addressed in the scenario:

1: Effective communication, consensus-building and negotiation skills are needed; leaders have to be willing to continuously examine their assumptions and beliefs; and barriers to achieving the vision have to be identified clarified, and addressed.

2: Consideration has to be given to adult learning, the change process for systems, organizations and individuals, and the principles of organizational development; multiple sources of information have to be used; and the responsibilities of all individuals have to be respected.

3: Decisions have to reflect organizational procedures at the school and district levels; human resources have to be managed and developed, and legal issues impacting school operations must be taken into consideration; risk is taken to improve schools; and effective conflict resolution skills are needed.

4: Conditions and dynamics of the diverse school community have to be recognized and respected.

5. A professional code of ethics and various ethical frameworks and perspectives on ethics are needed.

6: The political, social, cultural, and economic systems and processes that impact schools have to be considered; there has to be an understanding of principles of representative governance that undergird the system of American schools; and there is a need for ongoing dialogue with representatives of diverse community groups.

Reflective Questions

1. What effect did the political, social, and cultural aspects of the climate in the Bellwood School District have on the nature of the conflict that emerged?
2. If it is true that policy permitted the superintendent to take the personnel action described, what other actions might have been necessary to avoid the conflict that emerged?
3. What are some of the critical factors that must be considered in managing the type of conflict that has emerged in the Bellwood School District?
4. Based on your understanding of the ISLLC standards indicators, what are some of the actions a superintendent might take when board members publicly make critical statements about his or her effectiveness?
5. To what extent did the knowledge, disposition, and performance of the superintendent contribute to the conflict?

ADDRESSING THE CRITICAL ISSUES

Critical Factors Causing the Conflict

Superintendent Morgan established a goal of improving the delivery of instructional services to students. His process of achieving that goal included the appointment of an assistant superintendent of instruction and making various changes in the assignment of principals. He reviewed personnel files and selected individuals who he felt had the skills and experience necessary to meet his established goals. However, after the changes became public knowledge, some members of the board of education, individuals in the community, and personnel in the district expressed a different viewpoint regarding the goals of the superintendent and the approach he was taking to reach them. The goals of these individuals were not compatible with the goals of the superintendent.

When individuals and or groups in a school district have different goals from the superintendent, conflicts can emerge. That was the case in Bellwood; conflict emerged, and the sources of that conflict were role expectations and goal divergence.

Role Expectations

Quite clearly, the superintendent understood his role and had explicit expectations for his behavior as superintendent of the Bellwood School District. Self-expectations are influenced by the manner in which leaders perceive that they should behave (Gorton, 1987). However, some board members had developed a very strong negative feeling regarding the legitimacy of the superintendent's perception, and they were very intense in their feelings. Intensity may be defined in this situation as the extent to which individuals and/or groups believed that the actions taken by Superintendent Morgan should or should not have been taken, and that his behavior should have been different.

Superintendent Morgan's Expectations for Self

Superintendent Morgan felt strongly that he had performed his duties within the realm of policy, and once that had occurred, no other action was necessary. He was very intense in his feelings and did not display behavior that indicated that he had an understanding or was sensitive to the intensity of the feelings of some board members. Both self-expectations and intensity are factors reflected in the statement, "I will not speak to these charges. . . ." Such a statement challenged the compatibility between the superintendent's needs disposition and the intensity of the expectations some board members held for his role. Clearly this is not a statement that is made by a leader who recognizes and respects the legitimate authority of others or one who is committed to the ideal of the common good (Standard 5).

Superintendent Morgan had a perception of the role he should play as superintendent. Board members and other individuals in the school system also had expectations for their superintendent (his informal role). The differences in these expectations provoked conflict. The situation worsened when the conflict was not effectively diagnosed and the appropriate resolution strategy applied.

Divergent Goals: Another Source of Conflict

Another source of conflict was divergent goals as was characterized by the comments in the newspaper. These comments conveyed the opposing viewpoints and differences in goals that various individuals in the school district and in the larger community held regarding the appointment of personnel.

When reviewing the comments made by the Bellwood board members in the newspaper, one would quickly conclude that they were expressing dissatisfaction because of perceived unfair treatment and a pervasive element of injustice. Greenberg and Baron (1997), in explaining their proactive dimension of conflict, speak to the behavior individuals might display when they perceive the actions of others as being unjust and unfair. In such instances, the individual or group members make statements and take action in an effort to promote justice and create fair treatment. To minimize the negative effectiveness of these feelings, it is imperative that the leader become knowledgeable of the political, social, cultural, and economic systems and processes that impact schools and use these systems to promote the success of the school district (Standard 6).

Failure to Minimize the Dysfunctional Effects

In managing the conflict, Superintendent Morgan took the position that policy should prevail. However, this position was not acceptable to the opposing parties. Therefore, he failed to minimize the dysfunctional effects of the conflict. When two parties assume opposing points of view and use the power of their positions to prevail in their way of thinking, they are engaging in a power struggle, which erodes interpersonal relationships (Sashkin & Morris, 1984). Such was the case in the Bellwood School District when Superintendent Morgan held firm to the notion that policy gave him the authority to make his desired changes, in spite of the intensity of the opposing point of view. Effective communication no longer existed, which reduced the possibility of the conflict being resolved in a win-win manner.

Both the board and the superintendent have rights and responsibilities, and each is aware, or should be aware, of the position and power of the other. Therefore, the approach taken by Superintendent Morgan (power struggling) was likely to be the least effective approach in a situation of this nature. It cannot be overemphasized that when two parties engage in a power struggle as a method of resolving conflict, one will emerge as a winner and the other as a loser, as the major focus is on task completion and prevailing in one's position. Gorton (1987) writes that this is a very disruptive method that should be avoided if at all possible. Further, it should be noted that when such an approach is used, the losing party does not totally dismiss the conflict, but retreats, regroups, and returns after perceiving the timing is better to address the opposition (Barge, 1994).

Moving Toward Tranquility

Moving toward tranquility requires great effort and often a specific plan of action. The superintendent should attempt to engender a positive climate by refraining from making any comments that appear to hold a negative connotation. He should clarify his position and seek clarification from all board members regarding personnel matters. According to Covey (1989), an effective leader seeks first to understand and then to be understood.

In addition, the superintendent should be flexible in his mannerism, displaying a willingness to continuously examine his assumptions, beliefs, and practices (Standard 1). Following policy alone is not sufficient for effective leadership. The climate of the times, the norms of the district, and the individuals involved are all factors that influence action and must be given consideration. Given that his original intent was to enhance the quality of education in the district, he should not have allowed his behavior to be counterproductive to that intent.

In summary, a superintendent has to be sensitive to the environment of the school, and issues have to be resolved within the context of the prevailing climate. In today's educational climate, many superintendents are using shared decision making, collaboration, and other participatory governance models to address issues that have districtwide ramifications (Etheridge & Green, 1998). Rather than being adversarial, confrontational, and steadfast in their way of thinking, school leaders are turning to more cooperative and nonconfrontational approaches. Instead of using policies to defend their position, they are involving people in shaping their positions.

CHAPTER SUMMARY

Conflict can be defined as "the interaction of interdependent people who perceive opposition of goals, aims, and views, and who see the other party as potentially interfering with the realization of these goals" (Putnam & Poole, 1987, p. 352). It occurs in varying degrees in all organizations, as it is a normal part of social relations (Greenberg & Baron, 1997). It often occurs in today's schools as a result of change and the need for people to work in harmony.

Conflict that occurs in schools can be differentiated in two ways—context and content. The leader should seek to understand each of these areas and its implications for behavior in schools. Another type of conflict that frequently occurs in schools is role conflict. There are formal organizational roles and informal organizational roles, and the two must coexist. When they do not, conflict is likely to emerge.

If conflict occurs in schools, it must be assessed for direction, clarity, and intensity, then effectively managed. Therefore, leaders need knowledge of the principles of organizational development. For, if not managed effectively over time, conflict will erode the creative professional environment of a school and the faculty will not be able to see opportunities and collaborate with one another (Hanson, 1996; Ciancutti & Steding, 2001). Considering the effects of such an occurrence, the leader must be knowledgeable of strategies and skillful in processes that can be used in the effective management of conflict. Some identified approaches are avoidance, smoothing, bargaining, power struggle, and problem solving. The challenge for the leader is matching the appropriate approach with the situation.

There is no one right way to lead a school district or to eliminate all conflict. Nevertheless, when thought and consideration are given to the factors that impact a situation, optimal ways of managing conflict can be identified. One can reach the optimum by communicating effectively, making decisions with the involvement of appropriate individuals, and selecting appropriate strategies.

MOVING INTO PRACTICE

Review the scenarios in Chapter 6. Using the pros and cons of the various situations, identify several approaches that you would use to address the following issues in an actual school situation. Project yourself in the role of the principal and take care to formulate a rationale for your selected behavior.

◆ If you were principal of a middle school and half of your faculty wanted to have reading in the content areas for all students and the other half wanted self-contained remedial classes for only those students who needed assistance with their reading development, how would you resolve the conflict?

◆ In a high school where you serve as principal, several teachers want to move to a form of block scheduling. The majority of the faculty is convinced that block scheduling is a fad and that the benefits gained would not be worth the time invested in the change. After a negative vote of the faculty regarding the implementation of the concept, you learn that the original group of teachers has gone into the community and generated parental support for the concept. Parents have asked for a meeting with you to discuss block scheduling. You are aware that some parents are referring to you as the traditional administrator who is keeping their school in the dark ages. How would you resolve this conflict?

◆ Develop a conflict management strategy that you believe would be effective in managing the conflict that occurred in the Bellwood School District.

ACQUIRING AN UNDERSTANDING OF SELF

◆ Cite at least three of Principal Early's statements that would have made you uncomfortable had you been a member of the faculty at Lakeside.

◆ What is your style of managing conflict? When you resolve a conflict, what evidence do you secure to determine if your approach to conflict resolution is effective?

◆ Make a list of five educational activities that you feel are morally wrong, but that you have recently observed in a school situation.

◆ When you managed your last conflict, what strengths did you use? What would you do differently if you had to manage the same conflict again?

DEEPENING YOUR UNDERSTANDING

Now that you have read this chapter, visit the Companion Website for this book at **www.prenhall.com/green** *and take the Self-Assessment Inventory for this chapter.*

Completing this inventory will give you an indication of how familiar you are with the ISLLC Standards knowledge indicators that relate to this chapter.

SUGGESTED READINGS

Eller, J. (2004). *Effective group facilitation in education: How to energize meetings and manage difficult groups.* Thousand Oaks, CA: Corwin Press.

Kosmoski, G. J. & Pollack, D. R. (2000). *Managing difficult, frustrating, and hostile conversations: Strategies for savvy administrators.* Thousand Oaks, CA: Corwin Press.

Stephan, W. G. & Vogt, P. W. (Eds.). (2004). *Education Programs for improving intergroup relations: Theory, research, and practice.* New York: Teachers College Press.

AVAILABLE POWERPOINT PRESENTATIONS

 After completing this chapter, log on to the Companion Website for this book at **www.prenhall.com/green** *and click on the PowerPoint module.*

- Managing Conflict
- Theories On Conflict

WEBSITES

Managing Conflict
http://www.governorline.info/index.cfm?p=655

Conflict Management: Trends and Issues Alert
http://ericacve.org/docgen.asp?tbl=tia&ID=113

Conflict Management: Power Point
http://www.ais.msstate.edu/AEE/3803/Fall03pdfs/09-conflict.pdf

PRACTICE ISLLC EXAMS

 After reading this chapter, log on the Companion Website for this book at **www.prenhall.com/green** *to take the practice ISLLC exams.*

REFERENCES

Barge, J. K. (1994). *Leadership: Communication skills for organizations and groups.* New York: St. Martin's Press.

Barth, R. S. (1990). *Improving school from within: Teachers, parents, and principals can make the difference.* San Francisco: Jossey-Bass.

Berger, J., Zelditch, M., Anderson, B., & Cohen, B. P. (1972). Structural aspects of distributive justice: A status-value formulation. In J. Berger, M. Zelditch, & B. Anderson (Eds.), *Sociological theories in progress* (Vol. 2, pp. 21–45). Boston: Houghton Mifflin.

Campbell, R. F. (1968). Situational factors in educational administration. In R. Campbell & R. Gregg (Eds.), *Administrative behavior in education* (p. 264). New York: Harper & Row.

Ciancutti, A., & Steding, T. (2001). *Built on trust: Gaining competitive advantage in any organization.* Chicago: Contemporary Books.

Covey, S. R. (1989). *The 7 habits of highly effective people.* New York: Simon & Schuster.

Daft, R. L. (1999). *Leadership: Theory and practice.* Fort Worth, TX: Harcourt Brace.

David, G. (1994). School-based decision making: Kentucky's test of decentralization. *Phi Delta Kappa, 75,* 706–712.

Etheridge, C. P., & Green, R. (1998). *Union district collaboration and other processes related to school district restructuring for establishing standards and accountability measures.* (A technical report for the 21st Century Project). Washington, DC: National Educational Association.

Freedman, S. M., & Montanari, J. R. (1980). An integrative model of managerial rewards allocation. *Academy of Management Review, 5,* 381–390.

Fullan, M. G. (1993). *Change forces.* New York: Falmer Press.

Fullan, M. G. (1999). *Change forces: The sequel.* New York: Falmer Press.

Getzels, J. W. (1958). Administration as a social process. In A. Halpin (Ed.), *Administrative theory in education* (p. 153). Chicago: University of Chicago Midwest Administration Center.

Goodlad, J. I. (1984). *A place called school: Prospects for the future.* New York: McGraw-Hill.

Gorton, R. A. (1987). *School leadership and administration: Important concepts, case studies, and simulations* (3rd ed.). Dubuque, IA: McGraw-Hill.

Greenberg, J. (1996a). *Managing behavior in organizations.* Upper Saddle River, NJ: Prentice Hall.

Greenberg, J. (1996b). *The quest for justice on the job.* Thousand Oaks, CA: Sage.

Greenberg, J., & Baron, R. A. (1997). *Behavior in organizations.* Upper Saddle River, NJ: Prentice Hall.

Greenhalgh, L. (1986). SMR forum: Managing conflict. *Sloan Management Review, 27,* 45–51.

Gross, N. (1958). *Explorations in role analysis: Studies of the school superintendency.* New York: John Wiley.

Hanson, M. E. (1996). *Educational administration and organization behavior* (4th ed.). Needham Heights, MA: Allyn & Bacon.

Hoy, W. K., & Miskel, C. G. (1991). *Educational administration: Theory, research and practice* (4th ed.). New York: McGraw-Hill.

Katz, N., & Lawler, J. W. (1993). *Conflict resolution: Building bridges.* Thousand Oaks, CA: Corwin Press.

Leventhal, G. S. (1976). The distribution of rewards and resources in groups and organizations. In L. Berkowitz & E. Walster (Eds.), *Advances in experimental social psychology* (Vol. 9, pp. 91–131). New York: Academic Press.

Lindelow, J., & Scott, J. (1989). *Managing conflict in school leadership: Handbook for excellence* (pp. 339–355). Eugene, OR: Clearinghouse on Educational Management.

Lunenburg, F. C., & Ornstein, A. C. (1996). *Educational administration: Concepts and practices* (2nd ed.). Belmont, CA: Wadsworth.

Luthans, F. (1992). *Organizational behavior* (6th ed.). Princeton, NJ: McGraw-Hill.

March, J. G., & Simon, H. A. (1958). *Organizations.* New York: Wiley.

Martin, J. (1981). Relative deprivation: A theory of distributive injustice for an era of shrinking resources. In B. M. Staw & L. L. Cummings (Eds.), *Research in organizational behavior* (Vol. 3, pp. 53–107). Greenwich, CT: JAI.

Owens, R. G. (1991). *Organizational behavior in education.* Boston: Allyn & Bacon.

Owens, R. G. (1995). *Organizational behavior in education* (5th ed.). Boston: Allyn & Bacon.

Pondy, L. R. (1967). Organizational conflict: Concepts and models. *Administrative Science Quarterly 14,* 499–505.

Putnam, L. L., & Poole, M. S. (1987). Conflict and negotiation. In F. M. Jablin, L. L. Putnam, K. Roberts, & L. W. Porter (Eds.), *Handbook of organizational communication* (pp. 549–599). Beverly Hills, CA: Sage.

Rahim, A. (1986). *Managing conflict in organizations.* New York: Praeger.

Riley, R. (2002). Educational reform through standards and partnerships, 1993-2000. *Phi Delta Kappa, 83*(9) 700.

Sashkin, M., & Morris, W. C. (1984). *Organizational behavior: Concepts and experiences.* Reston, VA: Reston Publishing.

Sergiovanni, T. J., & Starratt, R. J. (1998). *Supervision: A redefinition* (6th ed.). New York: McGraw-Hill.

Southern Regional Educational Board (SREB). (2001). *Leading school improvement: What research says.* Atlanta, GA: SREB.

Thomas, K. (1976). Conflict and conflict management. In M. D. Dunnette (Ed.), *Handbook of industrial and organizational psychology* (p. 890). Chicago: Rand McNally.

Wexley, K. N., & Yukl, G. A. (1984). *Organizational behavior and personnel psychology.* Burr Ridge, IL: McGraw-Hill.

Witteman, H. (1990). Conflict and Cohesion in small groups in S. Phillips (Ed.), *Teaching how to work in groups* (pp. 84–111). Norwood, NJ: Ablex.

7

LEADING INSTRUCTIONAL CHANGE

When an individual assumes a leadership role in a school or school district, it is often expected that the individual will bring to that organization knowledge, expertise, and ideas that can be transformed into a shared vision for the enhancement of the school's programs and activities. This is especially true in today's schools, as leaders are being asked to assume the role of "Chief Learning Officer" and be held accountable for individual student achievement (Bottoms & O'Neill, 2001; Riley, 2002). Meeting these new expectations requires changing current school practices to ones that appear to be better in terms of enhancing academic achievement. Therefore, to be effective in today's schools, leaders must have knowledge and understanding of the change process for systems, organizations, and individuals (Standard 2). On a deeper level, it is essential for school leaders to be proficient in implementing significant change.

In this chapter, we explore the process of change, placing emphasis on the principal assuming the role of "Chief Learning Officer" and being willing to be held accountable for enhancing the academic achievement of all students. To that end, the focus is on instructional leadership and processes the leader uses in establishing learning communities, building capacity for change, and identifying positive and negative forces that influence the change process. Also, change theories are examined with the intent of providing the reader with a theoretical base for leading change in today's schools.

The scenarios in this chapter expose the reader to a process of establishing and implementing a shared vision and fostering a climate for student and staff professional growth. Given that schools are open social systems and forces in their internal and external environments influence the interactions between and among stakeholders, change is likely to impact the entire organization. For that reason, to some extent, all ISLLC Standards are addressed in this chapter. However, the primary focus is on Standards 1, 2, 3, and 4. It should be noted that such comprehensive reflections of the standards in the change process further emphasize the impact of change in schools.

The Concept of Instructional Change

When the leader attempts to alter the behavior, structure, program, purpose, or output of some unit of the school or school district, the leader is attempting to make a change. Change is a process, not an event; it can be planned or unplanned and can be influenced by forces inside and outside of the schoolhouse. Given that the focus of this chapter is instructional change, that is, change that leads to enhanced student achievement, our discussion will address planned instructional change.

The process of planned instructional change can be viewed in three steps (see Figure 7.1). The first step consists of establishing a clear sense of purpose—the vision and/or goals of the school. In essence, a determination is made of the standard of excellence the school staff desires to reach. In making this determination for a school or school district, guidance can be obtained from the response to two critical questions: "What do our students need to know and be able to do?" and "What kind of organization do I want this school to become?" For the most part, during this period of high-stakes testing and accountability, the first question is being answered by state and federal education agencies. Nevertheless, when the first question is answered or reaffirmed at the local level and the second question is answered by the school leader and shared by the faculty, greater commitment to achieving the desired outcome (the vision) is likely to be acquired from a faculty.

The second step involves assessing and determining the state of existing programs, or current reality. This step involves using assessment data to actually

FIGURE 7.1   Three steps in the change process as identified by Schmidt and Finnigan (1992)

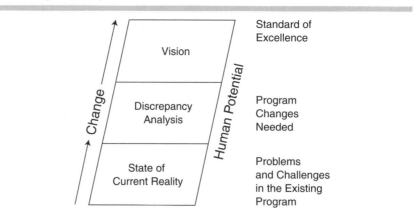

determine the strengths and weaknesses of the existing instructional program. The needed information can be acquired from report cards, achievement tests, state assessment measures, criterion referenced tests, and/or other planned assessment measures. The caution in acquiring information from these assessment tools is the need to disaggregate the data to the extent that a determination of students' needs can be individually and collectively determined schoolwide, by grade level, and by subject area.

Finally, a determination of what is needed in order to reach the desired goals is made. This step, often called a discrepancy analysis, assesses the difference between current reality and the stated goal (Schmidt & Finnigan, 1992). Imbedded in the process is the need to assess human potential (skills and attributes of faculty and staff) and draw conclusions about how to remove the discrepancy (decision making about programming) that existed between current reality and the desired goals (Schmidt & Finnigan, 1992).

For various reasons in schools, individuals have a difficult time accepting and adjusting to change. Therefore, in order for change to be effective and sustained, while minimizing disruption, the leader must be skilled in planning, implementing, and assessing the change process; then, the strategies employed must be carefully selected. In addition, prior to engaging in the change process, the leader should determine the magnitude of the change and the degree of difficulty involved in eliminating the discrepancy (Fullan, 1993). There are various theories and suggested practices that enlighten the approach leaders can take when attempting change, and in the following section, some of the most noted ones are reviewed.

Theories and Practices Informing Change

Change occurring in schools can be classified as either continuous, first-order change or discontinuous, second-order change (Meyer, Brooks, & Goes, 1990). Meyer and his associates report that continuous, or first-order, change occurs without a disruption to the system; the system remains stable (equilibrium is maintained), although some small modifications are made. With first-order change, the leader improves the efficiency and effectiveness of the school or program without extensively altering the manner in which teachers and students routinely behave, and upheaval and conflict are often avoided. With discontinuous, or second-order change, the equilibrium of the system is disrupted as the fundamental properties of the system are changed. The existing order is broken. New goals are established; the structure and programs change, and individuals have to perform differently. This type of change has proven to be very challenging in schools and is a major producer of resistance and conflict (Conley, 1997).

We witnessed second-order change in Chapter 2 when Principal Sterling (newly appointed principal of Frost Elementary School) attempted change, and again in

Chapter 6 when Principal Early (newly transferred principal at Lakeside Elementary) outlined to the faculty her expectations and intentions for change. In both instances, the leaders experienced resistance and conflict. The resistance and conflict occurred because in each instance, the leader was asking the faculty to make major alterations in the school structure, accept new programs, and perform differently.

First-order change occurred in Chapter 2 as Principal Johnson took action to change the school's science program. She changed the science program but did not substantially alter the way the faculty performed their roles. The science program was simply taken through a renewal process (change occurred to allow the faculty to teach a subject they were already teaching in a more effective manner). Principal Johnson introduced the idea and gradually took steps toward its implementation. Her practice followed the incremental decision-making model presented in Chapter 5. As Lindblom (1959) described, she made a series of decisions, and based upon the outcome of each, other decisions were made.

Determining the order of the change is very important, as it allows the leader to determine the extent to which the faculty and staff are ready for the change and what preparation is necessary before the change is undertaken. In essence, the leader can determine if the school has the capacity to make the desired change.

The Capacity for Change

When a school faculty is asked to make program changes, particularly if they run counter to the beliefs of some members, the changes are not likely to occur without disruption and/or conflict. This disruption and/or conflict can be minimized if the school has the capacity for the desired change (readiness of the school for the change process). Change capacity always influences the success potential of the change. This suggests that if the leader is desirous of making change that is effective and sustained and produces the least amout of conflict, the school's capacity for that change must be determined. Schmidt and Finnigan (1992) advise that in determining the school's capacity for change, leaders should consider:

1. the level of dissatisfaction the stakeholders are experiencing with current conditions
2. the short- and long-term costs
3. the extent to which individuals understand the vision to be achieved by the change
4. the consequences of the change
5. the degree of difficulty in making the change

Consideration should also be given to: (1) factors that influence the faculty's attitude toward the components of the change, (2) new information, if any, that will have to be learned, (3) identities that will be lost, and (4) new beliefs that will be formed.

Also, the amount of extra time and attention that will be required to implement the new program should be considered. People generally support change efforts if they believe current conditions need improving. However, they must also believe that achieving the vision will improve current conditions, that the desired change is realistic, clearly outlined, achieveable, and cost-effective (Schmidt & Finnigan, 1992).

When determining the school's capacity for change, of all items to be considered, the leader should perhaps be most concerned with the fear of failure that may exist among the faculty. Fear of failure is one of the major sources of resistance to change (Ryan & Oestreich, 1991). As a result of that fear, teachers might be prone to say, "I would have tried that approach; however, I was afraid it would not be considered the right approach; or we have always done it this way; or our former principal wanted us to do it this way" (Ryan & Oestreich, 1991). The idea is to have capacity for the desired change.

If a school does not have the capacity for the change, there are a number of actions that the leader can consider in building that capacity. A list of some of those actions appears in Table 7.1.

Change Agentry

Another theory relative to change and the capacity of the organization to make change is Fullan's (1993) Change Agentry Theory. As a part of this theory, Fullan advances four core capacities required by the change agent before attempting change in an organization: personal vision building, inquiry, mastery, and collaboration. He suggests that these core capacities must be compatible with institutional counterparts, which are shared vision building, organizational structure, norms and practices of inquiry, focus on organizational development and know-how, and collaborative work cultures (p. 12). He further theorizes that the change approach is dual, working simultaneously on the individual and institutional development, and the leader

TABLE 7.1   Actions that build a capacity for change

1. Establishing effective lines of communication between the school leader and the community
2. Securing community support for the change concept
3. Acquiring expertise in the new program concept
4. Driving fear out of the school
5. Working out collective bargaining regulations that facilitate change
6. Acquiring necessary approvals from the State Department of Education
7. Identifying sources of the necessary resources
8. Utilizing effective change strategies

SOURCE: This list was developed from various references reviewed in developing this chapter.

must be highly sensitive to the nature of the change and the change process. The following is a brief explanation of the four capacities offered by Fullan:

> *Shared vision:* The power for the change is provided through personal purpose. Every individual in the organization has a vision, and that personal vision causes individuals to raise questions about their roles in the change process and to take a stand for a preferred future. A shared vision is developed, and when the vision of the change is shared, change comes as a result of everyone fostering the change. This collective sense of purpose fosters power for deeper change.
>
> *Inquiry:* Through the process of inquiry, an individual internalizes norms, habits, and techniques for continuous learning. The individual continuously checks, views, and assesses the initial mental map to make sure it fits.
>
> *Mastery:* When individuals demonstrate an understanding and acceptance of new ideas and skills through their behavior, continuously clarifying what is important and learning how to see current reality more clearly, mastery has occurred.
>
> *Collaboration:* In order to collaborate, an individual needs to involve both attitude and ability.
>
> Collaboration involves the attitude and capacity to form productive mentoring and peer relationships, team building and the like. It consists of the ability to work in organizations that form cross-institutional partnerships such as school districts, university and school-community and business agency alliances, as well as global relationships with individuals and organizations from other cultures. (Fullan, 1993, p. 17)

With collaboration, skills, and relationships, individuals can learn and continue to learn what is necessary to improve the organization.

The net result of using the core capacities offered by Fullan is a positive step toward building a capacity for change and establishing learning communities in schools. Once a learning community has been established, if maintained, the likelihood of the school's achieving the vision that the change seeks is tremendously enhanced.

We will speak more about learning communities and change later in the chapter, but first, we review a popular theory that leaders might use to determine if a particular change should be attempted and the likelihood of its success.

Force Field Analysis

Kurt Lewin's (1951) Force Field Analysis theory of change is very applicable to school situations and can be used to assess the school's readiness for change, reduce conflicts, and enhance change effectiveness. Lewin theorized that the environment in which change occurs contains a force field. The field consists of two forces, which he categorized as driving and restraining. Driving forces move one toward the desired change, and restraining forces resist the desired change, inhibiting its attainment. In Lewin's theory, people are viewed as constantly seeking equilibrium between the power status of the two forces, which allows the status quo to be maintained in a frozen state of existence. Change causes a disruption in the balance of these forces. When one set of forces is substantially altered, reflecting a change in the power status of the other, the state of equilibrium is "unfrozen," and there is a break in the status quo, which prevails until a new state of equilibrium is established. When the change is completed, "freezing" occurs on a new level, thus establishing a new state of equilibrium between the two sets of forces. The change becomes the norm and remains such until the next change.

It is the power of these forces and their interaction relative to a particular change that determine the degree of difficulty a leader will experience in making that change. Lewin (1951) advises that if the driving forces far outweigh the restraining forces in power and frequency, the school leader might push the change forward, overpowering the resisting forces. However, if the reverse is true, and the restraining forces are much stronger than the driving forces, the school leader would be well advised to give serious consideration to abandoning the change. Lewin further advises that in making a change, it is far better to convert restraining forces to driving forces than simply increasing driving forces or overpowering restraining forces. A graphic analysis of the principles of this theory appears in Figure 7.2.

Given that change in schools is likely to meet with less resistance and there is likely to be less conflict in the school when restraining forces are converted to driving forces, the leader should consider this factor in pursuing change. For example, if the principal would like to change the first-grade reading program from a strong

Figure 7.2

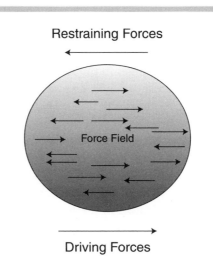

phonics-based approach to an exclusive whole language approach, and teachers are convinced that reading is best taught using a phonetic approach, they may resist the change and become a strong restraining force.

Changing to a new approach (a second-order change) would mean the teachers would have to adjust to a new way of teaching. Thus, they are likely to become a restraining force and remain such until they can see the benefit to be derived from the new method. Changing the program, in spite of the concerns of the first-grade teachers, could negatively impact the entire instructional program. However, if they could be persuaded (in a positive manner) to accept the new program approach prior to the change, not only would a restraining force be removed, but also a driving force would be added, as the teachers would likely become supporters of the change.

Assessing the force field provides the leader with an idea of the degree of difficulty that might be experienced in the change process. In that way, the leader can determine to some extent the likelihood of success. Only after it has been determined that change is promising, or leaders agree to take the risk of making change that is not promising, should they proceed.

Change Strategies

If the leader decides to proceed with a change, there are a number of strategies that can guide the leader through the process. Chin and Benne (1969) offered three: empirical-rational, normative–re-educative, and power-coercive. Using the empirical-rational strategy, the leader does not have to be coercive; the leader simply assembles and presents the necessary information regarding the desired change. Once the information is presented, the group selects the action suggested by the data. This strategy is based on the Theory Y assumption, which offers that people are rational and will select the best course of action when that action is justified with objective data.

If the group addressing the change is open to a consensus approach, the leader may elect to use the normative–re-educative strategy. Group activities are initiated to bring about changes in the norms of the group through changes in attitudes, values, skills, and relationships. This strategy facilitates the desired changes being made by the group, without the leader applying strong pressure. This concept was used in Chapter 5, Scenario 8, when the principal worked cooperatively with the faculty to revise the student recognition program.

The power-coercive strategy is used when the leader has a solid power base. This power may result from the leader's position, expertise, ability to punish or reward individuals, or a number of other sources. The key factor in using this strategy is the influence of the power of the leader over those with less power.

In bringing about change, the leader may choose either of these strategies or some combination of the three. The determining factors are likely to be the culture of the school, the leader's knowledge of the culture, and the leader's respect for it as a powerful force in the change process (Cusick, 1973).

The aforementioned theories, strategies, and practices are just four of the many that inform the process of change in schools. However, if they are utilized in an effective manner, they should greatly assist the leader in initiating, implementing, and sustaining change.

Instructional Leadership

Individuals providing the leadership for today's schools will need to be prepared to lead them through deep systematic change that affects every facet of school life and every segment of the community. In addition to having leadership ability, they will need to thoroughly understand the curriculum, as the fundamental assumptions, practices, and relationships that currently exist will necessarily have to change in ways that lead to improved and varied learning outcomes for all students (Bowman, 1999). "If schools are to be effective ones, it will be because of the instructional leadership of the principal" (Findley & Findley, 1999, p. 102).

The primary purpose for change in schools is to improve the instructional program and, in so doing, improve student achievement. When instructional change is offered in schools, most individuals will agree that instructional improvement is needed; however, there is still likely to be resistance. The resistance, more often than not, centers on the programs that will be changed, the process used to make the change, or the modified or new program. Resistance in these areas can be reduced, if not eliminated, provided the school has the capacity previously discussed. That capacity is likely to exist if the leader of the change process creates an environment wherein stakeholder involvement is respected and the programs being implemented are respected. Also, the programs being implemented must represent high-quality standards, expectations, and performances for all students (Standard 3). Having previously discussed change capacity, we now turn to stakeholder involvement in a learning environment where data are used to inform change that addresses the needs of all students.

Creating an Environment for Change

If schools make the kind of changes necessary to enhance the academic achievement of all students, the school leader will have to keep the focus on instruction and create a safe environment for teachers, using dialogue rather than dictates (Supovitz & Poglinco, 2001). They must be active, rather than reactive, assessing the environment, determining needs, and communicating those needs to stakeholders in a manner that enables them to acquire an understanding of the outcomes desired from students.

Change in Schools

Change in schools, in one way or another, affects teachers, as it often alters teaching practices in some manner. A change may be made in materials or structure (curriculum change); practices, behaviors, or skills (changes in teaching methods); or beliefs, rationales, or philosophies (orientation). Regardless of the area of change, teachers are affected, and their equilibrium will be disrupted. For example, if a teacher has been assigned to teach in a particular program, has become well versed in teaching that program, and has adequate plans, materials, supplies, and support, a request to change to a completely different program might meet considerable resistance. This resistance may involve a feeling of inadequacy on behalf of teachers relative to (a) their ability to teach the new program, (b) acquiring adequate materials for implementation of the new program, (c) relocating for program implementation, or (d) a combination of these concerns.

Resistance might also exist because teachers have a negative attitude about the new program, lack information about the positive aspects of the new program (particularly if new skills are required), or simply feel a concern over leaving one set of colleagues to work with another. Although the school leader might be able to identify a new program or mandate change in the use of materials and structure of an existing program, the leader is not likely to be able to mandate changes in the skills and/or beliefs of teachers and other personnel (Fullan, 1992). Therefore, to reduce some of the resistance to the change, increase the quality of decision making, and enhance successful implementation of the new program or activity, the leadership must establish an environment that fosters change.

Establishing an Environment That Fosters Change

To create an environment that fosters change, the leader must lead without dominating—facilitating the implementation of a vision, using a style that balances tasks and relationships, and fostering a readiness for change. The environment must foster "generative" thinking and involve stakeholders in a manner that promotes leadership opportunities throughout the learning community. Also, the personal values of the leader must be balanced with the diversity in the culture of the school, and the leader's style should evidence multidimensional leadership roles for teachers.

Leader Behavior in the Change Process

In the change process, school leaders might use one of two decision-making approaches: autocratic or participatory; both were discussed in Chapter 5. When an autocratic approach is used, instructions, purposes, and parameters are given to individuals to execute and implement. An example of a leader using an autocratic approach would be a principal of a high school who enters a faculty meeting and announces a change from the traditional scheduling format to block scheduling, then proceeds to pass out information that provides new course assignments, new time schedules, and new instructional locations. Fullan (1993) reports research that suggests the institutionalization of such change is very difficult. He further reports that school improvements that are significant and lasting can seldom be prescribed, mandated, or directed by agencies or individuals. In such a change, there may be several risk factors, for teachers may feel a sense of inadequacy or lack of preparation or they may fear the unknown or perceive a loss of power or control.

A change made using the participatory approach is likely to be received by stakeholders with less resistance. With the onset of the reform movement, much has been written about using a participatory approach and the advantages it offers for bringing about school change in an effective manner (Barth, 1990; Conley, 1997; Ryan and Oestreich, 1991; Short & Greer, 1997). The works of these individuals have produced such program concepts and practices as site-based management, shared decision making, participatory governance, and others that advocate leadership roles for teachers, placing them in a position to collaborate with school leaders in deciding how schools are administered. Also, these program concepts are consistent with the school of thought presented by writers and researchers who offer that the learning environment of the school needs to be one where responsibility is shared to maximize ownership and accountability (Goodlad, 1984; Sarason, 1996; Senge, 1990).

When a participatory approach is used, change is made in a manner that allows all individuals or persons desirous of the opportunity to assist in the change process; they feel valued, take ownership for implementation of the change, and are willing to assume responsibility for outcomes (Barth, 1990). Such was the case in Chapter 2, when Principal Johnson introduced the idea for a change in the science program at Walton Elementary School. The entire faculty was involved, and the change process moved in a positive direction. It was also evidenced at Frost when Principal Sterling received several volunteers for the second task force.

In summary, people are more likely to change when they share a compelling reason for the change that is being suggested. They need to own the change and feel that the leadership has demonstrated that they are serious about making the change and that it is going to be supported. Such behavior gives faculty members and other stakeholders a concrete picture of what the change will look like for them personally (Schwahn & Spady, 1998). Further, increased opportunities for teachers to lead enhance the internal capacity of the school for change and promote a "learning environment," wherein people continually expand their capacity to create the results they truly desire (Senge, 1990). In addition, the ISLLC Standards (1996) strongly support this approach and advocate models of collaboration that benefit the school community and ultimately our entire society.

Addressing the Needs of All Students

Individuals who lead today's schools must be committed to the education of all children and be able to share a vision of learning with the faculty and the larger community. They must also be able to create the kind of school climate wherein that vision can become a reality. As was initially stated at the beginning of this chapter, the purpose of school change, more often than not, is to improve the teaching and learning process. In addition, the major focus of ISLLC Standard 2 is teaching and learning. Thus, the questions regarding instructional change are: How do school leaders determine the areas in which to make the change, and what approach should they use? Several researchers and writers have responded to these questions, offering processes and models that have proven to be effective. The models and suggestions that follow will give the reader additional insight into practices and procedures that can be used in making instructional change that addresses the needs of all students.

Models in Practice

Marlow (1999) offers that to be effective in addressing the needs of all students, school leaders must (a) set and accept relevant role expectations in determining objectives of instruction; (b) establish knowledge objectives and skills that students should be expected to learn and which mutually reinforce each other; (c) lead the way in developing in students a positive attitude about learning, since quality attitudes help pupils to become increasingly proficient in attaining knowledge and skills; (d) ensure that learning opportunities capture pupils' attention, that the purpose of each lesson is stated, that students are motivated to learn, their different intelligences are nourished, and teachers are assisted in their pedagogical goals; and finally, (e) be prepared to teach a class, using the latest research and provide leadership in the school to help teachers use evaluation procedures.

Green and Etheridge (1999) found that a number of schools were achieving positive results in addressing the needs of all students. They reported that schools were achieving these results by:

1. Placing experienced leadership in the school
2. Creating an internal and external support system for the school leader
3. Developing an understanding of the change process and building collaborative relationships for change between and among all stakeholders
4. Establishing a single focus on teaching and learning which everyone supports;
5. Establishing a collaborative and cooperative culture and a value structure that respects individual capabilities
6. Acknowledging teachers as leaders and allowing them to inquire into program strategies and activities, and make recommendations regarding

standards, assessment measures, and the appropriateness of instructional materials and strategies for the students served

7. Allowing teachers to identify their professional development needs and design programs to address those needs

School leaders utilizing the model, practices, and procedures mentioned above are achieving positive results, and those results started with an assessment of current conditions and data analysis. Consistent with that practice, a factual assessment of current conditions, utilizing local criterion referenced and achievement data, national studies and reports, climate, and other inventories, should be the starting point of any major change effort.

Data-Driven Instructional Change

Change involving teaching and learning should be data-driven and contain certain elements, if it is expected to make a positive impact on student learning. Etheridge and Green (1998) interviewed individuals in six school districts who made instructional change to promote student learning and found the following steps were used and generated very positive results:

1. **A review and analysis of assessment reports**—Assessment reports were used to analyze student outcomes for several consecutive years. Reports from such measures as the Scholastic Achievement Test, Comprehensive Test of Basic Skills, American College Test, and TerraNova were used to acquire an understanding of the strengths and weaknesses in the instructional program. Scholarship reports, student interviews, teacher-made tests, criterion-referenced tests, and other assessment measures were also used for that purpose. Data generated by the assessment tools were disaggregated to obtain information concerning the academic progress of students by race, gender, grade level, and subject area. Students experiencing success and difficulty were identified, and the specific questions frequently missed and/or answered were noted.

2. **Assessment of current conditions**—Using data from the assessment analyses, a content analysis was conducted to determine the effectiveness of the curriculum. Teachers engaged in conversations raising questions about where the problematic concepts were taught, the amount of instructional time being devoted to the teaching of those concepts, the material used, and other curriculum content issues. Teachers also reasoned regarding the inability of students to apply concepts that were taught. Responses to these questions and other information acquired were used to inform the development of a school improvement plan.

3. **Review of content material**—At this point, the instructional review process became very focused. An analysis of all instructional material was

conducted to determine if the content material was aligned with concepts posing difficulty for students. The materials were also assessed to determine if they were effectively achieving what they were designed to achieve (program evaluation). In addition, instructional approaches were reviewed to determine if teaching styles matched learning styles and other aspects of learner needs. More importantly, this analysis was conducted to determine if there was a cause/effect relationship associated with the instructional material, teaching approaches, and the student's inability to master and apply the concepts identified by the assessment tools as being problematic.

4. **Broad-based review and discussion**—During this phase, parents, students, outside consultants, and other individuals were invited to participate in a series of group meetings and individual reaction sessions. These sessions were conducted to allow the decision-making team to capture and assess the perceptions, opinions, ideas, and suggestions of the invited individuals regarding student performance, school processes, student work activities, and home-related matters. At this point, all the players were engaged in conversations in an attempt to identify where the problems existed. Was it time on task, the amount of instructional time, teaching or learning styles, instructional materials, or instructional methods? Is there enough substance in the materials to address the problem areas? Once these conversations were held, decisions were made regarding what needed to be changed. The involvement of students was very important, as students specifically offered suggestions about their learning styles, teaching styles, and other factors they felt were affecting their success.

5. **Formulation of curriculum groups**—Once data were acquired regarding program areas needing change, broad-based committees were formed to review the data and make suggestions about the type of program changes that would likely increase student acquisition of the problematic concepts. The committees were very comprehensive, consisting of teachers of the focused grade level(s), those above and below the focused grade level(s), and parents and other individuals who may have had expertise in the area(s) being discussed.

6. **The plan for instructional improvement**—The committees designed a comprehensive plan for instructional improvement, often using one of the group decision-making techniques identified in Chapter 5. The plan necessarily was very comprehensive, including goals, objectives, human and material resources, a professional development plan, assessment tools, a time frame, and other components essential to effective implementation of the desired instructional change.

These six steps provide a definitive process to use in making change to improve instruction and enhance student achievement. In addition to these steps, the plan for change should include an evaluation component. Using an effective evaluation design, the leader can monitor the status of the change and determine its effectiveness.

Evaluating Change

As programs are designed and implemented, they must be monitored and assessed. The two forms of evaluation often associated with educational change are formative and summative. Formative evaluations acquire information about the program before it is fully implemented or during the refinement stage. This type of evaluation is conducted to ensure that there are no flaws in the program design and that the program is appropriate for the area of change. In some instances, the program changes are implemented as a pilot. In doing so, modifications can be made to the program in its early stages or prior to its full implementation. Summative evaluations address the totality of the program responding to the questions: Did the program do what it was designed to do? How effective was the program in achieving the goals for which it was implemented? In general, this type of evaluation is undertaken after the program has been operational for a specific period of time. When leaders make a summative assessment of a program or activity, formal surveys are prepared and administered to the faculty, and special tests are administered to students.

Leadership in Today's Schools

Today's school leaders who are effecting change with a minimum amount of conflict and disruption are using a participatory style of leadership and are skilled in securing the expertise and services of teachers, parents, and members of the community in support of the desired change (Standard 4). All stakeholders are invited to participate in school governance; instructional decisions are data-driven and made as close to the teaching and learning process as possible (Standard 1).

However, such actions require a change in the traditional roles of superintendents, central administrators, principals, and teachers (Etheridge & Green, 1998). The traditional top-down directive style of leadership must give way to the new form of participatory leadership, which requires collaboration (Fullan, 1999). This new thrust has been fostered through the implementation of national reform initiatives, such as the New American School Designs, College Board's Equity 2000, school site–based teams, school-based councils, and other school organizations that offer a forum for shared decision making.

The Scenarios

In Scenario 13, Principal Jones is charged with raising test scores in a school where the faculty members are complacent and do not fully accept or understand current reality. His disposition, understanding of information sources, and data collection and analysis strategies, as well as his ability to identify operational plans and procedures to achieve an established goal, are key factors in the change process. In addressing this scenario, a large number of ISLLC Standards indicators must be considered.

In Scenario 14, the reader will be able to follow the process a superintendent uses in developing a strategic plan. Management decisions are made to enhance learning and teaching, and the vision of the school district is communicated to all stakeholders. The reader will want to note the leadership behavior of both Superintendent Wallace and Director Clark as they both meet several ISLLC Standards indicators.

In both scenarios, change is attempted, involving a number of individuals. The reader might find it beneficial to compare the steps followed by each of the change agents in the scenarios with the strategies for change presented in the introductory material, as well as to identify the ISLLC Standards indicators met or not met by both change agents.

SCENARIO 13
JUST GET THOSE TEST SCORES UP

STANDARD 2

A school administrator is an educational leader who promotes the success of all students by advocating, nurturing, and sustaining a school culture and instructional program conducive to student learning and staff professional growth.

STANDARD 4

A school administrator is an educational leader who promotes the success of all students by collaborating with families and community members, responding to diverse community interests and needs, and mobilizing community resources.

Brady Jones, newly appointed principal of Eastern Hills Elementary School, left the superintendent's office somewhat perplexed but energized. The superintendent had shared with him that he was selected principal of Eastern Hills because he had placed a strong focus on instruction during his interview. The superintendent had further stated that he was very pleased that Mr. Jones had taken the assignment and intended to give him a free hand. "Just get those test scores up! Parents in the community have high hopes for their children now that you are principal," the superintendent had stated. "The last two principals were not instructionally oriented and spent most of their time on discipline and working with about 250 students (bussed into the school) who are in a special gifted and talented program; however, I am confident that you will address the needs of all students."

Principal Jones thought, "Only two weeks into my principalship, and the superintendent is expecting the implementation of a new instructional program to reduce the numbers of students who are unsuccessful on the state proficiency test." "Well," he said, "I have taken this job, and now I have to go to work."

Principal Jones went to his office and indeed he went to work. He called several teachers but found that most were on summer holiday or unavailable. However, he was able to contact six who said they had some free time and would be able to participate in an instructional planning session.

The six teachers were from various grade levels and disciplines, and Principal Jones considered this to be a plus. Over the next week for about two hours a day, working with the six teachers, he reviewed student records, proficiency test scores, state standards, discipline reports, attendance records, and curriculum guides. At the end of the week, Principal Jones thanked the teachers and informed them he would see them in September. The teachers left, feeling that Eastern Hills Elementary School was in for a major change.

Reviewing the data compiled over the past week, as well as the evaluation reports of the teachers, Principal Jones noted the following: Eastern Hills Elementary School was a large inner-city school of about 1,000 students. The school had a grade organizational structure of Pre-K–6. The fourth graders and the sixth graders take the state proficiency test (which is the Comprehensive Test of Basic Skills), and for the last five years, the scores at Eastern Hills have been the lowest in the district and close to the bottom in the state. For instruction, students are grouped and assigned to classes based on ability testing. They are then regrouped inside the classroom for instruction in reading, mathematics, science, and social studies.

The average teacher's tenure at the school is 15 years. However, there will be one new teacher who has recently moved into the district, and she was teacher of the year in her last assignment. Two other teachers have just been assigned to the school to fill positions that occurred because of retirements. The school is allotted 40 teaching positions from the state for every 1,000 students in grades 1–6 and a kindergarten teacher and an aide for every class of 25 kindergarten students. The local district funds one teaching position out of the local budget. His personnel report revealed the assignment of 37 teachers to the building with 3 teaching positions vacant.

THE STUDENT BODY

STUDENT ENROLLMENT 1,038

	Grade K	Grade 1	Grade 2	Grade 3	Grade 4	Grade 5	Grade 6	Total
Males	10	78	83	91	92	60	65	479
Females	15	94	96	98	93	88	75	559
Total	25	172	179	189	185	148	140	1038
African-Americans	3	48	55	63	58	21	12	260
Caucasians	21	118	118	118	120	120	120	735
Hispanics	1	6	6	8	7	7	8	43
Total	25	172	179	189	185	148	140	1038

THE FACULTY

There are 37 teachers (including 33 Caucasians, 3 African-Americans, and 1 Hispanic); average number of years in the profession is 26. The average number of years at Eastern Hills

Elementary School is 15. Subject area changes did not occur over the last 3 years; room assignment changes over the last 3 years were four. There are 4 teachers with less than 3 years of service, and there were no teacher transfers over the past 3 years. The teacher evaluations are excellent, and over the past 10 years, the state teacher of the year had been selected from the faculty four times. In addition, all teachers on the faculty are members of the local union, and the union president's wife teaches sixth-grade mathematics.

THE ORIENTATION MEETING

At the fall orientation meeting of the faculty, Principal Jones introduced the concept of "site-based management" to the faculty. He told the faculty that the concept was still in the planning stage, but he wanted the faculty to have some idea of what he believed should be the new thrust for Eastern Hills Elementary School and how the new concept could be utilized to improve instruction for all students. He said he had worked with several teachers over the summer and had identified three instructional goals for the school, but he did not want to present them until the faculty had been given time to review the site-based management concept and comment on its implementation. However, he said, "State proficiency scores are one of three major concerns that appear to need attention."

He also informed the faculty that parents, students, and members of the community would need to be involved in all instructional planning. Principal Jones then asked the faculty to meet in grade-level groups for 30 minutes to discuss his remarks and generate questions and concerns. The grade-level meetings were convened, and several teachers generated questions. When the faculty reconvened, Principal Jones asked for questions and comments. The following were offered:

Mrs. Walker of the math department, "I don't believe we can change the way we teach math; many of our students simply cannot learn the reasoning problems."

Principal Jones responded, "OK."

Mr. Clark, a teacher of social studies, "I am ready for a change, but some of the new concepts are foreign to me. Will we have adequate professional development activities?" Principal Jones replied, "The superintendent has advised that in the current budget there are no funds for additional professional development. However, he will provide staff time to draft federal grant proposals."

Mrs. Polls stated, "I understand that teachers who met with you this summer did not get paid. Is that not a violation of the union contract?"

Principal Jones replied, "That is a concern that I will have to review."

Mrs. Green commented, "I like what I have heard about site-based management; however, I don't quite understand how we can participate in all the meetings and teach the children all day."

Principal Jones responded, "With adequate release time, we can address that issue."

Mrs. Polls reflected, "Yes, we have been promised release time before, but it never came."

Mr. Frank questioned, "Are you aware of the attitudes of the children who attend this school, the daily discipline problems, the poor attendance rate, and the lack of parental involvement? We are currently doing all we can do, and I trust this is not another one of those educational reform efforts everyone is talking about."

Principal Jones responded, "Those are interesting comments, Mr. Frank, and I hope we can resist taking on some of the fads of which you speak."

Ms. Harris offered, "Principal Jones, there are three of us who have recently completed instructional seminars at the university, and in those seminars, we were introduced to several approaches that I believe would enhance instruction here at Eastern Hills. If you plan to form an instructional planning committee, the three of us would very much like to serve."

Principal Jones, "Thank you, Ms. Harris! After those comments, I believe this is an excellent time to pass out these committee lists and allow individuals to sign up for the committee of choice. I will review the list and speak with each of you individually, but now, let's have lunch."

When Principal Jones reviewed his phone messages at the end of the day, he noticed he had a phone call from the union president, requesting a meeting.

REFLECTIVE THINKING

The ISLLC Standards

The following are indicators of the ISLLC Standards addressed in the Scenario:

1: A vision of high standards will have to be shared by all stakeholders; information sources must be used; data collection and data analysis strategies are required; the leadership will have to accept responsibility for current conditions; the faculty will have to do the work required for high levels of personal and organizational performance; assessment data related to student learning will have to be used to develop the school's vision and goals; and barriers to achieving the vision must be indentified, clarified, and addressed.

2: Curriculum design, implementation, evaluation, and refinement strategies are required; principles of effective instruction will have to be used; consideration will have to be given to diversity and its meaning for educational programs; student learning as the fundamental purpose of schooling will have to have top priority; the principal will have to influence a culture of high expectations for self, students, and staff performance; and applied learning and motivation theories will have to be applied.

3: Human resources will have to be managed and developed; decisions that enhance learning and teaching will have to be made; and the principal will have to have knowledge of learning, teaching, and student development.

4: Consideration will have to be given to the conditions and dynamics of the diverse school community; diversity will have to be valued, noting the proposition that diversity enriches the school; the public must be kept informed of all changes; and the principal will need to share information about family and community concerns, expectations, and needs with the faculty.

5: The values of the diverse school community will have to be given consideration; the right of every student to a free, quality education will have to be accepted; and the prevailing values of the diverse school community will have to be examined and considered.

6: The law, as related to education and schooling, must be taken into account; the principal will need to recognize a variety of ideas, values, and cultures; communication concerning trends and issues will have to occur among the school community; then potential changes in the environment in which schools operate will have to be factored into the change process.

Reflective Questions

1. When Principal Jones assumed the principalship and approached the faculty for the first time at Eastern Hills Elementary, how would you characterize the school's change capacity?
2. How would you assess the approach used by Principal Jones when he introduced the concept of change to the faculty at Eastern Hills? Identify instances in the scenario that denote the manner in which the vision is being developed.
3. What models and strategies of change and conflict resolution would you utilize if you were principal in a similar situation?
4. What instances can you cite in the scenario that would serve as evidence that Principal Jones has knowledge and understanding of information sources, data collection, and strategies for program development.
5. What opportunities could Principal Jones provide for the faculty to develop collaborative skills?
6. What emerging issues and trends do you observe in the enrollment and test data?
7. What approach would you use to determine the types of instructional change strategies that would be best for the students of Eastern Hills? Identify where you would begin and define your position.

ADDRESSING THE CRITICAL ISSUES

Assessing Current Conditions

The new principal is coming into a school with a well-established organizational culture. The average teacher's tenure is 15 years. This would indicate a definite "This is the way we do things around here" attitude. A change would require members of the faculty to alter past practices. One major challenge would be getting the faculty to adopt new teaching approaches and overcome the tendency to want to return to previous practices. This type of resistance to change is cultural system resistance and is based on the premise that there is security in past practice (Tichy & Ulrich, 1984, p. 479). The responsibility for school improvement must be shared to maximize ownership and accountability, and this is most likely to occur when the faculty understands and accepts the problems that currently exist.

Sources of Resistance to Change

There are at least three sources of resistance to change at Eastern Hills. The first is a faculty ingrained in tradition. It is obvious from the comments made at the orientation session that some faculty members do not appreciate a need to change the existing instructional program. They appear to be safe and secure, or at least content with current conditions. Until the faculty accepts the notion that the current instructional program is not meeting the needs of all students, change will be difficult (Senge, 1990). A faculty that does not understand and accept the existing problems is not likely to be able to focus on what needs to be accomplished, develop an appreciation of the benefits to be derived from change, and reach a comfort level with the change (Sergiovanni, 1991).

A second source of resistance is characterized by the power of informal groups. There are at least two groups on the faculty (one group teaching gifted and talented students and another teaching in the traditional program), and it is highly possible that there are others. The group teaching gifted and talented students has acquired power as a result of having a common focus and will likely resist relinquishing that power.

When a faculty has ownership for the current state of existence, it is difficult for them to accept changing an instructional program that they have helped to create (Tichy & Ulrich, 1984, p. 479). Finally, only three teachers will be new to the school. If change is proposed, a large number of teachers, out of necessity, will need to participate in professional development programs to acquire skills in new programs and instructional practices. Their technical skills will need to be enhanced.

A third source of resistance is composed of those who favor ability grouping. If ability grouping is discontinued, the change will raise concerns among faculty members who subscribe to homogeneous grouping. These individuals are likely to become restraining forces in the change process. Providing for a wide range of individual differences in their classrooms may prove to be challenging for teachers who have grown accustomed to teaching ability-grouped classes. In addition, there are parents who support the concept of homogeneous grouping and believe their children benefit most when they are grouped in such a manner. If change is offered, some parents are also likely to become a restraining force.

Building a Capacity for Change

Although change appears to be needed at Eastern Hills, the school in its current state does not have the capacity for the needed change. Three barriers that are most obvious are (a) lack of a clear vision of the needed change, (b) lack of faculty support for the change, and (c) insufficient funds for the needed professional development.

Nevertheless, with effort and using the appropriate strategies, a capacity for change can be developed. Change will not come quickly, rather it will require time or task, an adequate assessment of student needs, and the alignment of human and material resources with those needs. Also, the principal will need to develop an understanding of the culture of the school, be considerate of the values, skills, and motivation of individuals currently affiliated with the school, and have patience sufficient to allow them to develop an understanding for the need to change.

Developing a Vision of the Needed Change

The first step in building the change capacity is developing a shared vision for the school. This is least likely to occur by placing blame on any individual or on teachers who teach at a particular grade level. Rather, relevant data pertaining to students and their families will have to be compiled and used in developing a vision, mission, and goals for the school.

Accomplishing this task will require skills in the areas of group dynamics and instructional planning. Therefore, the leader will need to unite the faculty and develop a collaborative working relationship among them. The greater the assistance from individuals trained in group dynamics and instructional planning, the more likely the faculty will develop a collaborative relationship, share the vision, and facilitate successful change.

Analyzing the Data

An analysis of data across grade levels in reading, language, and math indicates that percentile scores are at or slightly below the national average. Using this data, only the second and third grades can be assessed from 1999 to 2002. During those years, in the area of language, the scores of students increased in grades three and four. However, there was a decline in the scores of both groups in grades five and six. This decline occurred between 1995 and 1996. A further drop is observed for these students in 1997. The trend appears to be reflected in the area of language. The language scores for many students tend to increase in grades three and four and decrease in grades five and six.

THE COMPREHENSIVE TEST OF BASIC SKILLS SCORES

TOTAL READING IN PERCENTILES

Grades	1999	2000	2001	2002
2	41	44	40	40
3	60	43	46	44
4	48	57	42	41
5	61	42	52	35
6	44	54	39	42

TOTAL LANGUAGE IN PERCENTILES

Grades	1999	2000	2001	2002
2	40	45	50	56
3	47	47	38	47
4	55	69	51	54
5	56	60	59	41
6	46	59	54	52

TOTAL MATH IN PERCENTILES

Grades	1999	2000	2001	2002
2	34	34	39	32
3	62	50	49	50
4	42	55	43	38
5	54	54	60	44
6	48	75	56	59

Formulating the Plan

An analysis of the test results reveals regression in student reading scores at the fourth-grade level, continuing through grade six. They also reveal a regression of student language scores in grades five and six. There is a need to improve instruction in both of these areas, and the entire faculty should be involved in the alteration of existing programs and instructional strategies and/or the development of new program concepts. Giving consideration to this factor in filling the three vacant positions, the principal would greatly benefit the school by employing teachers who are skilled in teaching reading and language arts and could couple those skills with providing teacher leadership for instructional improvement.

In summary, the new principal of Eastern Hills Elementary has accepted a very challenging assignment. However, with effective planning and involvement of the right individuals, he should be able to move the school forward. When change occurs in schools, all role groups should be involved. There are a number of role groups who will have a strong interest in any change taking place at Eastern Hills and will want to participate in the process. Therefore, a school improvement team should be created, and the team should consist of representatives from all concerned role groups—teachers, parents, students, central office personnel, and state instructional department personnel. Once the school improvement team is organized, it should be commissioned to develop a plan for school improvement. The plan should consist of the following items:

1. Needs assessment
2. Shared vision
3. Shared mission
4. Schoolwide goals and expectations for all students
5. A list of programs that need to be modified or replaced
6. A list of new instructional programs that address the needs of all students
7. A list of needed professional development program activities
8. An implementation plan that includes assessment tools that will generate pupil and program data that can be used to make revisions to the instructional program

When the initial planning process is completed, team members should become partners in the implementation of the plan and in making decisions about the administration of the school. With the establishment of a team, decision quality and acceptance are likely to be enhanced, for collaborating with others on change strengthens the partnership and enhances the likelihood of the school achieving its desired goal (Fullan, 1993).

SCENARIO 14
THE STRATEGIC PLANNING PROCESS

STANDARD 1

A school administrator is an educational leader who promotes the success of all students by facilitating the development, articulation, implementation, and stewardship of a vision of learning that is shared and supported by the school community.

In the fall of 1998, with Mr. Clark coordinating the process and the superintendent serving as a member of the committee, the district began developing a strategic plan that would propel the district into the 21st century. Care was taken to place individuals who represented the diversity of the district on the committee. Thirty-nine individuals, half district personnel (teachers, administrators, students) and half community members (business affiliates, religious leaders, parents, and city government), formed the strategic planning committee. First, they met for several days in very intense sessions to identify operational procedures. An outside consultant was invited to provide training in the art of collaboration. Rules were established, and everyone agreed to follow the rules, respecting the right of individuals to disagree and foster a difference of opinion. After the collaboration training was concluded and operational procedures were in place, Superintendent Wallace offered comments to the committee regarding her view of district needs, passed out material on state and national standards and assessment measures, and spoke to current trends in educational reform. She concluded her remarks by acknowledging Director Clark's leadership skills and voicing support for him in the position of coordinator.

Operating on the assumption that everyone's views were important and had a meaningful role to play, the planning committee used a modified Delphi technique to generate information from all segments of the school community for inclusion in the strategic plan. From the process, which took several months, a mission statement that incorporated the core values of the district was developed. The committee distributed the statement and sought and received district and communitywide acceptance before continuing with the strategic planning process. The mission statement read as follows: "It is the mission of the Arrowhead Consolidated School District to teach all students to the fullest extent, instilling in them a passion for learning and a readiness to pursue their personal careers in a manner that will enhance our democratic society." This mission emerged from the values that the committee identified from a values clarification study conducted throughout the district. The following core values emerged from the study:

1. Families are the foundation of the community, and parents and community members should participate in the educational process.
2. All individuals are accountable and responsible for their choices and actions.
3. All individuals have values.
4. All individuals have the capacity for continuous growth and development.
5. Honesty and integrity are central to building and maintaining trust and relationships.
6. Diversity is a strength that enriches a community.
7. People working together toward a common goal are more likely to accomplish that goal.
8. Schools should prepare students to be contributing members of society.

To achieve this mission, the planning committee identified five goals to be achieved by the year 2007:

1. Improve the readiness level of all students.
2. Improve educational outcomes at every school.
3. Improve staff effectiveness by providing professional development programs that are tailored to the needs of teachers in individual schools.
4. Strengthen parent and community participation in the educational process.
5. Design an open assessment process to measure student progress and make curriculum decisions.

After getting districtwide acceptance of the mission statement, the list of districtwide goals was agreed upon and under the leadership of building principals, local site-based councils were established for each building. The councils consisted of administrators, teachers, staff, students, parents, and other representatives of each local school community. The councils then worked within each school to establish local school goals that were aligned with the district goals. The attainment of the local goals was facilitated by the establishment of school committees in the areas of curriculum, resource allocation, and professional development.

After the planning process was completed to foster effective communication, the superintendent provided periodic written updates to every board member. In addition, she met weekly in face-to-face meetings with the board president and had monthly meetings with every board member. In almost every instance, staff made presentations with Mr. Clark taking the lead. Full disclosure was practiced with the board and the community.

REFLECTIVE THINKING

The ISLLC Standards

The following are indicators of the ISLLC standards addressed in the scenario:

1: A vision of high standards will have to be shared by all stakeholders; information sources must be used; data collection and data analysis strategies are required; each faculty will have to do the work required for high levels of personal and organizational performance; assessment data related to student learning will have to be used to develop their school vision and goals; and barriers to achieving the vision will have to be identified, clarified, and removed.

6: The law as related to education and schooling must be taken into account; the principal will need to recognize a variety of ideas, values, and cultures; communication will have to occur among the school community concerning trends and issues; and potential changes in the environment in which schools operate will have to be factored into the change process.

Reflective Questions

1. What activities in the planning process adhered to the knowledge indicators of ISLLC Standard 1?
2. Can you cite statements in the scenario that would provide evidence that Superintendent Wallace believes in the inclusion of all members of the school community in developing plans for the district?
3. Now that local councils exist at each building, reflecting on the performance indicators of ISLLC Standard 2, what are the implications for the authority, roles, and responsibilities of the central staff? Is there reason to believe that ownership and accountability for student success will be maximized?
4. How would you rate the amount of collaboration that occurred between and among administrators, teachers, and community stakeholders? Did the planning process give credence to individuals and groups whose values conflicted? What approach would you use to ensure stakeholder involvement in a strategic planning process?
5. Identify theoretical information from the introductory section of this chapter and Chapter 2 and relate that information to passages in the scenario in a manner that will verify that appropriate procedural steps were followed in establishing the strategic plan.

ADDRESSING THE CRITICAL ISSUES

Utilizing Appropriate Styles and Strategies

When engaging in the process of change, effective school leaders conduct inquiries into best practices and select successful models of school reform. These models suggest that the leader should subscribe to collaboration, open communication, trust, and shared accountability (Conley, 1997). From all indications, Superintendent Wallace subscribed to collaboration and used a participatory style of leadership. Her attitude indicated a respect for diversity, and she was concerned with the composition of the committee.

Her approach was well designed; using a participatory leadership style and establishing a committee with a diverse composition are very important characteristics of an effective strategic planning process. However, the implementation model is also critical; one might have an outstanding plan, but without an implementation model supported by participants who have a commitment to its success, the plan is likely to be extremely difficult to implement, and therefore of little value. Conley (1997) reports that two strong components of successful restructuring efforts are a change in the roles of principals and teachers and a commitment from all stakeholders.

Utilizing the Expertise of Stakeholders

Standard 2 places major emphasis on teaching and learning. In fact, it requires the principal to lead in ensuring that the educational needs of all students are met. Developing a plan for instructional improvement, within itself, will not necessarily meet this standard or have a positive effect on the teaching and learning process. As was discussed in Chapter 5, one must be concerned with both decision quality and acceptance. Consequently, select involvement in the planning process is tantamount to achieving the desired outcome. It is evident that Mr. Clark and the superintendent are aware of this point, as both community and school personnel were involved in the planning process. However, whereas the involvement of parents is an important factor and is likely to yield great results in terms of improving instruction in schools, they are not directly delivering instruction to children. On the other hand, involving teachers in a manner that allows them to utilize their expertise in resolving problems that affect student learning can have a very positive effect on students.

Teachers know their students, are aware of a variety of ways to teach them, and can identify and remove barriers to learning. The primary leadership for bringing about improvements in a school district should come from the educational level where the change is to take effect (Barth, 1990). Therefore, the greatest benefit to be gained relative to teaching and learning is to involve teachers in a new, empowered role.

Using Data to Inform Change

School leaders should have various means of determining if programs are working and if the diverse needs of students are being met. To that end, frequent assessments should be made of pupils and programs to acquire data that can be used to make changes for instructional improvement (Standard 1). Without sufficient data to drive decisions, change is not likely to be focused and can become educated guesses at best. In Arrowhead, a key program component was missing from the plan, and the assessment component of the plan should identify the missing component.

The Missing Component

The plan started with a focus on the values of the community and acquired a strong commitment from all stakeholders, and a component for local school implementation was also outlined. What appears to be missing is a plan to facilitate professional development. Professional development is key to change effectiveness. Many programs are designed in an excellent manner. However, without an effective professional development component, successful goal attainment may never become a reality, as teachers may not have skills sufficient to implement the new concept. Consequently, to be effective, the plan must include a professional development component.

In summary, the successful development of a strategic plan in Arrowhead resulted from hard work. Also, people in the internal and external environment realized that in order for students to achieve curriculum standards, everyone in the district had to rally around a single focus. Throughout the process, the leadership respected individuality and diversity, addressing the unique needs of each section of the community.

Superintendent Wallace chose to place Director Clark in a highly visible role in the district, one with major responsibility. Then, she supported him in that role. The community, as well as Director Clark, could see that the superintendent respected his expertise and trusted him to do the right thing. Although she demonstrated many indicators of the ISLLC Standards, quite clearly she demonstrated that she was committed to trusting people and their judgment and involving stakeholders in management processes, two indicators of Standard 3.

CHAPTER SUMMARY

Individuals who make changes in today's schools need knowledge, understanding, and commitment. They need knowledge of change processes for systems, organizations, and individuals, an understanding of organizational stakeholders, and a commitment to addressing the needs of all constituent groups (Standard 2).

Change is a process, not an event; it can be planned or unplanned and can be influenced by forces inside and outside of the organization. The change process can be viewed in three steps: (a) establishing a vision, (b) determining the state of existing programs, and (c) determining what is needed to reach the desired vision (Schmidt & Finnigan, 1992). As these steps are taken, the leader or change agent needs to be sensitive to human potential in the organization and the general capacity of the organization to address change because either of these factors can negatively impact the change process.

A number of theories and processes inform change in schools. Three worthy of note are Kurt Lewin's Force Field Analysis; Chin and Benne's empirical-rational, normative–re-educative, and power-coercive strategies; and Fullan's Change Agentry Theory. Any of these theories or strategies can assist the leader through the change process. However, prior to engaging in the change process, it is advisable for the leader to determine if the change to be made is a first-order or second-order change and the extent to which the organization has the capacity to make that change. If the change capacity does not exist, the emergence of conflict is almost a certainty.

In addition to assessing the capacity of the organization to engage in change, the leader will need to determine if the change is best made using an autocratic or participative approach. Knowing which approach to use can influence the degree of success and the extent to which the change is likely to be accepted.

In a learning organization, one individual does not administer a school district; rather, a combination of individuals work cooperatively, each bringing their skills to the table and debating the merits of their position in a collegial manner. If the desired change is to be effective, not only must leaders influence individuals to do things they do not want to do, but they must also focus on intangibles that create commitment and values. They must exude confidence in others and give them authority to make decisions in a participatory manner. In today's schools, fair process and sound implementation plans are keys to success. When leaders value diversity, are committed to fostering programs that address the needs of all students, and include all stakeholders in the process, change is being made in accordance with standards for effective leaders (Standards 2 and 4).

MOVING INTO PRACTICE

Review the scenarios in Chapter 6, using the pros and cons of the various situations, and identify several approaches that you would use to address the following school-related issues in an actual school situation. Project yourself in the role of the principal or superintendent and take care to formulate a rationale for your selected behavior.

◆ You have just been appointed superintendent of a large urban school district that is faced with declining achievement scores. The community is very diverse, and the scores are identifiable by ethnic group and by socioeconomic status. The community is very upset, as the school district has always had a fine reputation, and for that reason, the city has been able to attract a large number of corporate headquarters. You have been asked to change the climate in the district and to design programs that will increase student achievement. Describe the action steps you would take to fulfill your charge. Take care to reflect various change strategies in your plan and highlight procedures you would use to sell your ideas and, at the same time, minimize conflict.

◆ Outline the strategies you would use to create and implement a school improvement plan. Support your selected strategies with change theory.

ACQUIRING AN UNDERSTANDING OF SELF

◆ What is equity?

◆ What meaning do you give to "lifelong learning for self and others"?

◆ How would you determine the services to provide for students who have lower test scores than their counterparts?

DEEPENING YOUR UNDERSTANDING

Now that you have read this chapter, visit the Companion Website for this book at **www.prenhall.com/green** *and take the Self-Assessment Inventory for this chapter.*

Completing this inventory will give you an indication of how familiar you are with the ISLLC standards knowledge indicators that relate to this chapter.

SUGGESTED READINGS

Baker, B.D. (2004). *The ecology of educational systems: Data, models, and tools for improvisational leading and learning.* Upper Saddle River, NJ: Prentice Hall.

Fullen, M. (2002). *Leading in a culture of change.* New York: Wiley

Fullen, M. (2001). *Leading in a culture of change: Being effective in complex times.* San Francisco, CA: Jossey-Bass.

Goldenberg, C. (2004). *Successful school change.* New York: Teachers College Press.

AVAILABLE POWERPOINT PRESENTATIONS

After completing this chapter, log on to the Companion Website for this book at **www.prenhall.com/green** *and click on the PowerPoint module.*

• The Change Process

• Closing the Achievement Gap

• Enhancing the Teaching and Learning Process

WEBSITES

No Child Left Behind
http://www.ed.gov/nclb/landing.jhtml

Data Driven Decision Making
http://3d2know.cosn.org/

Change Management: Force Field Analysis
http://www.accel-team.com/techniques/force_field_analysis.html

Leading and Managing Change
http://www.homebiznews.ca/Change.html

PRACTICE ISLLC EXAMS

After reading this chapter, log on to the Companion Website for this book at **www.prenhall.com/green** *to take the practice ISLLC exams.*

REFERENCES

Barth, R. S. (1990). *Improving school from within: Teachers, parents, and principals can make the difference.* San Francisco: Jossey-Bass.

Bowman, R. (1999). Change in education: Connecting the dots. *The Cleaning House, 72,* 298–299.

Bottoms, G., & O'Neill, K. (2001). *Lending school improvement what research says: A review of the literature.* Atlanta, GA: Southern Regional Education Board.

Chin, R., & Benne, K. D. (1969). General strategies for effective changes in human systems. In W. G. Bennis, K. D. Benne, & R. Chin (Eds.), *The planning of change* (2nd ed.). New York: Holt, Rinehart & Winston.

Conley, D. T. (1997). *Roadmap to restructuring: Charting the course of change in American education.* Eugene: University of Oregon (ERIC Clearinghouse on Educational Management).

Cusick, P. A. (1973). *Inside high school.* New York: Holt, Rinehart.

Etheridge, C. P., & Green, R. (1998). *Union district collaboration and other processes related to school district restructuring for establishing standards and accountability measures.* (A technical report for the 21st century project). Washington, DC: National Educational Association.

Findley, B., & Findley, D. (1992). Effective schools: The role of the principal. *Contemporary Education, 63*(2), 102–104.

Fullan, M. G. (1992). Overcoming barriers to educational change. In Office of Policy and Planning (Eds.), *Changing Schools Insights* (pp. 11–19). Washington: DC: Office of Policy and Planning.

Fullan, M. G. (1993). *Change forces.* New York: Falmer Press.

Fullan, M. G. (1999). *Change forces: The sequel.* New York: Falmer Press.

Goodlad, J. I. (1984). *A place called school: Prospects for the future.* New York: McGraw-Hill.

Green, R. L. & Etheridge, Carol (1999). *Building collaborative relationships for instructional improvement.* Education *120* (2), 388–396.

Interstate School Leaders Licensure Consortium of the Council of Chief State School Officers. (1997). *Candidate information bulletin for school leaders assessment.* Princeton, NJ: Educational Testing Service.

Lewin, K. (1951). *Field theory in social sciences.* New York: Harper & Row.

Lindblom, C. E. (1959). The science of muddling through. *Public Administrative Review, 19,* 79–99.

Marlow, E. (1999). The principal and curriculum development. Retrieved September 26, 2002 from Electronic Data Resources Service (ED437719).

Meyer, A., Brooks, G., & Goes, J. (1990). Environmental jolts and industry revolution: Organizational responses to discontinuous change. *Strategic Management Journal, 11,* 93–110.

Riley, R. (2002). Educational reform through standards and partnerships, 1993-2000. *Phi Delta Kappa 83*(9), 700.

Ryan, K. D., & Oestreich, D. K. (1991). *Driving fear out of the workplace: How to overcome the invisible barriers to quality, productivity, and innovation.* San Francisco: Jossey-Bass.

Sarason, S. (1996). *Revisiting the culture of the school and the problem of change.* New York: Teachers College Press.

Schmidt, W., & Finnigan, J. (1992). *The race for the finish line: America's quest for total quality.* San Francisco: Jossey-Bass.

Schwahn, C. J., & Spady, W. G. (1998). *Total leaders: Applying the best future-focused change strategies to Education.* Arlington, VA: American Association of School Administrators.

Senge, P. M. (1990). *The fifth discipline: The art and practice of the learning organization.* New York: Doubleday.

Sergiovanni, T. J. (1991). *The principalship.* Needham Heights, MA: Allyn & Bacon.

Short, P., & Greer, J. T. (1997). *Leadership in empowered schools: Themes from innovative efforts.* Upper Saddle River, NJ: Merrill/Prentice Hall.

Supovitz, J. A. & Poglinco, S. M. (2001). *Instructional leadership in standards-based reform.* Philadelphia: Consortium for Policy Research in Education.

Tichy, N. M., & Ulrich, D. O. (1984). The leadership challenge: A call for the transformational leader. In D. A. Kolb, J. S. Osland, & I. M. Rubin (Eds.), *The organizational behavior reader* (6th ed., pp. 476–486). Upper Saddle River, NJ: Prentice Hall.

APPENDIXES

THE INTERSTATE SCHOOL LEADER LICENSURE STANDARDS AND INDICATORS

Standard 1

A school administrator is an educational leader who promotes the success of all students by facilitating the development, articulation, implementation, and stewardship of a vision of learning that is shared and supported by the school community.

Knowledge Indicators

The administrator has knowledge and understanding of:
▲ learning goals in a pluralistic society
▲ the principles of developing and implementing strategic plans
▲ systems theory
▲ information sources, data collection, and data analysis strategies
▲ effective communication
▲ effective consensus-building and negotiation skills

Disposition Indicators

The administrator believes in, values, and is committed to:
▲ the educability of all
▲ a school vision of high standards of learning
▲ continuous school improvement
▲ the inclusion of all members of the school community
▲ ensuring that students have the knowledge, skills, and values needed to become successful adults
▲ a willingness to continuously examine one's own assumptions, beliefs and practices
▲ doing the work required for high levels of personal and organization performance

Performance Indicators

The administrator facilitates processes and engages in activities ensuring that:
▲ the vision and mission of the school are effectively communicated to staff, parents, students, and community members
▲ the vision and mission are communicated through the use of symbols, ceremonies, stories, and similar activities
▲ the core beliefs of the school vision are modeled for all stakeholders
▲ the vision is developed with and among stakeholders
▲ the contributions of school community members to the realization of the vision are recognized and celebrated

▲ progress toward the vision and mission is communicated to all stakeholders

▲ the school community is involved in school improvement efforts

▲ the vision shapes the educational programs, plans, and activities

▲ the vision shapes the educational programs, plans, and actions

▲ an implementation plan is developed in which objectives and strategies to achieve the vision and goals are clearly articulated

▲ assessment data related to student learning are used to develop the school vision and goals

▲ relevant demographic data pertaining to students and their families are used in developing the school mission and goals

▲ barriers to achieving the vision are identified, clarified, and addressed

▲ needed resources are sought and obtained to support the implementation of the school mission and goals

▲ existing resources are used in support of the school vision and goals

▲ the vision, mission, and implementation plans are regularly monitored, evaluated, and revised

Standard 2

A school administrator is an educational leader who promotes the success of all students by advocating, nurturing, and sustaining a school culture and instructional program conducive to student learning and staff professional growth.

Knowledge Indicators

The administrator has knowledge and understanding of:

▲ student growth and development

▲ applied learning theories

▲ applied motivational theories

▲ curriculum design, implementation, evaluation, and refinement

▲ principles of effective instruction

▲ measurement, evaluation, and assessment strategies

▲ diversity and its meaning for educational programs

▲ adult learning and professional development models

▲ the change process for systems, operations, and individuals

▲ the role of technology in promoting student learning and professional growth

▲ school cultures

Disposition Indicators

The administrator believes in, values, and is committed to:

▲ student learning as the fundamental purpose of schooling

▲ the proposition that all students can learn

▲ the variety of ways in which students can learn

▲ lifelong learning for self and others

- professional development as an integral part of school improvement
- the benefits that diversity brings to the school community
- a safe and supportive learning environment
- preparing students to become contributing members of society

Performance Indicators

The administrator facilitates processes and engages in activities ensuring that:
- all individuals are treated with fairness, dignity, and respect
- professional development promotes a focus on student learning consistent with the school vision and goals
- student and staff feel valued and important
- the responsibilities and contributions of each individual are acknowledged
- barriers to student learning are identified, clarified, and addressed
- diversity is considered in developing learning experiences
- lifelong learning is encouraged and modeled
- there is a culture of high expectations for self, students, and staff performance
- the school is organized and aligned for success
- technologies are used in teaching and learning
- student and staff accomplishments are recognized and celebrated
- multiple opportunities to learn are available to all students
- curricular, co-curricular, and extra-curricular programs are designed, implemented, evaluated, and refined
- curriculum decisions are based on research, expertise of teachers, and the recommendations of learned societies
- the school culture and climate are assessed on a regular basis
- a variety of sources of information is used to make decisions
- student learning is assessed using a variety of techniques
- multiple sources of information regarding performance are used by staff and students
- a variety of supervisory and evaluation models are employed
- pupil personnel programs are developed to meet the needs of students and their families

Standard 3

A school administrator is an educational leader who promotes the success of all students by ensuring management of the organization, operations, and resources for a safe, efficient, and effective learning environment.

Knowledge Indicators

The administrator has knowledge and understanding of:
- theories and models of organizations and the principles of organizational development

▲ operational procedures at the school and district level
▲ principles and issues relating to school safety and security
▲ human resources management and development
▲ principles and issues relating to fiscal operations of school management
▲ principles and issues relating to school facilities and use of space
▲ legal issues impacting school operations
▲ current technologies that support management functions

Disposition Indicators

The administrator believes in, values, and is committed to:
▲ making management decisions to enhance learning and teaching
▲ taking risks to improve schools
▲ trusting people and their judgments
▲ accepting responsibility
▲ high-quality standards, expectations, and performances
▲ involving stakeholders in management processes
▲ a safe environment

Performance Indicators

The administrator facilitates processes and engages in activities ensuring that:
▲ knowledge of learning, teaching, and student development is used to inform management decisions
▲ operational procedures are designed and managed to maximize opportunities for successful learning
▲ emerging trends are recognized, studied, and applied as appropriate
▲ operational plans and procedures to achieve the vision and goals of the school are in place
▲ collective bargaining and other contractual agreements related to the school are effectively managed
▲ the school plant, equipment, and support systems operate safely, efficiently, and effectively
▲ time is managed to maximize attainment of organizational goals
▲ potential problems and opportunities are identified
▲ problems are confronted and resolved in a timely manner
▲ financial, human, and material resources are aligned to the goals of schools
▲ the school acts entrepreneurially to support continuous improvement
▲ organizational systems are regularly monitored and modified as needed
▲ stakeholders are involved in decisions affecting schools
▲ responsibility is shared to maximize ownership and accountability
▲ effective problem-framing and problem-solving skills are used
▲ effective conflict-resolution skills are used

- effective group-processes and consensus-building skills are used
- effective communication skills are used
- there is effective use of technology to manage school operations
- fiscal resources of the school are managed responsibly, efficiently, and effectively
- a safe, clean, and aesthetically pleasing school environment is created and maintained
- human resource functions support the attainment of school goals
- confidentiality and privacy of school records are maintained

Standard 4

A school administrator is an educational leader who promotes the success of all students by collaborating with families and community members, responding to diverse community interests and needs, and mobilizing community resources.

Knowledge Indicators

The administrator has knowledge and understanding of:
- emerging issues and trends that potentially impact the school community
- the conditions and dynamics of the diverse school community
- community resources
- community relations and marketing strategies and processes
- successful models of school, family, business, community, government, and higher education partnerships

Disposition Indicators

The administrator believes in, values, and is committed to:
- schools operating as an integral part of the larger community
- collaboration and communication with families
- involvement of families and other stakeholders in school decision-making processes
- the proposition that diversity enriches the school
- families as partners in the education of their children
- the proposition that families have the best interests of their children in mind
- resources of the family and community needing to be brought to bear on the education of students
- an informed public

Performance Indicators

The administrator facilitates processes and engages in activities ensuring that:
- high visibility, active involvement, and communication with the larger community is a priority
- relationships with community leaders are identified and nurtured

▲ information about family and community concerns, expectations, and needs is used regularly

▲ there is outreach to different business, religious, political, and service agencies and organizations

▲ credence is given to individuals and groups whose values and opinions may conflict

▲ the school and community serve one another as resources

▲ available community resources are secured to help the school solve problems and achieve goals

▲ partnerships are established with area businesses, institutions of higher education, and community groups to strengthen programs and support school goals

▲ community youth and family services are integrated with school programs

▲ community stakeholders are treated equitably

▲ diversity is recognized and valued

▲ effective media relations are developed and maintained

▲ a comprehensive program of community relations is established

▲ public resources and funds are used appropriately and wisely

▲ community collaboration is modeled for staff

▲ opportunities for staff to develop collaborative skills are provided

Standard 5

A school administrator is an educational leader who promotes the success of all students by acting with integrity, fairness, and in an ethical manner.

Knowledge Indicators

The administrator has knowledge and understanding of:
▲ the purpose of education and the role of leadership in modern society
▲ various ethical frameworks and perspectives on ethics
▲ the values of the diverse school community
▲ professional codes of ethics
▲ the philosophy and history of education

Disposition Indicators

The administrator believes in, values, and is committed to:
▲ the ideal of the common good
▲ the principles in the Bill of Rights
▲ the right of every student to a free, quality education
▲ bringing ethical principles to the decision-making process
▲ subordinating one's own interest to the good of the school community
▲ accepting the consequences for upholding one's principles and actions

▲ using the influence of one's office constructively and productively in the service of all students and their families

▲ development of a caring school community

Performance Indicators

▲ The leader examines personal and professional values.

▲ The leader demonstrates a personal and professional code of ethics.

▲ The leader demonstrates values, beliefs, and attitudes that inspire others to higher levels of performance.

▲ The leader serves as a role model.

▲ The leader accepts responsibility for school operations.

▲ The leader considers the impact of one's administrative practices on others.

▲ The leader uses the influence of the office to enhance the educational program rather than for personal gain.

▲ The leader treats people fairly, equitably, and with dignity and respect.

▲ The leader protects the rights and confidentially of students and staff.

▲ The leader demonstrates appreciation for and sensitivity to the diversity in the school community.

▲ The leader recognizes and respects the legitimate authority of others.

▲ The leader examines and considers the prevailing values of the diverse school community.

▲ The leader expects that others in the school community will demonstrate integrity and exercise ethical behavior.

▲ The leader opens the school to public scrutiny.

▲ The leader fulfills legal and contractual obligations.

▲ The leader applies laws and procedures fairly, wisely, and considerately.

Standard 6

A school administrator is an educational leader who promotes the success of all students by understanding, responding to, and influencing the larger political, social, economic, legal, and cultural context.

Knowledge Indicators

The administrator has knowledge and understanding of:

▲ principles of representative governance that undergird the system of American schools

▲ the role of public education in developing and renewing a democratic society and an economically productive nation

▲ the law as related to education and schooling

▲ the political, social, cultural and economic systems and processes that impact schools

▲ models and strategies of change and conflict resolution as applied to the larger political, social, cultural and economic contexts of schooling
▲ global issues and forces affecting teaching and learning
▲ the dynamics of policy development and advocacy under our democratic political system
▲ the importance of diversity and equity in a democratic society

Disposition Indicators

The administrator believes in, values, and is committed to:
▲ education as a key to opportunity and social mobility
▲ recognizing a variety of ideas, values, and cultures
▲ importance of a continuing dialogue with other decision makers affecting education
▲ actively participating in the political and policy-making context in the service of education
▲ using legal systems to protect student rights and improve student opportunities

Performance Indicators

The administrator facilitates processes and engages in activities ensuring that:
▲ the environment in which schools operate is influenced on behalf of students and their families
▲ communication occurs among the school community concerning trends, issues, and potential changes in the environment in which schools operate
▲ there is ongoing dialogue with representatives of diverse community groups
▲ the school community works within the framework of policies, laws, and regulations enacted by local, state, and federal authorities
▲ public policy is shaped to provide quality education for students
▲ lines of communication are developed with decision makers outside the school community

Source: Interstate School Leaders Licensure Consortium Standards For School Leaders. Council of Chief State School Officers, 1996. Washington, DC.

It cannot be emphasized too much that these standards are used as a basis for the design of a number of leadership preparation programs and assessment instruments. Of particular interest is their use in the standards-based assessments instruments designed and administered by Educational Testing Services. A portion of the content of those assessment instruments contains scenarios and vignettes. Therefore, the reader may find the following on scenarios helpful as a practice activity for that assessment.

ADDITIONAL SCENARIOS FOR ANALYSES AND REFLECTIONS

Chapter 2

THE NEW FOURTH-GRADE TEACHER

Mrs. Williams has served as principal of Jacksonville Elementary School for 15 years. She is an experienced principal and realizes the benefits to be derived from involving her faculty and staff in the selection and orientation of new personnel.

It was just 3 weeks prior to the end of the school year when the registrar provided her with the estimated student enrollment figures for the next school year. According to the numbers received, she will need an additional fourth-grade teacher. Currently, the fourth-grade faculty consists of three teachers who have their own styles, and there is very little cooperative teaching or interaction among them.

Following her practice of involvement, Mrs. Williams informed the teachers that an additional fourth-grade teacher was needed and that she wanted them to participate in the selection process. She also asked one of them to volunteer to serve as mentor to the newly employed teacher. The current fourth-grade teachers showed little interest in the new position, acquiring knowledge of how it would affect their grade level, or being included in the selection process. Each of the teachers offered reasons for not being interested in accepting the assignment. "I have a computer club to organize and maintain next year, so I won't have the time," said one teacher. Another teacher remarked, "I am doing an inclusion class next year, and I will also have a student teacher." The third teacher stated, "I have been assigned Parent's Night, and the planning of that activity is going to really take a lot of extra time."

Concerned about the situation, Mrs. Williams replied, "All fourth-grade teachers will serve on the selection committee; I will look over everyone's obligations and assign one of you the mentoring responsibility." Fully respecting the wishes of the current faculty members, but being in a situation where she needed a mentor for the incoming teacher, she exercised her authority in order to implement one of her proven leadership concepts. The selection process began and within 3 weeks, the position was filled. Although each of the fourth-grade teachers had reasons for not volunteering to accept the commitment of mentoring the new teacher, one of the teachers received the assignment. The teacher receiving the assignment was not pleased with the principal's decision; however, he agreed to it.

The new school year began with the assigned fourth-grade mentoring teacher and the newly employed teacher working together. The new teacher was acquainted with policies, schedules, activities, and procedures of the school. Aware of the lack of motivation the senior teacher showed for mentoring the new teacher, Mrs. Williams closely supervised the process and often stopped in to check on how the mentoring was progressing.

REFLECTIVE THINKING

1. Identify several factors that would serve as a basis for a characterization of the existing state of the fourth-grade faculty.
2. At Jacksonville Elementary, what might be occurring that would influence faculty members to resist serving on a selection committee and mentoring a new colleague?
3. Which adult learning and professional development models would best inform the actions needed in this scenario?
4. Identify the system, organization, and individual change process that Mrs. Williams might have used to influence the participation of her faculty without making a direct assignment.
5. Using the Vroom-Yetton model, give a theoretical rationale for why Mrs. Williams should be concerned with the decision she made. In addition, cite the decision rule that is most applicable.
6. What long-term provisions could Mrs. Williams make to sustain an effective mentoring program?

Chapter 3

THE NEW PRINCIPAL AT EVANS MIDDLE SCHOOL

Janice Freeman has served as principal of Evans Middle School for three months. When she accepted the assignment, the superintendent informed her that the enrollment at Evans was increasing at an average of 15 students per grade level each year. However, budget constraints would not allow additional staff. He also stated that he was aware of her creativity and felt that she would be able to design a program plan to serve students at Evans in a manner that would allow achievement to continue at the level of excellence that parents had come to expect.

Principal Freeman, challenged by the information received from the superintendent, began to ponder how to deliver the same quality of service with additional students and no additional staff. As she deliberated the issue, many ideas came to mind. The one that seemed most appropriate for the situation was team teaching. She thought that by implementing this concept she could capitalize on the strengths of each teacher, have larger classes, and thereby address the increase in enrollment. Also, this concept would allow teachers to select a schoolwide theme and work together in departments, thereby easing the workload. More to the point, team teaching was a concept that she loved, had worked with as a teacher, and had always stated she would implement if she became principal.

Although energized by the notion of implementing the concept, Principal Freeman is somewhat concerned about how the faculty will react to her plan. She realized from past meetings that several factions exist within the faculty. There is a core group of influential teachers who seem to be somewhat skeptical of her ideas. In addition, there is a group that has no ambition, always needs directions, and has to be coerced to teach their classes. She wonders if this group will be able or willing to take on the challenge of implementing such a concept in the time allotted.

Principal Freeman is also aware of a parent group that is not particularly fond of new instructional program ideas; they feel it is unsettling to the children. Then there is the union. As she pondered the concept she thought, "Maybe I can just direct the teachers to implement the concept; after all, the superintendent is expecting me to come up with a new program. I do have one group of teachers who has really been supportive and seems to be enthusiastic and eager for new program ideas. I can depend on them to assist me."

Nevertheless, she realized that it is important for new ideas to be presented in a way that will gain the most support and leave the entire faculty with a positive outlook for the school year. Her basic concern is how best to approach the faculty in the upcoming meeting.

REFLECTIVE THINKING

1. What barriers to student learning are identifiable in the scenario?
2. Do the concerns expressed by Principal Freeman indicate a particular theoretical persuasion? What management decisions must she make if her primary concerns are teaching and learning?
3. What are some reasons you would give for advising Principal Freeman to consider the feelings of teachers prior to presenting the concept in an open faculty meeting? What adult learning and professional development models might she consider?
4. What are some strategies that you would recommend for Principal Freeman to use in establishing an effective working relationship between the various groups of teachers? Base your response on factors that are relevant to a principal desirous of formulating faculty teams and using professional development as an integral part of school improvement.

Chapter 5

STEVEN AND HIS KNIFE

Steven is a seventh grader at Harrison Middle School. He lives with his grandmother and two younger brothers. His grades are below average, and he is often sent to the principal's office for behavior problems. Steven has missed 20 days of school, and it is only the beginning of the second semester. His grandmother has been called several times because she is listed on school records as Steven's legal guardian. Steven's mother has recently made two trips to the school for conferences with the principal. In each of these conferences, she suggested that school personnel did not provide Steven with the assistance he needed to be successful. She also requested that the principal contact her when there was a problem with Steven.

On Wednesday afternoon during his math class, Steven was showing off a knife to some of his classmates. It caused such a disruption that the teacher, Mrs. Adams, went to the back of the room to find the cause of the commotion. She saw the knife and immediately asked Steven to hand it over to her. He gave her the knife, and they proceeded to the principal's office.

Mrs. Adams explained the incident involving Steven to the principal. She stated that she had confiscated the weapon and immediately brought Steven to the office because she knew the school had a zero tolerance policy regarding weapons on school premises. Mr. Jordan (principal) excused Mrs. Adams and proceeded to talk with Steven about the incident. Steven explained that he was not going to hurt anyone. Rather, he said he had found the knife, thought it was cool, and wanted to show it off to his friends. Mr. Jordan explained to Steven that the school had a zero tolerance policy regarding weapons on school property and asked if he was aware of that policy. Steven said that he was aware and understood that he would be punished. Mr. Jordan, having addressed situations of this nature on several previous occasions, believed that he knew when students were really troublemakers. He looked at Steven, advised him that he had two weeks of detention, and sent him back to class.

During the next two hours, Mr. Jordan tried to contact Steven's mother three times but was unable to do so. Steven's mother was extremely hard to reach, for she worked two jobs and was seldom home. Had he been able to contact her, his plans were to ask her if she was aware that her son was carrying a weapon and had the weapon in school. It was also Mr. Jordan's intention to ask her if she had given him permission to possess the knife. Mr. Jordan was never able to reach Steven's mother.

At the end of the school day, Mr. Jordan held a second conference with Steven. After this conference, he felt that Steven really understood the policy and did not have bad intentions. Mr. Jordan placed the knife in a box on his desk and explained to Steven that if he were ever caught on school property with a weapon again, the zero tolerance policy would be applied, and he would receive severe punishment. Steven nodded in agreement, said that he understood and that he would never bring a weapon to school again.

Just as the conference was concluding, Mr. Jordan's secretary called him to speak with a parent who had been waiting for some time. In a rush to meet with the parent, he did not notice that Steven lifted the knife from the box on his desk.

During his walk home from school, Steven got into a fight with Bob, a classmate. It started out as name calling, but then became physical. During the course of the fight, Steven stabbed Bob with the knife. Bob was not killed but did suffer serious injuries. His family pressed charges, and Steven was taken to the juvenile detention center.

The same afternoon, after receiving the news from a number of sources, Superintendent Walker asked Principal Jordan to meet with him in his office. However, before Mr. Jordan arrived, Superintendent Walker received several calls from the news media, board of education members, and parents. The calls all contained a large outcry for disciplinary action against Mr. Jordan. In between calls, Superintendent Walker reviewed the outstanding record of Principal Jordan and discussed the board's policies on student discipline, attendance, and administrative personnel procedures with the Directors of Student Services and Human Resources. All policies were clear, and even though the board had a zero tolerance policy regarding weapons on school premises, action regarding personnel who failed to implement the policy was at the discretion of the superintendent.

When Mr. Jordan reached the office of the superintendent, he provided Superintendent Walker with a full explanation of what had occurred. The superintendent listened, seemed satisfied, and said to Mr. Jordan, "I will review the matter and meet with you again within the next several days." As Mr. Jordan was about to leave the superintendent's office, three additional calls were received. After completing the third call, Superintendent Walker turned to Mr. Jordan, advised him that he was on suspension with pay and was not to return to Harrison until further notice.

REFLECTIVE THINKING

1. From the scenario, cite factors that would support the notion that the disposition of Principal Jordan influenced or did not influence the quality of his decision. Specifically identify the ISLLC Standards indicators in the content of the scenario.
2. What are some of the critical decision factors that appear not to have been considered by Principal Jordan?
3. Which of the decision-making models described in this chapter would least likely produce the outcome described in the scenario?
4. Is there ever a time when a principal is justified in exercising flexibility in the implementation of school policy? Provide a rationale for your response.
5. One of the ISLLC indicators states, "Families should function as partners in the education of their children." Subscribing to this indicator, what was the appropriate action for Principal Jordan to take? Justify your response.
6. In what manner did each of the school leaders allow the power of his position to influence the decision he made? What influences impacted the decisions, their quality, and acceptance?
7. Who is likely to be liable in a situation of this nature and why?

Chapter 7

ASSESSING STUDENT ACHIEVEMENT AT CENTRE CITY HIGH SCHOOL

Mr. Adams's first year in the principalship was school year 1999–2000 when he became principal of Centre City High School (CCHS). CCHS has 1,500 students in grades 9–12 and is located in the metropolitan area of a large urban city. When Mr. Adams accepted the assignment, the high school was in the middle range of student achievement when compared to the other high schools in his system. CCHS's population is 85% African American, 10% Caucasian, 4% Hispanic, and 1% Asian. Most of the parents are working, and many of the homes are single-parent homes. The school's free and reduced lunch percentage is 85%, making it a Title I school.

In July of 2000, the summer after Mr. Adams's first year, he was informed by the State Department of Education that CCHS was placed "on notice" for school year 2000–2001 and if the school shows no improvement, it would be placed "on probation." The state accountability model calls for placing high schools "on notice" according to the following criteria:

- Achievement criteria—achievement levels in Algebra I End of Course, 11th grade writing, and ACT composite: *Schools identified as on "The List" had below average achievement in two or more of these areas.*
- Growth factors

  1. Positive value added (meeting predicted targets)
  2. Closing the achievement gap by a reduction in the number/percentage of students in below average group
  3. Positive trend in reducing dropout rate: *Schools identified as on "The List" failed to meet one or more of the growth factors.*

Schools showing no improvement after two years of probation are subject to a state takeover.

Mr. Adams determined that the school was placed "on notice" because of (a) below average achievement on the Algebra I Gateway Test and 11th Grade Writing Test and (b) no positive trend in reducing the dropout rate. Mr. Adams informed all the teachers and held a few meetings with the Algebra I and English 11 teachers to offer support and discuss the problem.

Unfortunately, in September of 2001, Mr. Adams was informed that Centre City High School showed no improvement and was "on probation." After looking at the data carefully, Mr. Adams has noticed that although the total failure rate of the Gateway Algebra I Test is 49%, when the data is broken up by standard and honors classes, the story is very different. Forty-three percent (43%) of the students in Standard Algebra I are failing, while only 5% of the Honors Algebra I are failing.

Other information Mr. Adams learned is as follows:

	STANDARD ALG I	HONORS ALG I
Enrolled 9th graders	360	90
Enrolled 10th graders	100	0
Total Number of Students	460	90
Passing Gateway	198	85
Percent Passing	57.0%	94.4%
Failing Gateway	262	5
Percent Failing	43.0%	5.6%

The school's average failure rate for Algebra I is 28%, which means that approximately 154 students will fail the Algebra I course for the year. If that average holds true, there are approximately 113 students who will fail the Algebra I Gateway Test but pass the Algebra I class.

Mr. Adams begins to analyze the data a bit more and learns that there are two honors algebra teachers, Mr. Brown and Mr. White. Mr. White teaches one Honors Algebra I and Geometry the rest of the day. However, Mr. Brown teaches two Honors Algebra I and three Standard Algebra I. The percentage of his regular students passing the Gateway Algebra I Test is no different than any other Standard Algebra I class (Jones—five classes, Williams—five classes, and Clark—three classes). Mr. Adams also noticed that the percentage of Mr. Brown's Honors Algebra I class passing the Gateway Algebra I Test is lower than the other Honors Algebra I class.

The Writing test is falling out the same way: There is a huge difference in the passing rate between the standard and honors English classes.

	ENGLISH 11 STANDARD	ENGLISH 11 HONORS
Students	304	76
Passing Writing	192	72
Percent Passing	63.2%	94.7%
Failing Writing	112	4
Percent Failing	36.8%	5.3%

Mr. Adams decides to break the data down by teacher. Ms. Green teaches all three honors English 11 and two Standard English 11. Data shows a higher percentage of her standard students pass the 11th Grade Writing Test than standard students in other teachers' classes.

Breakdown of Data for Standard English 11 and Writing Test

	GREEN	MILLER	SMITH
Number of Classes	2	5	3
Number of Students	60	150	94
Students Passing Writing	48	90	54
Percentage Passing	80.0%	60.0%	57.0%
Students Failing Writing	12	60	40
Percentage Failing	20.0%	40.0%	43.0%

The newspaper has been profiling those schools that remained on the list for a second year because after the third year, the school faces state takeover. Phone calls to the school from concerned parents and community members are beginning to come into the office. Mr. Adams has even had some parents discuss transferring their students to an optional school or county school in order to get a better education. Some parents just want their child transferred to another teacher.

What's a principal to do?

REFLECTIVE THINKING

1. How would you characterize the cause of the existing conditions of the school?
2. What are the key issues in this scenario?
3. What are some instructional strategies that could be used to raise academic achievement among all student groups?
4. Identify the leadership approach that you would use to display leader behavior that is fair and equitable.
5. List in sequential order the steps you would take to save the school from state takeover.

INDEX